CONTEMPORARY THEOLOGIANS

CONTEMPORARY
THEOLOGIANS

by james bacik

THE THOMAS MORE PRESS
CHICAGO, ILLINOIS

ISBN 0-88347-233-3

For my sister,
Barbara Bacik Tyrrel
whose inspiring dedication and loving generosity
shine through the faces of
David, Martin, Christopher and Kathryn
revealing again the graciousness of the Mystery.

Publication of this volume of
BASICS OF CHRISTIAN THOUGHT
is made possible in part by a
ROBERT E. BURNS GRANT
from the Claretian Fathers and Brothers

contents

introduction

THIS BOOK IS INTENDED FOR ALL THOSE who want to participate more fully in the great conversation about the religious concerns which tug at the mind and heart. It does not presume any particular background, but requires only an interest in the deep questions of life. It is written from the practical perspective of personal development and service to others rather than from a more speculative viewpoint. The book functions as an invitation to dialogue with the great religious thinkers of our time.

The drive to understand ourselves and our world is deeply rooted in our minds and hearts. We are infinite questioners charged with the task of interpreting our experience and coping with the challenges of life. Some of our concerns are implicitly religious. Thus we wrestle with questions of ultimate concern, search for an encompassing purpose and probe the mystery dimension of life. Our questioning also includes concerns which are more explicitly religious. We must work out, for instance, our relationship with God, Christ and the church.

It is possible to neglect or repress these religious concerns for a time. They remain in our hearts, however, always prepared to spring into awareness. Sometimes the events of life, both joyful and tragic, thrust them upon our conscious life. On other occasions they appear quietly and naturally as part of our cultural heritage and psychic makeup. Whatever the precise catalyst, the religious dimension of the great conversation eventually comes to our attention and we are challenged to respond with intelligence and courage.

As we engage these deeper concerns of life, we do well to turn to the outstanding theologians and religious thinkers who have helped shape the discussion. Their personal triumphs and struggles can inspire us as we try to cope with our own problems. Their revealing perspectives and penetrating insights can challenge our narrowness and guide us on the human journey. By passing over to their viewpoints and retrieving their ideas, we can learn more about ourselves and the religious questions which engage our attention.

In these chapters, we will encounter 20 contemporary religious thinkers who have made important contributions to the great conversation. Most are professional theologians, and all have written incisively on theological matters. We want to enter emphatically into their world so that we can make greater sense of our own. Our intent is to make their key ideas and insights available for reflection on our current experience. Our examination is neither exhaustive nor critical but focuses, instead, on the positive contributions these individuals have made to particular questions. Each chapter begins with a current religious concern and presents the author's ideas as a response to it. The chapters include biographical material which provides a context for interpreting the writer's thought.

The selection of the religious thinkers to be included in this book obviously reflects my own history, assumptions and interests. Since my training is in systematic theology, I have decided not to include important moral theologians such as Bernard Haring or biblical scholars such as Rudolph Bultmann. The strong Catholic representation on the list reflects my lifelong immersion in the Catholic community. The exclusion of some prominent religious thinkers including Dietrich Bonhoeffer, Jürgen Moltmann, Wolfhart Pannenberg, Nikolai Berdyaev, and Abraham Heschel, was dictated by space limitations as much as personal preference. A similar book written a few years from now would surely include John Dunne, David Tracy, Gabriel Moran, Harvey Cox and Michael Novak, as well as other younger theologians. The predominance of male authors is not so much a matter of choice as a sad commentary on our patriarchal society and its sexist bias which must be overcome to unleash the creative talents of all.

In my explanations of these authors, I have tried to be faithful to the dynamics and the thrust of their thought. Nevertheless, my perceptions are surely influenced by my own theological position which was shaped largely by the great German Jesuit theologian Karl Rahner. The appearance of Rahner in the first chapter helps to clarify some of the assumptions I bring to my treatment of the other authors. We could imagine each chapter as a dialogue between the interested reader and a significant thinker, moderated by a Rahnerian theologian.

Practical interests have dictated my treatment of the content of each author's thought. I have tried to discover and examine key ideas and enduring insights which can direct spiritual growth and pastoral practice. From the pastoral perspective, there is limited value in a negative critique of these great thinkers, although each chapter at least indicates some major criticisms of their work. On the other hand, a positive retrieval of pastorally relevant ideas makes the dialogue with each author more stimulating because the topic touches genuine concerns. When possible, I have tried to relate the central ideas of these writers with their personal stories and life experiences. If these correlations can be made clear, their thought becomes more concrete and more readily applicable to the life situations of people today.

While the chapters of the book are autonomous units which can be read separately, the sequence and the groupings of the authors also have importance. The first grouping contains the three giants of Catholic systematic theology, Karl Rahner, Bernard Lonergan, and Yves Congar, all born the same year, 1904. They are followed by four more systematic theologians who have worked out of the broad Catholic tradition, Hans Urs von Balthasar, Edward Schillebeeckx, John Macquarrie and the youngest of the group, Hans Küng. Next comes Karl Barth and Paul Tillich, the two most influential Protestant theologians who produced multi-volume summaries of Christian theology. Reinhold Niebuhr and John Courtney Murray are then linked together as public theologians. They did not produce complete systematic theologies but made great contributions to the public discourse about religious matters. They are followed by four political and liberation theologians, Johann Metz, Gustavo Gutierrez, Rosemary Ruether, and Martin Luther King, all of whom speak for the oppressed and mobilize the Christian tradition in the struggle for justice. The next grouping consists of authors who were not professional theologians but exercised great influence on religious thought: Alfred North Whitehead, a mathematician and philosopher of religion who spawned the movement known as process theology; Jacques Maritain, a Catholic philosopher who led the neo-Thomistic revival in our century; and Teilhard de Chardin, a religious visionary who exercised great influence on contemporary Catholic thought. Finally, Martin Buber and Mohandis Ghandi, influential thinkers who represent religious traditions other than Christianity, complete our list.

I have added a postscript which attempts to put some order into 20th-century religious thought. After recounting the influence the 20 authors have made on my ministry, I have organized them into five models (classical, experiential, liberation, public and interfaith) constructed from a pastoral perspective. This analysis not only helps us locate each thinker in a larger context but highlights again the immense resources contained in contemporary religious thought for inspiring and guiding our personal growth as well as our service to the world.

We can mine the riches of this collective resource by entering into open dialogue with the thought of the individual authors treated in the following chapters. Through a searching examination of their lives and relevant ideas, we can indeed participate more fully in the great conversation which always takes us back to inherently interesting religious concerns.

CHAPTER 1

Karl Rahner
finding god in daily life

THE POET RILKE suggested that if our daily round seems unrewarding, we should not blame it but rather ourselves for failing to evoke the riches found in it. We sense wisdom in this statement, but we also know all too well the problems of daily life: boredom with routine, doubts about meaning, impatience with progress, and temptations to escape. Certain cultural trends intensify the problem. Science and technology tend to become idols which replace a religious sense of life. Our language is impoverished, and it is difficult to speak in depth about the great human realities such as death, love, freedom and sexuality.

When the mysterious depths of ordinary experience are eclipsed, then the human spirit cries out for something more. The current interest in the occult and in extraordinary religious experience is not surprising in our culture. This is, however, simply another way of denigrating the ordinary and escaping from the everyday. In this situation, many of us sense the need for guidance if we are to evoke the riches hidden in our daily lives.

My mind instinctively turns to the great German Jesuit theologian Karl Rahner(1904-1984) to serve as our guide in this effort to discern the divine presence in our ordinary experience. Karl Rahner was well-suited for this task by virtue of his natural instincts as well as his professional training. He was born March 5, 1904, in Freiburg, Germany, the second son of a German professor and his dutiful wife. His family life, steeped in traditional Catholic piety, helped him develop his intuitive sense that all human beings are essentially oriented to the ever mysterious God. In 1922, Karl, following in the footsteps of his older brother Hugo, entered the Jesuit novitiate in Feldkirch, Austria. Through his Jesuit training, especially the Spiritual Exercises of Ignatius, he sharpened his sense of finding God in all things. During his seminary training, he recognized the limitations of his required courses in Thomistic philosophy and, therefore, spent a good deal of time assimilating the thought of more modern authors, especially Immanuel Kant, the 18th-century philosopher who accomplished a "Copernican revolution" by placing the human knower in the center of his philosophy, and Joseph Maréchal, a 20th-century Belgian Jesuit who tried to overcome the limitations of Kant's approach by emphasizing that human beings are dynamic seekers after knowledge.

AFTER BEING ORDAINED A PRIEST IN 1932, Rahner did graduate studies in philosophy at Freiburg from 1934 to 1936. His doctoral dissertation, which interpreted the Thomistic analysis of human knowing in light of the more contemporary approaches indicated by Kant and Maréchal, was rejected by his teacher Martin Honecker because it strayed too far from traditional Thomism. Fortunately, Rahner later published this work in 1939 as *Geist in Welt* (English translation, *Spirit in the World)*, and it was recognized by many scholars as a genuine contribution to a philosophical understanding of human knowing. During his Freiburg years, Rahner had the opportunity to participate in the seminars conducted by Martin Heidegger, the German existentialist philosopher. Rahner usually played down the influence of Heidegger on his thought. Once when I questioned him about this, he responded sharply by asking me how much Heidegger had ever written on God, Christ, church and the sacraments. He then sat back in his chair as though the question was settled. Actually, Rahner did assimilate Heidegger's key understanding of human beings as infinite questioners as well as important aspects of his analysis of death. Furthermore, the vivid descriptions of common human experience which appear throughout Rahner's writings reflect Heidegger's philosophical method commonly called "phenomenology."

After failing to get his doctorate in philosophy, Rahner went to the University of Innsbruck in Austria where he completed a doctorate in theology in one year. His dissertation was "On the Origins of the Church from the Side of Christ" and included a discussion of the Sacred Heart of Jesus—a theme which appears periodically in his writings. In 1937, Rahner began teaching theology at the University of Innsbruck, but the following year the Nazis suppressed the theology faculty. Some of the professors, including his brother Hugo, went to Switzerland, but Karl remained in Innsbruck. On August 15, 1939, he made his final vows as a Jesuit. Later that year, when the Nazis ordered him out of the Tyrol, the Archbishop of Vienna invited him to come to Vienna to work in their Diocesan Pastoral Institute. He was comparatively safe there and periodically went off to lecture in other cities. In the summer of 1944, the Gestapo became more active in Vienna and Rahner left for rural Bavaria where he stayed until August of 1945 when he went to Munich to do pastoral work. In 1948, he returned to Innsbruck where he taught theology until 1964. During this time, he was incredibly productive. He lectured before large audiences and wrote ground-breaking articles. He participated in scholarly discussion groups on important topics such as religion and science, and edited major projects,

"If there is any path at all on which I can approach You, it must lead through the very middle of my ordinary daily life. If You have given me no single place to which I can flee and be sure of finding You, then I must be able to find You in every place in each and every thing I do. In your love all the diffusion of the day's chores comes home again to the evening of Your unity, which is eternal life."

— Meditations and Prayers

including the encyclopedia *Sacramentum Mundi*. Much of his time and energy was expended at the Second Vatican Council where he served as a peritus, giving lectures to the bishops and helping to draft some of the major documents.

His work during this period also brought him into conflict with the Roman Curia. He was denied permission to publish a book on Mary, forbidden to speak on the topic of concelebration, and was directed in 1962 to submit everything he wrote to preliminary censorship in Rome. This ban was effectively lifted when Pope John XXIII appointed him as an official peritus for the council. In 1964, Rahner left Innsbruck for the University of Munich to take over the chair of philosophy and religion, formerly held by Romano Guardini. This move, greatly desired by Rahner, did not work out very well. When the theology faculty refused to allow him to work directly with theology students, he decided to go to the University of Münster to serve as professor of dogmatics—a position held from 1967 until his retirement in 1971. During his retirement years he remained very active, lecturing around the world and continuing his prolific writing. His eightieth birthday brought a great outpouring of affection and praise from friends and colleagues. He died shortly afterward on May 30, 1984. His final hours were peaceful as this energetic man who knew well the darkness and anxiety of life prepared to hand himself over to the Gracious Mystery.

While Rahner was clearly one of the great speculative theologians in Christian history, I am convinced that he is an excellent practical guide for our spiritual journey through daily life. There is no doubt that he was a theologian's theologian, but he also has a valuable message for the average person. It is true that his academic articles are often difficult to decipher, but he has also written popular pieces and preached simpler sermons which speak directly to the heart of ordinary people. Although he treated a wide range of esoteric theological questions, he also consistently responded to the real problems of the contemporary world. To me, Karl Rahner appears, in the midst of all his speculative brilliance, as a theologian for the average person. He is an insightful interpreter of common human experience and a resourceful guide in the struggle to discover meaning in our ordinary activities and purpose in our daily routine. He shows us how the Christian tradition can illumine our common journey and offer us practical advice on how to respond faithfully to the call of the great God. Let us further explore the ways he helps us appreciate the ordinary by examining his personal and pastoral approach to theology.

I FIRST MET KARL RAHNER in September of 1974 in Munich, when I sought his advice on a book I was writing about his theology. There was clearly an aura of greatness around the man, but he also struck me as very ordinary. There was a simple, straightforward, down-to-earth side to him which I found very attractive. His emotions surfaced easily. He began our first conversation by reminding me sternly that we didn't have much time to talk and declaring, jokingly, that books on his theology were like the sands of the seashore. During our conversations he became warmer and even shared with me some off-the-record personal opinions about other theologians. By the end of this first visit, he put his arm around me and asked that I pray for his happy death.

As I learned in subsequent visits, Rahner was like an old shoe in his Jesuit residence. He was seldom the center of attention and preferred to withdraw into the background. The common ordinary things of life fascinated him. One day on a walk we stopped into a gathering place for young people and he immediately began asking about how they prepared and served the food. His piety was basic and traditional. He said private masses and prayed the Rosary regularly. I heard him preach on Holy Thursday in his own Jesuit house. He

"The depths in us are not pools of stagnant bitterness but the waters of infinity springing up into eternal life. It is easy to stir up the slime; but it needs faith to see behind and through all these dark forces a much more powerful force—the power of the presence of the Holy Spirit."

—On Prayer

read a short homily which was both simple and inspiring. My impression of him was that he liked earthy people and avoided individuals who tended to be pompous. I once asked him what his own greatest religious experience was and he replied, "immersion in the incomprehensibility of God and the death of Christ." I then asked whether this occurred in prayer and meditation. He answered quickly and pointedly, "No, in life, in the ordinary things."

Thus, my own limited contacts with Rahner convinced me that he has a message for ordinary persons because he himself retained the common touch despite his brilliance and fame. His writings, often subtly autobiographical, can illumine our daily lives because he habitually saw the hand of God in his own life. He is a theologian for the average person because he never forgot that we all make the journey of life together in response to the call of God.

RAHNER CONTINUES TO BE SUCH A HELPFUL GUIDE for our spiritual quest because of his consistent emphasis on the pastoral side of theology. He was a professional theologian of the highest order. His unpublished lecture notes for the theology classes he taught early in his career reveal a wide-ranging grasp of the Judeo-Christian tradition as well as a keen sense of the biblical basis for church teaching. His later writings often assumed this background without explicitly mentioning it. He wrote scholarly articles on an amazing variety of dogmatic questions, and he participated in the great dialogues between East and West, religion and science, Christianity and Marxism, theology and philosophy. David Tracy has described him as one of the four or five most influential theologians in the history of Catholic thought. The list of his books and articles, including translations and various editions, runs to over four thousand items. His influence on current theologians is vast and deep.

Yet throughout this whole prodigious theological project, Rahner's concern was always pastoral. Theology for him was not a speculative exercise but a means of relating the Christian tradition to real life. His guiding principle, often repeated, was that the more scientific theology is, the more pastoral it will be. The more it searches out the real questions of the current age and explores the rich resources of the Christian tradition, the more practical it becomes. The more truly competent a theologian is, the better spiritual guide he or she will prove to be. Rahner serves our needs so well because he was extremely good at his craft. He is helpful in discerning meaning in ordinary experience because he possessed a vast knowledge of the theological tradition. In his hands, theology became a way of opening up the mysterious depths of human existence and of pointing to a God who makes all of our knowing and loving possible and meaningful.

The last time I saw Karl Rahner was in December of 1977. He had graciously written the introduction to my book, *Apologetics and the Eclipse of Mystery* (Notre Dame Press, 1980), which makes use of his seminal ideas on promoting dialogue with the secular world. I wrote him a note the day I left Munich, thanking him for enabling me to be a Catholic with intellectual honesty and for showing me a way to achieve greater personal integration in my life. He has performed a similar service for countless others, including those who have never heard his name but have benefited indirectly from his pastoral approach to theology. His thought is in the air and permeates the writings of other theologians. It filters into religious education programs, homilies and lectures. The essential message, derived from Rahner, is that theology must be pastoral. This means that it must help us understand the depth dimension of our common experiences and enable us to live our everyday lives more responsibly.

FROM THE VERY BEGINNING OF HIS CAREER, Rahner was interested in religious experience as the basis for theological reflection. In his earliest articles, he examined the notion of the spiritual senses in Origen and Bonaventure in order to learn more about our inner capacities for discerning the workings of the Spirit. Already in 1937, he published an inspiring collection of simple prayers (*Encounters with Silence*, Newman Press, 1960) which reflected both his original intuition that we are all oriented to an inexhaustible mystery, and his personal struggles with the incomprehensible ways of this mystery which we call "God." His doctoral dissertation which, as we saw, was rejected but later published in English as *Spirit in the World* (Herder and Herder, 1968), argued that all of our questioning and knowing demands an infinite horizon as a condition of its possibility. In other words, our ordinary activities of learning and growing in self-knowledge already involve the presence of God, who enables, guides, and fulfills them.

"We are all pilgrims on the wearisome roads of our life. There is always something ahead of us that we have not yet overtaken. When we do catch up with something it immediately becomes an injunction to leave it behind us and to go onwards. Every end becomes a beginning."

—Meditations and Prayers

In his next book, *Hearers of the Word* (Herder and Herder, 1969), he argued that we need to be on alert for a word from the Lord; and that any divine communication would occur, not through abstract ideas, but in our concrete history—or, as we would say today, our daily experience. These seminal ideas on religious experience were then played out in numerous articles, lectures and homilies which have been collected in his 21 volumes of *Theological Investigations* and in more popular books such as *The Eternal Year*, (Helicon, 1964), *Opportunities for Faith* (Seabury, 1974), and *Christian at the Crossroads* (Burns and Oates, 1975). Finally, in his great masterwork, *The Foundations of Christian Faith* (Seabury, 1978), he brought together in one volume his organic approach to the major theological questions, beginning with the human experience of orientation to the inexhaustible mystery addressed by Jesus as "Father."

Thus we see that in his whole theological project, Rahner has always been concerned with uncovering the depth dimension of human existence and relating it to various aspects of the Christian tradition. He has done so in stimulating homilies which shed the light of the Gospel on common concerns, in popular talks which manifest the relevance of Christian doctrines for real life, and in technical articles which often contain vivid descriptions of the graced condition of human existence. Rahner speaks to us today precisely because he remained attuned to the changing questions posed by life in the contemporary world and analyzed them from a theological viewpoint solidly rooted in the Christian tradition.

With some sense of Rahner's general contribution to the spiritual quest of ordinary people, let us now examine some of his particular insights which can guide us in evoking the riches present in our daily lives. My experience in teaching Rahner's theology suggests that the best way of doing this is by analyzing and applying his systematically developed thought in *Foundations of Christian Faith*. While this book is difficult reading, especially in the early chapters, it deserves careful study because it provides such a helpful overview of how Christian doctrines can illumine ordinary experience. Serious readers will find helpful guidance in *A World of Grace*, edited by Leo O'Donovan, in which various Rahnerian scholars provide a chapter-by-chapter commentary on *Foundations*.

The Experience of Mystery

RAHNER'S STARTING POINT and the consistent foundation for his whole theology is an analysis of human beings as positively oriented to mystery. All of our knowing and loving are only intelligible on the condition that we are sustained and drawn by a source and goal which always exceeds our grasp. For example, there is a longing in the human heart for a love which is both totally satisfying and finally imperishable. This desire, however, is constantly frustrated. There are no perfect lovers. Our desires exceed all possible fulfillment on this earth. This raises the question of meaning and absurdity. Is there a final fulfillment for our longings, or are we doomed to eternal frustration? Believers claim that there is a goal for our strivings which will totally satisfy our desires.

We can call this goal the "Holy or Gracious Mystery." The word "mystery" suggests that while we know something of this goal, it remains ultimately beyond our comprehension and control. Problems can be analyzed and solved. Mystery, even when revealed, is finally inexhaustible, ultimately incomprehensible, and essentially unsolvable. The terms "gracious" and "holy" suggest that the mystery is trustworthy and well-disposed toward us. It brings to imagination a sense of tenderness, care, and love. All human beings are in the hands of the gracious mystery. Believers call this mystery "God," and Christians address this God as "Father."

THIS EXPERIENCE OF MYSTERY IS COMMON to all people, and it forms a deep bond of solidarity within the whole human family. Our essential interdependence as human beings is revealed in our common quest for knowledge and love. Teamwork makes sense because we face the common task of extending and deepening our knowledge. Love, which involves mutual giving and receiving, draws us out of our selfishness and into life-giving relationships. We do not make the journey alone; we search out the mystery in the company of others. We seek love and treasure friendship. In short, we are oriented to mystery, but always as social creatures and interdependent persons.

"Almighty God can it be that You are my true home? Are You the One who will release me from my narrow little dungeon? Are you merely unrest for the restless soul? Must every question fall dumb before You, unanswered?"

— Encounters with Silence

This theological anthropology, developed in detail by Rahner, puts us on solid ground in our effort to find meaning in our ordinary experience. His careful philosophical analysis, which supports his intuitive sense of our orientation to mystery, guards us against simplistic and faddish approaches to religious experience. For example, Rahner's anthropology enabled him to recognize quickly the essential fallacies of the Death-of-God movement. Those steeped in his theology also have a perspective for assessing the claims of individuals who speak about direct and unambiguous messages from God. Rahner's insistence on the interdependent character of human existence prevents us from thinking of ourselves as isolated individuals seeking after privileged messages from the deity. Positively, it reminds us of the commonness of human experience and the need for communication with fellow searchers. Dialogue based on our participation in the human adventure is a great tool for sharpening our awareness of our final goal. Thus, our interdependence enables us to explore together our common human experience for intimations of the gracious mystery.

Rahner's notion of the incomprehensibility of God, which echoes the best of the Christian tradition, including Aquinas, rules out any effort to control God or to program religious experience. Since God's ways are finally inscrutable, it is impossible to claim that our particular way of approaching the deity is the only way. When we realize that the mystery is beyond all of our images, the folly of erecting idols and of turning finite realities into absolutes becomes more obvious. For example, participating in a prayer group, walking in the woods, or making a Marriage Encounter may bring some individuals closer to God, but none of these activities can claim to be the answer for everyone. The sacraments have a great power to focus the joys and sorrows of our daily lives, but they remain only one of many vehicles of God's grace. The Bible has a remarkable capacity to illumine and guide human existence, but it only partially reveals the source of all truth. Rahner's insistence on the incomprehensibility of the gracious mystery frees us to find God in the most ordinary of situations, and at the same time it guards us against setting up our own perceptions as the final word.

Dimensions Of Sin

IN OUR DAILY LIVES, we come to know the ambiguous character of our search for God. We live in a world that is a mixture of grace and sin. The human situation is flawed, and the evil tendencies of our hearts are real. As Rahner says, we are radically threatened by sin and guilt. Thus we must deal with systems which oppress people and with unjust structures which render whole groups powerless. We know the temptation to live for self rather than for God; and, at times, we choose the self-contradictory stance of saying "no" to the very source of our being. Sin is an abiding dimension of human existence, and we must take it into account as we probe our ordinary experience. Subtle manipulation can enter into the most intimate relationships. Family life can breed its own brand of insensitivity. Work can inspire a destructive competitive attitude. Leisure can devolve into culpable escapism. In short, the everyday world knows its share of sin and vice.

Rahner's analysis of the dark side of human existence suggests that the search for God in ordinary life cannot be pursued in a spirit of naive optimism. We need, rather, a sober realism which recognizes the power of the dehumanizing forces which threaten us. Thus we are called to find meaning in a daily routine which can indeed be deadening. Our charity must be exercised in family situations which try our patience. Our task is to fight injustice even in the face of powerful systems of oppression. We have to learn to maintain a prayerful, reflective spirit despite the demands and frustrations of our daily work. In all our ordinary activities, grace and sin contend. Our hope is based on the abiding presence of the Holy Spirit, who energizes us for our daily tasks and guarantees the final meaning and triumph of all our good efforts.

Uncreated Grace

IN *FOUNDATIONS,* Rahner develops a theology of grace and revelation. Christianity affirms our hope that the rule of mystery over our lives is both gracious and personal. The great God wills the salvation of all people (1 Timothy 2:4), and to this end has entered a process of self-communication to the whole of creation and to all human beings. Retrieving elements of the scholastic tradition, Rahner calls this totally gratuitous divine self-giving "uncreated grace." This self-communication as offered produces our positive orientation to the mystery. It also causes a universal revelation which can be described as an inner word echoing in the call of conscience and as an interior light illuminating our intellect. When we heed this call and accept God's self-giving, we are transformed or divinized. This justifying grace brings us into a new relationship with the Father, initiates the process of putting on the mind of Christ, and makes us responsive to the promptings of the Spirit.

From this perspective, grace, though free, is not rare. We live and move and have our being in one graced world. God's grace permeates the whole of the cosmos and all dimensions and aspects of human existence. Only sin, personal and social, can screen out the power of God's self-giving. Thus all things are potentially revelatory. Personal relationships, the beauties of nature, the burden of our own freedom, being in love, falling into sin, belonging to a community, fighting injustice—these and all the elements which make up our daily lives can serve as catalysts for a deeper understanding and appreciation of our relationship to the deity. At the same time, it is clear that no particular created reality can exhaust or control the gracious mystery which has communicated itself to us. We come to know God in and through the experiences of life and are called to respond to the divine in our daily activities. As Rahner summarizes it, the experience of self is the experience of God.

This theology of grace and revelation has prompted Rahner to examine the depth dimension of many common activities, such as laughing, working, playing, eating, sleeping, moving about, and sitting down. For example, in *Everyday Faith* (Herder and Herder, 1968) he points out that wholesome laughter flows from a proper perspective on life as well as from a sense of empathy and affection for others. He then relates this to the biblical suggestion that God laughs because he recognizes the ultimately successful outcome of an historical process currently filled with darkness and chaos. A careful reading of Rahner's vast writings reveals his amazing capacity to probe the depths of ordinary human experience. He, in turn, inspires us to take a closer look at our own daily routine which seems so mundane and yet contains surprising depths.

The Final Word

IN HIS THEOLOGY, Rahner emphasizes that divine grace seeks visibility and a full human response. The inner word of universal revelation strains toward an outer word which makes it concrete and particular. God's self-communication, which has created the world and divinized human beings, strives for full expression in history. Christians claim that divine self-giving and human receptivity have met completely, definitively and irrevocably, in Jesus of Nazareth. He is God's final word to us and, at the same time, the most obedient and responsive of all human beings. He is the greatest prophet and the best example of complete humanity. He is the absolute Savior and the wisest of teachers. In his death, he definitively surrendered himself to the mystery he addressed as "Abba." Through his Resurrection, God has vindicated his claim and guaranteed the ultimate triumph of his cause.

Rahner's Christology, which forms the core of his *Foundations*, helps to illumine and transform our experience. The historical Jesus portrayed in the gospels reveals the true nature of human existence. His parables enable us to perceive the hidden depths of ordinary life and call us to live more fully in accord with the surprising ways of God. His miracles remind us that healing is available and transformation possible, even in the face of the dark and demonic forces which threaten us on the common journey. The Scriptures, which witness to Christ, provide us with ideals which guide us in discerning the truth and encourage us in seeking the good. Finally, through the death and Resurrection of Jesus Christ, we are able to believe what we desperately hope to be true—that love is stronger than death, that our ordinary activities have ultimate meaning, and that there is a final purpose to our lives.

Thus, brief examination of *Foundations* suggests the power of Rahner's theology to help us understand and transform our ordinary experiences. He, of course, has much more to say to ordinary people; and we will continue to learn from him in the years ahead. Other religious thinkers may have more extensive analyses of aspects of human experience. We can think of Martin Buber on personal relationships, Gustavo Gutierrez on the experience of liberation, and Paul Tillich on cultural trends. Karl Rahner, however, remains the great interpreter of ordinary experience. His organic and comprehensive theology keeps calling us back to the task of evoking the riches found in our daily life, which is always sustained and guided by the Gracious Mystery.

Discussion Questions

1. What are the most troublesome obstacles for you in relating your belief to ordinary life?

2. How do you understand Rahner's statement that his greatest religious experience was "immersion in the incomprehensibility of God and the death of Christ"?

3. What are the main components of Rahner's thought and how do they affect his theology of the ordinary?

4. How could Rahner's insights help enrich your everyday life?

Suggested Readings

Prayers for a Lifetime (Crossroad, 1984). A simple way to enter into Rahner's complex thought which contains the twelve prayers originally published in *Encounters with Silence* (now out of print).

Foundations of Christian Faith (Crossroad, 1978). Difficult reading but the best single-source summary of Rahner's comprehensive and organic thought.

A World of Grace, edited by Leo O'Donovan (Seabury, 1980). A valuable chapter-by-chapter commentary on Rahner's *Foundations*.

The Rahner Reader, edited by Gerald McCool (Seabury, 1975). A fine selection with a helpful introduction by the editor.

Bernard Lonergan
achieving personal development

OUR MATERIALISTIC, SUCCESS-ORIENTED CULTURE places great emphasis on the external world of money, status, and power, while often neglecting the inner world of emotion, imagination, and reflection. The superficiality of this prevailing utilitarian philosophy has helped foster a counter-movement with a renewed concern for personal development. Thus our culture has produced a vigorous self-growth movement manifested in greater interest in self-help books, popular psychology, fitness programs, meditation techniques, holistic spirituality, and a host of other therapeutic approaches. While we can laud this movement for challenging the superficiality of the dominant culture, we should also question its tendency toward excessive individualism, faddish approaches, and shallow uses of the religious traditions.

In trying to overcome these narrow and superficial tendencies, we will find helpful guidance in the systematic approach to personal development advocated by Bernard Lonergan (1904-1984), one of the giants of 20th-century Catholic theology. This reserved, intense, brilliant scholar spent his adult life in academic environments, working out methodologies to guide human growth and theological reflection.

Born in Canada in 1904, Lonergan attended Jesuit schools in Montreal and entered the Society of Jesus in 1922. He studied philosophy in England from 1926 to 1930, followed by a three-year teaching stint in Montreal. After his ordination to the priesthood in 1936, he began doctoral studies in theology at the Gregorian University in Rome, completing his work in 1940. During the next thirteen years he taught theology in Jesuit seminaries in Canada before returning to the Gregorian, where he served as professor of theology for twelve years. In 1957 he published his great work, *Insight: A Study of Human Understanding* (Philosophical Library, 1957), which explored in great detail and depth the unvarying patterns he discerned in the process of human knowing. This work established his scholarly reputation and helped secure his appointment as an expert consultant at the Second Vatican Council. After surgery for lung cancer in 1965, Lonergan continued his teaching career at Regis College in Canada and at Boston College until his retirement in 1983, a year before his death.

"From a casual viewpoint, one would say that first there is God's gift of his love. Next, the eye of this love reveals values in their splendor, while the strength of this love brings about their realization, and that is moral conversion. Finally, among the values discerned by the eye of love is the value of believing the truths taught by the religious tradition, and in such tradition and belief are the seeds of intellectual conversion."

— Method in Theology

During this period, despite his health problems, Lonergan published his other famous work, *Method in Theology* (Herder and Herder, 1972), which offers a highly structured approach to the theological enterprise, based on an analysis of its eight interlocking functions.

While Lonergan never received a great deal of popular acclaim during his lifetime, he did exert great influence within the ranks of professional theologians. The highly respected theologian David Tracy, commenting on Lonergan's unparalleled interdisciplinary work, described him as "the greatest Catholic theologian North America has produced." Lonergan is often compared with the other giant of 20th-century Catholic theology, Karl Rahner. Their perceptions of each other are revealing. During a 1970 interview, Lonergan commented succinctly: "Rahner emphasizes mystery a lot. I have a few clear things to say" (*A Second Collection*, p. 229). Rahner, who seldom discussed theological questions directly with Lonergan, once indicated to me in a private conversation that, while he respected Lonergan greatly, he felt he had overemphasized method to the neglect of substance.

Lonergan did indeed concentrate on questions of methodology, while Rahner explored the mystery dimension of a whole range of theological topics. It is, however, Lonergan's attention to process, patterns, approaches, and systems which make him valuable as we explore the question of personal development. He invites us to take seriously our own experience, to explore the way we function as knowers and lovers, and to discern the patterns involved in human growth.

The Transcendental Precepts

LONERGAN SUGGESTS four general principles, or "transcendental precepts," to guide our development: be attentive by openly probing the full range of your experience; be intelligent by cultivating an inquiring mind and gaining insight into your experience; be reasonable by marshalling evidence and judging the validity of your insights; be responsible by acting on your valid insights. He also helps us understand the dynamic interplay among these four transcendental precepts. He cautions us, for example to keep the second and third steps in proper sequence by making sure we understand the relevant data and the possible alternatives on particular questions before making a judgment about them. By providing these general guidelines and inviting us to apply them to our concrete experience, Lonergan helps us avoid scattered and superficial approaches to personal development.

By the time *Method in Theology* appeared in 1972, Lonergan was making extensive use of the notion of "conversion" to interpret all aspects of human development. The word "conversion" is, of course, highly charged today because of its associations with evangelical Christianity. As a result, many people associate it with a sudden, once and for all turning from sin to a reborn life of commitment to God. This understanding puts emphasis on the private moment of encounter with God in the explicitly religious realm. Lonergan, on the other hand, understands "conversion" in a broader way, as a new beginning, a fresh start which leads to an ongoing process of growth in the intellectual, moral, and religious dimensions of life.

This interpretation of the conversion process is rooted in various aspects of Lonergan's philosophical anthropology. We are, first of all, self-transcendent creatures, called to strive always for more knowledge, better values, and deeper love. Thus, while a conversion experience may be concentrated in a clear moment of decision, it is rooted in a continuing process of growth.

Second, our existence is composed of emotional, intellectual, and religious dimensions. We can, for example, feel sad over suffering and rejoice in ac-

"Besides conversions there are breakdowns. What has been built up so slowly and so laboriously by the individual, the society, the culture, can collapse. . . . Values have a certain esoteric imperiousness, but can they keep outweighing carnal pleasure, wealth, power? Religion undoubtedly had its day, but is not that day over? Is it not illusory comfort for weaker souls, an opium distributed by the rich to quiet the poor, a mythical projection of man's own excellence into the sky?"

— Method in Theology

complishment; ask questions and find solutions to problems; commit sins and act virtuously; search for ultimate meaning and utter prayers of gratitude. Conversions can occur initially in any of these dimensions, as we decide against stagnation and for progress in a particular area of our lives. Since the dimensions are interrelated and ultimately united in our single consciousness, we can achieve a fully authentic life only through conversion in all dimensions.

Finally, according to Lonergan's understanding of human existence, we are, at the same time, unique individuals and social creatures who function in various communities and institutions. Thus conversion, which is intensely personal, is not purely private. It brings insights which can be communicated and commitments which demand common action. A personal moral conversion, for example, may move an individual to join with others to work for social justice. Moreover, continued growth may depend on the challenge and support provided by various communities and associations.

Lonergan is also well aware that human existence is not a one-way process of growth. In addition to conversions, there are breakdowns. Our emotions can take us in destructive directions by prompting choices of pleasure over goodness. Self-deception can cloud our intellect and reinforce irresponsible decisions. Sin can impair our loving relationships with God and other people. Conversions call for continued effort, precisely because they are fragile and can be reversed.

Lonergan often insisted that his carefully worked out method should not be followed slavishly, but should function as a catalyst for creative responses. Thus, inspired but not constrained by Lonergan and borrowing suggestions from his many followers, let us explore four types of conversion: affective, intellectual, moral, and religious. This approach invites personal reflection and suggests Lonergan's enduring value as a guide for personal development.

Valuable Emotions

AFFECTIVE CONVERSION leading to a healthy emotional life is crucial to full human existence. Our feelings provide us with an initial response to the value and worth of persons and things. When we meet good persons, for example, our initial attraction prompts us to find out more about them in hopes of furthering the relationship. Emotions also help us focus our decisions and actions. Persons who feel great fear and revulsion over the prospect of nuclear war may be prompted to devote their time and energy to the peace movement.

On the other hand, emotions which are not properly handled can be destructive. Those who simply ignore their emotions are in danger of becoming cold, insensitive individuals who cannot relate in a truly human way. Repressing negative feelings often causes fatigue and bottles up positive emotions as well. Without an adequate understanding of the affective life, individuals are subject to self-deceptions and mysterious compulsions. Decisions dictated by hidden emotions are often flawed because they reflect unexamined and biased assumptions. When persons fail to search out the source of their deepest joys and most threatening anxieties, their religious lives suffer because they have neglected matters of ultimate concern.

Learning to deal with our emotions in a consistently healthy way requires a systematic effort. We must be in touch with what we are actually feeling in a given situation, instead of falling into a programmed response dictated by others' expectations. It is vital to recognize in ourselves strange or embarrassing emotions while searching for constructive ways to release them.

Precise identification and accurate naming of a wide variety of nuanced feelings provide us with greater power to deal with them. We should learn to distinguish, for example, positive and negative emotions elicited by objects, the intense and subtle feelings accompanying personal relationships, the often contradictory emotions attached to important symbols, and the affective states which motivate our behavior. It is especially important to differentiate appropriate and inappropriate emotional responses as a first step in managing and transforming those which are excessive or disproportionate. Honest communication about our feelings is also helpful both in identifying them and in finding healthy ways of acting on them. Such disclosures should always be governed by the law of charity, which looks to the well-being of others as well as ourselves. I find this analysis exemplified by the story of a middle-aged man suffering from anxiety and fatigue who consistently repressed his anger. After recognizing the destructive effects of this habitual repression, he decided to deal more openly with this frightening emotion. As a test case, he purposely confronted a co-worker who often angered him with his overbearing attitude. The encounter helped clear the air and convinced the man of the wisdom of this more open approach. He began to pay greater attention to all of his emotions by regularly sharing and discussing his feelings with his wife. This whole process of affective conversion has proven to be liberating and energizing for him and is now an important part of his quest for full personal development.

Quest for Wisdom

IN A CULTURE which oscillates between a narrow rationalism and a soft romanticism, intellectual conversion is difficult but vital. We need to embark on a lifelong quest for wisdom which rises above both scientism, with its exclusive emphasis on the empirical method, and the new romanticism, with its celebrations of feelings and intuition to the exclusion of reason and logic. Wise persons who are intellectually converted recognize that knowledge does not arise simply from isolated observation of the objective world presented to the senses. They realize that knowledge grows within a community and that much of what we accept as true is based on faith. For them, knowledge develops from making valid judgments about the meaning of experience.

Wise persons seek an integrated understanding of life, which combines the theoretical with the practical, self-fulfillment with a concern for the common good, and knowledge of the highest principles with the light of love. Those who possess wisdom make good dialogue partners and constructive participants in a pluralistic society, because they seek truth without pretending to monopolize it. In short the life of wisdom represents the ideal toward which intellectual conversion tends.

The process unleashed by a decision to seek wisdom involves various tasks. In general, we are called to be more attentive to our experience. Those who are tempted by their busy routines to concentrate almost exclusively on practical and utilitarian concerns must pay special attention to the spiritual dimension of their experience. This could be done by keeping a journal, meeting with a spiritual director, engaging in serious conversation with a friend, and meditating regularly. Those who feel bored with themselves or limited by their lack of knowledge need to find intellectual stimulation by various means such as reading a good book, taking a course, meeting new people, and accepting new challenges. Intellectual conversion can be triggered and fostered by new experiences as well as by greater awareness of familiar routines.

THE QUEST FOR WISDOM ALSO MOVES US to criticize all the forms of anti-intellectualism in our culture, including misgivings about intellectuals among ordinary people, the denigration of theology among religious enthusiasts, and the disdain for reason within the popular self-improvement movement. Converted persons understand that intelligence is a broader capacity than is reason, with its narrow focus on logical analysis. They cherish and foster the power of intelligence to probe, understand, and judge all aspects of our experience. Wise persons thus expose the limitations of anti-intellectualism by demonstrating that intelligence is a great ally in the process of personal development.

Wisdom can be cultivated. Some individuals make progress by concentrating on thoroughly understanding an idea or a proposition before making a judgment about it. A close reading of classic texts not only puts students in touch with the ideas of great thinkers but also teaches the art of critical thinking. In ordinary conversation, we have many opportunities to pass over to another person's viewpoint in order to catch the emotional tone and personal context of his or her comments. Finally, careful analysis of one of our particular failures in life often brings unexpected insights, reminding us in the process of the importance of using intelligence to transform our negative experiences.

An important aspect of wisdom is the ability to recognize the limitations of our insights. Not every bright idea proves to be valid or accurate. Thus we must learn to make reasonable judgments about our insights into the meaning of experience. In this way, intellectually converted persons acquire a sense of pluralism by recognizing the relativity of their own positions. They realize that much of knowledge is based on faith and that on many questions human beings cannot achieve absolute certitude but must rely on convergent probability. The quest for wisdom moves them to respect new data, to weigh all the evidence, and to revise judgments when necessary.

Individuals who tend to be opinionated and leery of pluralism can learn to be more tolerant and open-minded. Through wrestling with the great questions of meaning and purpose, we learn to accept the mysterious character of human existence which provides no simple and final answers to the matters which concern us most. By studying the history of disputed questions, we come to appreciate the diversity of opinion which has always characterized the human search for truth. Through travel, learning another language, and meeting people from diverse backgrounds, our horizons are broadened and our viewpoints are relativized. A healthy sense of self-criticism enables us to recognize the limitations of our own positions and to stay open to truth wherever it is to be found.

The decision to seek wisdom sets us on an exciting but demanding adventure. We are called to stay alert though tempted by indifference, to ask probing questions though prone to complacency, and to admit our mistakes though fearful of embarrassment. Nonetheless, intellectual conversion can bring a deep joy and quiet delight as we expand our horizons, sharpen our insights, and improve our judgments. Through this process we prepare ourselves to cooperate with others who treasure wisdom, so that we can move forward together on the journey toward greater maturity.

Turning to Goodness

AUTHENTIC PERSONAL DEVELOPMENT also requires moral conversion, in which we choose to pursue goodness and virtue even when they conflict with pleasure and satisfaction. Children who naturally seek self-gratification need rules and regulations to control their behavior. Individuals striving for genuine adulthood must assume greater responsibility for their actions based on inner convictions, moral principles, and habitual attitudes. Even after we have chosen to strive for goodness over satisfaction, we must still live out this decision in the real world of conflicting values and cultural bias. This requires constant attention to the task of ordering and focusing our values as well as unmasking societal contradictions and imbalances. Moral conversion requires a change of heart which moves us to constructive action in accord with our ideals. It is a decision to be faithful to the transcendental principle: be responsible.

In order to live out our decision for goodness, we must move beyond legalism to a generous love. Legalism, which suggests a slavish adherence to external laws out of fear of punishment, leads to a minimalistic and negative morality. The Catholic legalist, for example, who goes to mass primarily out of fear of mortal sin, may worship in routine fashion and never discover the inherent

> *"Religious conversion is being grasped by ultimate concern. It is other-worldly falling in love. . . . It is revealed in retrospect as an undertow of existential consciousness, as a fated acceptance of a vocation to holiness, as perhaps an increasing simplicity and passivity in prayer."*
>
> — Method in Theology

value of wholehearted participation in the liturgy. Morally converted persons strive to act out of love without counting the cost. They come to know the truth of Karl Rahner's maxim that "love is true to itself only if it is prepared to give more tomorrow than today."

Enlightened individuals who appreciate the way authoritarianism can impede human growth are sometimes tempted to swing from legalism to antinomianism, in which a "do your own thing" morality prevails. Genuine moral conversion, however, calls us to avoid such a pendulum swing and to concentrate instead on developing a responsible freedom. Responsible behavior demands fitting responses to the call of God, the wisdom of the past, the needs of our neighbors, and the ideals in our hearts. Persons who have achieved authentic freedom do not follow their whims, but act on insight. Their moral decisions flow from intelligent consideration of many influences, including their intuitive responses, their own character traits, the consequences of their acts, the circumstances constituting the situation, and the example of good persons who have acted virtuously in similar situations.

Given our contemporary awareness of injustice and the nuclear threat, the process of moral conversion today must lead to the development of a social conscience which rejects ethical privatism and joins the struggle for liberation. Believers encased in privatism are concerned with saving their own souls by loving God and avoiding personal sins. Converted persons today must develop a broader vision, recognizing that love of God is essentially linked with love of neighbor; that sin has a social dimension because it fosters unjust structures and dehumanizing systems; and that work for justice is an essential element in spreading the gospel. The decision for goodness furthers the cause of authentic personal development, but always within the larger context of concern for the well-being of the whole human family.

Moral conversion prompts us to overcome vices which retard our growth and to cultivate virtues which give us the assured capacity to respond constructively in changing circumstances. Individuals who have made progress in the moral life are not always in a grim fight with their destructive tendencies. On the contrary, through discipline and the repetition of fitting behavior they often are able to perform good actions with little effort and great delight. Their strengths become integrated into a harmonious pattern so that virtue is second nature for them. The decision to pursue constructive values over pleasure inaugurates a lifelong effort to cultivate a whole range of virtues which facilitates a life of high idealism and service to others.

Furthermore, moral conversion encourages persons to appreciate the wisdom and ideals of their formative traditions, to immerse themselves in the life of a community, and to contribute to the good of the various associations which make partial claim on them. The moral life, even at its highest stages of development, is not confined to acting on general principles discerned by rational deduction but always includes a communal dimension. I recall a woman committed to the peace movement explaining how she was influenced by her parents, who preferred conflict resolution to the use of force; by the scriptures which proclaim peacemakers blessed; and by the leaders of her church who have called for an entirely new attitude toward war. She continues to be sustained in her efforts by the peace organizations she has joined, by the liturgy she attends weekly, by her friends who are also committed to the cause, and by her religion which teaches her that peacemaking is valuable even when results are meager. As the example suggests, moral conversion is clearly a call to live out a life story which reflects the best of communal ideals and is nourished by community life.

He Who Shared Our Lot

RELIGIOUS CONVERSION is at the very center of the process of personal development. Our efforts to achieve affective integration, to attain wisdom, and to live out our ideals are always limited, incomplete, and filled with failures.

Thus our never-satisfied drive for self-transcendence raises for us the question of ultimate meaning and absolute value. Through religious conversion, we come to the conviction that life has meaning despite all of the absurdity which surrounds us, and that love will triumph despite all the evils which threaten us. We sense that the mystery which encompasses our existence is ultimately gracious, even though it remains incomprehensible. Our center of gravity has shifted from ourselves to the mystery which, paradoxically, forms the very center of our being.

GENUINE RELIGIOUS CONVERSION IS EXPERIENCED not as a personal achievement, but as the work of God who first loves us. We find ourselves in the hands of one who loves us without restriction or condition. This experience has the power to transform and liberate us. It calls us to surrender ourselves totally, to turn from sin to righteousness, to strive wholeheartedly for holiness, and to put aside idols by making God our ultimate concern. To undergo religious conversion is to fall in love with God. This free gift sets us on a lifelong journey filled with challenges and opportunities. Despite our sins, we believe we are loved. Despite our limitations, we know we must continually strive to deepen and extend our love for God and others.

For us Christians, religious conversion, which we believe is available to all human beings, is focused and mediated by Jesus Christ. He is the parable of God's love who teaches us about divine fidelity. He is life-giving spirit who floods our hearts with divine love. Individuals who experience Christian conversion accept Jesus Christ as the final prophet and absolute savior. They commit themselves to him, attempting to live out his message in their daily lives. It is in Christ that they perceive most clearly the unconditional character of God's love and experience most profoundly the call to make a wholehearted response. For Christians, religious conversion is not a theoretical acceptance of a new worldview or an intellectual adherence to a more enlightened theology. It involves, rather, a personal dedication to Jesus Christ, who shared our lot completely and triumphed over its worst evils.

Christian conversion calls for a total-person response which unifies and brings to a higher synthesis all aspects of personal development. Dedication to Jesus, who cast out the demons, frees us to face our most threatening emotions confident that they cannot destroy us and can even be mobilized for our personal growth. Handing our lives over to Christ, who addressed God as "Abba," enables us to surrender ourselves to the gracious mystery who calls each one of us to strive intelligently and wholeheartedly for full personal development.

This examination of conversion as the key to personal growth reflects one of the enduring contributions of Bernard Lonergan. His often difficult, tightly structured, and highly impersonal masterworks have a paradoxical power to encourage us to take hold of our lives rather than drift along, and to structure our spiritual growth rather than follow the latest trends. In this way we are open—as Lonergan often insisted—to the generous love of God "poured into our hearts by the Holy Spirit" (Romans 5:5).

Discussion Questions

1. How have you been influenced by the cultural movement which stresses self-growth and personal development?

2. What influence did Lonergan's training and life as a Jesuit have on his thought?

3. What is Lonergan's understanding of conversion and how does it guide personal development?

4. How would you apply Lonergan's advice to your own life?

Suggested Readings

Insight: A Study of Human Understanding (Philosophical Library, 1957). A detailed and demanding treatment which gives the philosophical foundations for Lonergan's thought and invites readers to probe their own process of knowing.

Method in Theology (Herder and Herder, 1972). Provides a systematic method for doing theology which appeals to professional theologians more than average readers.

Collection, edited by Frederick Crowe and Robert Doran (University of Toronto Press, 1988). Contains essays on a broad range of topics, including love and marriage and the role of the university, some of which are more readable than his major works; the introduction by Crowe is helpful in understanding Lonergan's thought.

The Achievement of Bernard Lonergan, by David Tracy (Herder and Herder, 1970). An excellent exposition of the dynamics of Lonergan's thought.

CHAPTER **3**

Yves Congar

revitalizing
the ecumenical movement

SIGNS OF WHAT YVES CONGAR called "ecumenical passion" are hard
to detect these days. Many of us recall the excitement when we first got involved
in the ecumenical movement. Living room dialogues, common services, covenant
relationships, pulpit exchanges, and ecumenical conferences provided stimulating
opportunities to get to know Christians from other traditions and to discover
the wide areas of agreement we share. Today much of the excitement has
gone out of the movement. We have cooperated enough to realize one another's
strengths and weaknesses, and learned enough to be beyond any great surprises
about similarities and differences. Despite the great progress made by theologians
in solving disputed questions, church leaders maintain a cautious reserve thereby
delaying progress toward institutional unity. Not surprisingly, committed
ecumenists often experience great frustration as they encounter such obstacles
to the full expression of Christian unity.

On the other hand, many Christians never experienced this initial
surge of interest in ecumenism.
Some continue to live a narrow
denominational life with no interest
in dialogue with different Christian
traditions. Others, especially young
people, simply assume an easy
tolerance toward those who belong
to different denominations. They
have little sense of the history of
Christian divisions and believe that
separated churches should unite immediately without worrying about
theological differences or historical

disputes. Thus, from various perspectives, the ecumenical movement appears
to be at a standstill, lacking both energy and motivation to fuel a fresh start.

In this situation, we would do well to consider again the life and thought
of the great French Dominican theologian Yves Congar, generally regarded as
the leading Catholic ecumenical theologian of the 20th century. Born in 1904,
the same year as two other Catholic theological giants, Karl Rahner and Bernard
Lonergan, he has outlived them both, although very poor health prevents him
from writing anymore.

Congar himself has told the story of the development of his ecumenical
vocation in the preface to his book *Dialogue Between Christians* (Newman

*"The substance and truth of the unity of the church is
made up in and by Jesus Christ. All the images by
which the New Testament expresses it convey this. The
New Testament speaks of the church as a building, a
vine, a flock, a bride, a body, always in relationship to
Jesus Christ. But the Christ is only the cornerstone of a
single construction; he is the only stem of a single vine,
the shepherd of a single flock, the husband of a single
wife, the head of a single body which is organically one."*

— Diversity and Communion

Press, 1964). Fortunate to have had open-minded parents with a broad circle
of acquaintances, he grew up with many Protestant and Jewish friends. In
1914, when he was 10 years old, his parish church near Sedan, France, burned
down. For the next six years, the Catholic community worshipped in a neighboring Protestant chapel at the kind invitation of the pastor. This gesture fired
Congar with a desire to make some return to the Protestants for all he had
received from them. At the age of 21 he decided to become a priest, and
in 1925 entered the Dominican order.

Shortly before his ordination, Congar had a deep and formative religious
experience. While meditating on the 17th chapter of John's Gospel, which
includes the priestly prayer of Jesus, he recognized his vocation "to work for

the unity of all who believe in Jesus Christ." This became the driving force of his life. He was totally committed to breaking down the barriers which divide Christians and responding to the priestly prayer of Jesus that all his followers might be one. From then on, his burning desire to bring separated Christians together dominated his scholarly and pastoral work. Despite many hardships, misunderstandings, and frustrations, this saintly man and eminent scholar has remained faithful to his ecumenical vocation throughout his whole life.

Congar's passionate commitment reminds us of our own vocation to be ecumenically-minded Christians. The prayer of Jesus for unity sets a task, not just for a few elite specialists, but for all Christians. Long-standing divisions and deep-seated prejudices can be overcome only if ordinary people respond to the promptings of the Holy Spirit. Christian witness in the world will be enhanced if believers can work cooperatively on behalf of peace and justice. The scandal of division will be overcome only if large numbers of Christians refuse to live as narrow-minded individuals locked into a denominational mind-set.

Congar insisted that when we behave as though the divisions in the Christian world are inevitable, we become co-responsible for the continuing separation. He also reminds us that "the whole Church is answerable for the ecumenical effort. To a tiny and yet very real extent, the issue is in the hands of one parishioner in some remote village" (*Ecumenism and the Future of the Church*, The Priory Press, 1967, p. 125). Thus, Congar's ecumenical passion becomes a pointed challenge. Each one of us has the ability to bring new life to the ecumenical movement.

A Theology of Ecumenism

CONGAR LIVED OUT HIS ECUMENICAL VOCATION primarily as a theologian, and deserves to be classed with the giants of the 20th century. Although he taught at the Dominican seminary at Le Saulchoir for 17 years and published extensively, he never received the recognition accorded to his great contemporaries Rahner and Lonergan. His books have not been as readily available in English as even those of lesser European theologians. Perhaps this is because his carefully-balanced approach did not produce startling results, or because he lacked an integral philosophical system which would have given more coherence to his vast theological project. Professional theologians, however, have long recognized his great significance, including his influence on the Second Vatican Council as well as his ground-breaking contributions to the ecumenical movement. Richard McBrien, for instance, has called him the most distinguished ecclesiologist of this century, and probably since Trent.

Congar has indeed addressed the major questions of his day with great courage, responding to them with a sure grasp of the history of Christian thought. Throughout his career he worked long hours and produced over 1,600 books and articles. Many of his writings were directly concerned with ecumenism, such as his extremely influential classic work, *Divided Christendom: Principles of a Catholic Ecumenism* (London: G. Bles, 1939); his historical study of the split between the Eastern and Western churches, *After Nine Hundred Years* (Fordham Press, 1959); his collections of essays, *Dialogue Between Christians* (Newman Press, 1966) and *Ecumenism and the Future of the Church* (The Priory Press, 1962); and his final book on the topic, *Diversity and Communion* (Twenty-Third Publications, 1982). Even when he addressed other major topics such as the church, the laity, tradition, and the Holy Spirit, the ecumenical question was never far from his mind. Always concerned with furthering dialogue among Christians, he tackled the most difficult disputed questions and openly discussed the most controversial Catholic doctrines.

In his work, he drew heavily on the thought of Thomas Aquinas and the church Fathers. His method was primarily historical, which helped him bring modern questions into perspective. He insisted that theology must be historical; and he criticized others, including Karl Rahner, for not taking enough interest in the actual history of the ecumenical movement. He remained remarkably self-critical throughout his life, and was willing to adjust his views according to new data and contemporary developments. He criticized his own masterwork, *Divided Christendom*, because it was too influenced by scholastic Thomism and liberal Protestantism and did not appreciate sufficiently the active missionary orientation proposed by the forerunners of the World Council of Churches. Despite a crippling disease of the bone marrow in his later years, he continued his theological labor, completing at the age of seventy-six his three-volume work, *I Believe in the Holy Spirit*. This left him with the final task, as he himself said, of uniting his sufferings to the chalice of Jesus.

MANY OF CONGAR'S CONTRIBUTIONS to ecumenical theology have worked their way into the books and articles of other theologians as well as official church documents, such as the Vatican II Decree on Ecumenism. Moreover, his writings continue to be valuable because they provide a historical context and depth of analysis matched by few others. He helps us understand the truly destructive character of longstanding divisions among Christians. Continued separation creates a psychological outlook or false consciousness in which we no longer sense the terrible sin and scandal involved and simply accept divisions as normal. This creates a climate in which prejudice can flourish unchecked by personal interaction and genuine dialogue. The whole church suffers because the various traditions undergo a distinct historical development

"One cannot avoid seeing the church as plenitude. The unity which Jesus asks for the church in his 'high-priestly prayer' is that of a unity of plenitude, the image of unity existing between Father and Son. It is not a union woven by poverty, by reduction to a single element. Pluralism will find a place there."

— Diversity and Communion

without benefit of the corrective provided by other traditions, and without being able to contribute their new insights and practices to the collective consciousness of the larger faith community. Thus, disunity not only weakens the church's witness to the world, but also retards its inner growth and makes distortions inevitable

As all ecumenists must, Congar struggled throughout his life with the question of unity and diversity. He placed the question in an eschatological framework by insisting that the limited unity already given at Pentecost will achieve its perfection only at the end time, as a gift of God. This context enables us to keep two points in fruitful tension: first, our ecumenical activity is an important ingredient in the dynamic development of the church toward its fullness; and second, we cannot expect a utopian union on earth, but must await a final fulfillment in heaven as a result of God's saving action.

The unity we seek is found, not in a dull uniformity or in rigid doctrinal formulas, but in the rich and diverse life of the church members who are committed to Christ in faith. Unity is not the victory of one denomination over others, but the victory of Christ, who prayed that his followers might be one. This unity must be social and visible, but it will always be deficient and incomplete.

Thus the church must always be reforming itself, as Congar insisted and the Second Vatican Council affirmed. The church is a living organism, and its unity flows from the inner life of the Spirit and from the common faith in Jesus Christ.

Within this unity Congar wants to celebrate pluralism and diversity. All his research, as he himself stated, was devoted to demonstrating that diversity is compatible with communion. For him, pluralism does not imply merely

"As to the Catholic church, the terms metanoia, reform, 're-reception' represent more than a programme: they are already facts. The moves everyone needs to make are primarily spiritual. The dialogues and explanations are necessary, but they must be backed up by a great vitality of prayer and love."

— Diversity and Communion

difference or dispersion, but a healthy differentiation of something held in common. Christians hold a common faith in Christ; but this faith can be expressed in a great variety of pieties, creeds, doctrines, theologies, and lifestyles—all of which can enrich the total understanding of what it means to be a Christian. We should not just tolerate this kind of diversity, but encourage it.

In this regard Congar calls upon Rome to adopt "a genuine policy of non-uniformity at the center, which will take into account national peculiarities and needs and deal with peoples according to their special genius and tradition" (*Divided Christendom*, p. 104). Congar based his proposal on earlier tradition. In 601, for example, Pope Gregory the Great advised Augustine of Canterbury, who was about to embark on his missionary journey to England, to "choose from each of the different churches, whatever is pious, religious, just, draw them together and use them to establish a custom in the spirit of the Angles" (quoted in *Diversity and Communion*, p. 25). Christianity is lived out in diverse spiritual worlds, which are composed of distinct aggregates of ideas and values capable of nourishing our consciousness and giving meaning to our lives. Individuals and churches should demonstrate respect for these distinct spiritual worlds by entering into dialogue with them in a search for a truth greater than any one community possesses.

The problem of how to relate unity and diversity in the one Christian church is complex and admits of no easy answers. Congar came to recognize that reunion could not be viewed as the return of the prodigal son; nor could it involve Orthodox, Anglicans and Protestants in a denial of their distinctive histories, doctrines, and practices. On the other hand, he was not completely happy with the Lutheran notion of reconciled diversity, which he thought failed to recognize the unity of the church already given as God's gift.

The traditional notion of sister-churches reuniting appealed to him. In discussing the split between East and West, he expressed the desire that the one church would begin to breathe again through its two lungs. The reunited church would be healthier and richer than any existing church. It would concentrate on the fundamentals of the faith and respect the notion of a hierarchy of truths, which is based on the idea that some doctrines are more significant than others because they are closer to the foundations of Christianity (*Decree on Ecumenism*, #11). Embracing the developed traditions of the sister-churches and refusing to impose unnecessary burdens on them, this church would strive to be faithful to the gospel so that it could be a united force for good in the world. Congar's own sense of unity is expressed in the phrase "diversity in communion," which suggests that the one church is an organism living the life of the triune God, and that the diverse traditions within the one church are united in the life of faith and charity.

East Versus West

NOT ONLY DOES CONGAR OFFER general principles to guide us in our ecumenical efforts, but he also helps us understand the specific issues involved in the divisions among Christians. He has written perceptively, for example, on the historical causes of the split between the Roman Catholic and the Orthodox churches and has offered helpful suggestions on achieving reunion.

He points out that almost from the very beginning, the churches of the East and West tended to go in different directions. This tendency was intensified by political factors, such as Constantine's shift of the capital of the empire to Byzantium; by cultural trends, including the emphasis in the West on analysis and reason, while the East stressed synthesis and mysticism; and by ecclesiological differences, especially the West's insistence on starting with the universal church and papal primacy, while the East preferred beginning with autonomous local churches which together form the Body of Christ. Congar's full historical analysis makes it clear that the split between East and West did not occur simply over the famous *filoque* controversy, which was a theological dispute about the proper way to understand the relationship between the Holy Spirit and the Father and the Son. In addition, the mutual excommunications of 1054 appear not so much as the beginning of a schism, but as an abortive effort at reunion which failed to overcome divisions rooted in political disputes and cultural differences.

Congar, who had many contacts with Orthodox leaders and theologians, thinks that an understanding of the eastern concept of uncreated grace is the key to entering their spiritual world. In their way of thinking, the ultimately mysterious God communicates to us his very self, not merely a grace which he creates. The gift totally transforms or divinizes us. The process is completed in the Resurrection and celebrated especially in the feast of Easter, which illumines the whole cosmos and brings an optimistic and joyful sense to human existence. Orthodox liturgical celebrations, which embody and carry on a living tradition, highlight the mysterious character of the hidden God, as well as the nature of the church as a spiritual communion.

Congar said late in his life that after more than fifty years of careful study, he was convinced that at the sacramental level the East and West are the same church (*Diversity in Communion*, p. 73, ff.). They are simply complementary ways of living out the Christian identity. This implies, of course, that we in the West will find corrections and enrichment from dialogue and cooperation with our sister-churches in the East. For example, our tendencies toward rationalism, legalism, and secularism will surely be challenged by their mystical sense of the divinization of the whole world. Congar's extensive writings on the Catholic-Orthodox dialogue are a rich resource which could be tapped for years to come. This brief summary merely suggests the immense contribution he has made to this and other substantive ecumenical questions.

Patience and Prayer

YVES CONGAR INSTRUCTS US, not only as an ecumenical theologian, but as man of ecumenical virtue. He lived out and taught a spiritual ecumenism which emphasizes the need for prayer and inner conversion in the pursuit of Christian unity. In the midst of many hardships and intense criticism, he found a way to combine courage with loyalty, and activity with patience.

After teaching theology for eight years, Congar was drafted into the French army in 1939. One year later he was captured by the Germans, spending the next five years in various prison camps. Containment, however, could not quench his spirit. On numerous occasions he tried to escape, but was always apprehended. He adopted a militant anti-Nazi attitude and gave lectures in the camps opposing their ideology. During this time, he experienced an exhilarating sense of solidarity with other courageous prisoners, but he was also disillusioned with the anti-Catholic prejudice he discovered among ordinary Protestants. This whole experience taught him in a new way the importance of inner attitudes in pursuing

"Rahner thinks that in terms of dogma union is possible between the Protestants of the great churches and Rome. I would not disagree."

— Diversity and Communion

his ecumenical vocation. He found that he could not harden his heart against one group, the Nazis in this case, and remain as open and loving toward others as he was before.

Congar recognized the need for a "global attitude of peace, openness, and love" which could guide his thinking even when ecumenical dialogue demanded criticism and rejection of false views. He had learned what I would call the dialectical virtue of committed-openness, which roots us firmly in our tradition and thereby frees us to make careful and open-minded judgments about the truth claims of others.

Throughout his life, Congar stressed the need for inner conversion in pursuit of Christian unity. While individuals and churches further the cause by being more responsive to the call of Christ and the message of the Gospel, unity is fundamentally the gift of the Holy Spirit. Prayer, which is like the breathing of the soul in union with God, is effective because it attunes us to God's will. Thus we are transformed and become better instruments of the Spirit, who wills the unity of all. Prayer *for* our Protestant and Orthodox friends also makes us aware of the truth and goodness they possess. Prayer *with* them, as Congar himself experienced, banishes distrust and establishes a bond of communion. Prayer cannot replace doctrinal discussions, but it does create a less polemical and more congenial atmosphere for dialogue.

The annual Week of Prayer for Christian Unity (January 18-25), begun in

1908, had immense significance for Congar. Each year, beginning in 1936, he preached special sermons during this week officially devoted to prayer for the unity God wants by the means he wills. The ground-breaking conferences he gave in Paris during the Unity Week of 1936 formed the basis for his classic work *Divided Christendom*. In 1954, the ninth centenary of the split between the Eastern and the Western churches, he preached in the historical centers of Eastern Christianity, including Constantinople, Alexandria, and Jerusalem. For Congar, the Week of Prayer for Unity was always a special time of grace for the churches. These weeks sparked some of his finest contributions to the ecumenical movement and gave public expression to his conviction that prayer in common was essential in the process of Christian reunion.

Congar felt, too, that the virtue of active patience was crucial to his own ecumenical work. This "habit of the heart" is based on the two-fold conviction that in great matters delay is part of the maturation process and that the God in charge will ultimately accomplish his gracious design. In the saying of the apostle Paul that "patience breeds hope" (Romans 5:4), Congar saw the profound truth that genuine hope grows out of suffering and frustration. The cross is always the necessary condition of God's final victory.

Congar knew this kind of suffering firsthand, especially in his relationship with church leaders. In 1939, just a few years after the publication of *Divided Christendom*, he was called to Paris by the master general of the Dominican order and informed of serious difficulties with his book. From then until the time of Pope John XXIII and the vindication of his views at the Second Vatican Council, Congar was in constant trouble with reactionary forces in the Roman Curia. Sometimes the problems were intense. "From the beginning of 1947 to the end of 1956," he wrote, "I knew nothing from that quarter but an uninterrupted series of denunciations, warnings, restrictive or discriminatory measures, and mistrustful interventions" (*Dialogue Between Christians*, p. 34). As a result, he was forced to curtail his ecumenical activities, to leave his teaching position for a period of time, and to submit all of his writings to Rome.

Solvable in Principle

THUS THIS LOYAL, obedient, careful scholar knew the sufferings of the cross precisely because of his commitment to his ecumenical vocation. His active patience, however, fueled his hope by keeping him from growing bitter and by enabling him to perceive and appreciate the positive developments in the ecumenical movement. He could rejoice that many of his insights were enshrined in the Vatican II Decree on Ecumenism and that his labors had helped bring us to the point where, as Karl Rahner contends, all the theological differences among the main Christian churches are now solvable in principle. Despite these promising developments, he well understood the remaining obstacles to reunion and was able to continue his own efforts toward that goal. In sum, Congar, in his life and teaching, reminds us that prayer, openness, and active patience are always necessary in working for the Christian unity which eludes us on this earth but will finally be God's gift to us at the end time.

Yves Congar once said, "I have lived the drama of disunion and the promise of unity intensely in my heart and prayer" (*Dialogue Between Christians*, p. 20). He did so live, and in the process he has given us the immensely valuable gift of insight and inspiration for carrying on the struggle for Christian unity. If we could appropriate some of his ecumenical passion and virtue, we would be in a far better position to do our small but important part in revitalizing the ecumenical movement.

Discussion Questions

1. What is the story of your own participation in the ecumenical movement and how would you describe your current interest?

2. How did Congar's life experience prepare him for his ecumenical vocation?

3. What did Congar mean by "unity in diversity" and how did he apply it to the major ecumenical questions?

4. What shape and direction would ecumenism today take if we took Congar's teachings seriously?

Suggested Readings

Diversity and Communion (Twenty-Third Publications, 1982). A fine sampling of Congar's most mature thought on a wide range of ecumenical topics.

Divided Christendom: Principles of a Catholic Ecumenism (London: G. Bless, 1939). His influential classic work on ecumenism.

Dialogue Between Christians (Newman Press, 1964). The preface contains his autobiographical notes on the development of his ecumenical vocation.

I Believe in the Holy Spirit, 3 vol. (Seabury, 1983). An excellent example of Congar's ability to place current questions in an historical context.

CHAPTER 4

Hans Urs von Balthasar

a contemplative spirit

THE MODERN WORLD OFFERS severe challenges to those struggling to maintain a contemplative spirit which is receptive, integrated, and serene. Our fast-paced life, with its daily demands, leaves little time for quiet reflection. Our technological society, with its penchant for specialization, has impaired our ability to see life whole. Our success ethic, with its utilitarian goals, tends to diminish our appreciation of beauty.

Within the church, similar trends can undercut the contemplative aspect of Christian life. At times, liturgy is so concerned with forming community that it fails to create a reflective mood for worshipping God. Believers, passionate about peace and justice, are tempted to neglect private meditation and prayer. Efforts to explain and justify the faith are sometimes excessively rationalistic, thereby diminishing the beauty and integrity of the Christian message. In short, it is not easy to be a contemplative Christian in our world today.

The whole life project of the prolific Swiss Catholic theologian Hans Urs von Balthasar (1905-1988) constitutes a comprehensive and insightful response to this loss of the contemplative spirit in the modern world. Drawing on his vast knowledge of the Judeo-Christian tradition and Western culture, Balthasar has produced a grand and integrated synthesis of the Christian faith which directs our attention to the glory of the triune God manifested in Jesus Christ and reflected in the beauty of the world.

Moreover, this brilliant theologian, reflecting the depth and style of his own spiritual life, encourages us to contemplate the God revealed in this grand vision, to join ourselves in prayer with Jesus Christ, the definitive Word of God, and to be responsive to the promptings of the Holy Spirit living within us.

Fathers of the Church

LET US BEGIN our analysis of Balthasar's great theological synthesis by briefly examining his life, especially his encounters with great religious thinkers, past and present, who helped form his vision. Balthasar was born August 12, 1905, in Lucerne, Switzerland. His family had been involved in the cultural and political life of the country for generations. From his parents, he gained respect for learning and an appreciation for culture, including a love of music which led him to become an accomplished pianist. After studying in a Benedictine school in Switzerland and with the Jesuits in Austria, he entered the University of Zurich in 1923, where he studied German literature and philosophy. While doing his doctoral studies, he made a retreat based on the Spiritual Exercises of St. Ignatius, during which he felt a clear call to become a priest. In response, he entered the Society of Jesus soon after completing his doctorate in 1928. During his thirty-day Ignatian retreat, "the good hand of God" seized him, as he reported later, turning him away from the subjective emphasis on personal development fostered by his intellectual training, toward a more objective outlook based on the Christian belief that God takes the initiative by calling his people to discipleship. This deep religious experience was a decisive factor in grounding and shaping his theological project.

After the usual two-year novitiate, Balthasar studied philosophy for three years at Berchmanskollege, a Jesuit school outside Munich. This was followed by four years of theological studies at Lyons, France, where he encountered the great patristics scholar Henri de Lubac. He imparted to Balthasar an appreciation of the Fathers of the Church, those great thinkers such as Origen and Augustine whose contemplative reading of the Scriptures gave them an integral understanding of the Christian faith, centered on the redeeming love of God which is mediated to the whole world by the Word made Flesh. Throughout his long theological career, Balthasar remained faithful to this great vision of the Fathers.

Balthasar was ordained a priest in 1936, worked for a few years in Munich on the editorial staff of an influential Jesuit periodical and, in 1940, became a chaplain to students in Basel, Switzerland. This last move brought him into contact with Adrienne von Speyr, a Swiss physician who became a convert to Catholicism under his direction. In turn, Adrienne, a genuine mystic, shared at length with him her spiritual reflections, especially on the passion, death, and descent into hell of Christ. Through these extensive conversations, she exerted a tremendous influence on his subsequent writings, causing him to comment later that her work and his own were "two halves of a whole which, at center, has but one foundation." Together they became convinced that the Lord was calling them to found a secular institute which would enable lay people to live the life of the traditional vows in the context of their activities in the world. Since his Jesuit superiors disapproved of doing this within the

"Contemplation's object is God, and God is triune life. But as far as we are concerned, we only know of this triune life from the Son's incarnation. Consequently we must not abstract from the incarnation in our contemplation."

—Prayer

framework of the order, Balthasar, with great reluctance, left the Society in 1950 and founded the Community of St. John, in Basel, which he led and directed. From this base he poured himself into writing, editing, and publishing. In 1988, he was designated as a cardinal by Pope John Paul II, but died June 26, shortly before he was to be officially installed at the Vatican.

During his years in Basel, Balthasar had frequent contact with Karl Barth, the great Protestant neo-Orthodox theologian, who also exerted great influence on his theological development. With Barth, Balthasar insisted on both the transcendence of God who always takes the initiative in the divine-human relationship and the centrality of the crucified Christ who remains our savior and model. Balthasar's book, *The Theology of Karl Barth*, originally published in 1951, was considered by the great Protestant theologian to be one of the finest studies of his thought.

Balthasar's religious vision was also formed by his creative dialogues with the great thinkers from the past: the Eastern Fathers, especially Origen; medieval theologians, including Aquinas and Bonaventure; founders of religious orders, primarily Ignatius; and literary figures ranging from Dante to Hopkins.

Balthasar's brilliant rereading of these authors was grounded in his remarkable ability to capture the unique core, impulse, and dynamic direction of the thought of each of these dialogue partners.

Aesthetic Perspective

ENRICHED BY THESE dialogues with figures from the past and present, Balthasar began his own project "to render the Christian message in its unsurpassable greatness." In undertaking his task, Balthasar explicitly separated himself from his former collaborator Karl Rahner who, according to Balthasar, erred by seeking "to demonstrate how closely Christian truth conforms to the profoundest and boldest hopes and expectations of mankind." Balthasar was disappointed by such efforts to make the Christian message relevant for the contemporary world, including his own work, *The God Question and Modern Man*, originally published in 1956. Therefore he aligned himself with Louis Bouyer and others who "feel overwhelmed by the Word of God" which appears as "unmistakably unique," like a great work of art by Bach or Mozart. From

"Furthermore, at each instance of contemplation, the love of God . . . plays an utterly fresh, original and inimitable melody upon the instrument of Christ's life."

—Prayer

this perspective he was determined to present the Christian faith as a whole so that people today could contemplate its beauty and splendor.

Thus, in the late 1950s, a plan for a vast theological trilogy formed in his mind. Since he did not publish the first volume until 1961 when he was already fifty-six, he never expected to complete the project. However, blessed with good health and a long life, he was able to finish the 14th and final volume in the original German series shortly before he died at the age of eighty-two.

This brilliant synthesis is divided into three major parts, following the traditional scholastic teaching that being as a whole possesses the transcendental characteristics of beauty, goodness, and truth. The first part, comprised of seven volumes in the English translation, under the general title *The Glory of the*

Lord: A Theological Aesthetics, develops Christian theology from the often neglected perspective of the beautiful. Balthasar insists that this aesthetic perspective is the proper starting point, because it brings back the classical balance to theology by encouraging us to contemplate God's glory, objectively and definitively manifested in Christ, before beginning to discuss the ethical implications and the truth claims of the Christian faith. This first part of the trilogy, which constitutes Balthasar's most distinctive contribution, offers his clearest guidance for rediscovering a healthy contemplative spirit in the modern world.

In the second part, Balthasar proposes a theological dramatics which examines Christianity from the ethical perspective of the good, revealing us as participants in the great drama of salvation directed by the loving God. Finally, in the last part of the trilogy, Balthasar presents a theological logic which analyzes, from the logical perspective, the truth claims surrounding the appearance and action of God in history.

Even without mastering all the volumes in this immense work, it is possible to get a sense of Balthasar's distinctive aesthetic vision of Christian revelation which can encourage our contemplative response. He continually insists that we see and appreciate the Christian faith as a whole before beginning to analyze it. All aspects of Christian life—reading the Scriptures, participating in the liturgy, spreading love in the world, and reflecting theologically—should work together to sharpen our vision of the loving triune God manifested in Jesus Christ, the Word made Flesh.

The Glory of God

FOR BALTHASAR, God comes to us, primarily, not as the master of the truth or the redeemer offering all good gifts, but rather as the Glorious One, displaying and radiating the splendor of divine love. Glory is the most divine of God's attributes. The God of splendor took the initiative in creating and redeeming the world in order to manifest his glory. In the Bible, the theme of God's glory plays a central role, forming a backdrop against which other biblical teachings, such as creation and redemption, can be more clearly seen. The Hebrew Scriptures perceive the glory of Yahweh, in special phenomena such as the pillar of fire which led the Israelites in the Exodus and the brilliant luminous cloud described by the prophet Ezekiel (1:28). This glory of God visibly manifested in the world calls the people to a life of praise and worship.

While, according to Balthasar, the Hebrew understanding of glory became increasingly vague throughout their history, the Christian Scriptures recognized God's glory as definitively and concretely manifested in the human form of Jesus Christ. The form of Christ is uniquely attractive because in him a perfect balance and harmony exists between the infinite divine splendor and the human form manifesting it. Jesus is the most integrated of human beings because his whole being and purpose is to be a vehicle of divine grace and the epiphany of the Father's love. Through the life and death of the Word made Flesh, "the true God is heard, seen and touched." As a genuine man, Christ is "the perfection of creatureliness" and "the archetype" of fulfilled humanity. As the Word Incarnate, he radiates the glory of the Father and the light of the Holy Spirit. As the God-man, he is the inner norm of history and the unique source of ultimate meaning.

HEAVILY INFLUENCED BY THE NEW TESTAMENT theology of Paul and John, Balthasar puts great emphasis on the obedient death of Jesus Christ as the decisive revelation of God's glory. Jesus as a man of faith is totally obedient to the will of the Father and completely transparent to the radiance of the Spirit. He lives in perfect accord with the divine plan and gives absolute precedence to following the Father's direction and timetable rather than his own wishes and rhythms. Thus, his faithful obedience takes him to the decisive hour of the passion in which "the whole power of sin spends its fury on him." The descent of the Word into human existence is complete and total, carrying the Incarnate One into the finality of death. Jesus, "stripped by the cross of every power and initiative of his own," descends into hell to be in solidarity with those estranged from God. The divine condescension is completed as "eternal love descending into the uttermost darkness."

The eyes of faith, however, perceive that this descent into darkness issues in the ascent to glory. The Father raised the Son to life, bringing him back to himself so that together they might send the Holy Spirit into the church and the world. In contemplating the cross of Christ, the believer sees the divine splendor most clearly revealed. Good Friday and Holy Saturday make possible the joy of Easter and the illumination of Pentecost.

To contemplate the full mystery of the Word made Flesh is to perceive the beauty of the divine plan. Jesus Christ is the "concrete universal"—a particular historical person in whom the whole meaning of human history is summarized and fulfilled. The Word has been present from the beginning of creation, giving intelligible structure to the universe and gathering the whole of reality around the Father's redeeming love. The Incarnate Word, Jesus Christ, is "the way, the truth and the life." He is the absolute unique savior who is able to preserve, integrate, and fulfill all the truth, goodness, and beauty found in redeemed creation. Reflection on the concrete and universal character of the Word of God reminds us that the whole world was created and redeemed to manifest the glory of the Father and to reflect the radiance of the Spirit.

The Spirit establishes an intrinsic bonding between Christ and the church. The church is a community, or network of individuals, empowered by the Spirit to put on the mind of Christ by living as his disciples. Through the action of the Spirit, the various relationships of the historical Jesus with his followers are continued and extended to the church, constituting her life and structure. The most significant disciple relationship is represented by Mary, the Mother

"Unavoidably, the life of contemplation is an every-day life, a life of fidelity in small matters, small services rendered in the spirit and warmth of love which lightens every burden."

—Prayer

of Jesus, who, in her total receptivity and openness, is the "principal and exemplar of the response of the entire church." In other words, the church necessarily has a "Marian structure," which means that all the members are called and empowered by the Spirit to live in a loving and receptive relationship to Christ as did Mary. The church also reflects and makes available the specific characteristics of other disciples, such as the servant leadership of Peter and the tender love of John.

Balthasar's understanding of the relationship between Christ and the church is reflected in his two favorite biblical images, the Body of Christ, which suggests that the church is identified with the Lord as his extension and manifestation, and the Bride of Christ, which indicates that it is the recipient of the Lord's love and care. United with the head and treasured by the Bridegroom, the church has the task of radiating the divine glory and splendor in the world.

In the sharing of the Eucharistic meal, Christians celebrate this intimate union of Christ and the church, which is called to manifest the beauty of his form. As a memorial meal, the Eucharist recalls the self-surrender of Jesus at the Last Supper, which issued in the birth of the church and continues to constitute the community of faith. Furthermore, in the Eucharist, the risen Christ is really present as promise of the eternal banquet of joy and the final revelation of the radiant glory of the triune God.

Thus we see that Balthasar's theological aesthetics, which examines the form of God's appearances, is at once comprehensive and integrated, universal and particular, trinitarian and Christocentric. He creates a sense of symmetry by balancing the descent of the Incarnate Word to the darkness of hell with the ascent of the whole of creation to the light of heaven. In this grand and beautiful vision, the glory of God is manifested to us in the Incarnate Word, radiated to the world by the church and celebrated in the Eucharist by Christians. By examining Christian revelation from the aesthetic perspective, Balthasar hopes to attract our gaze, stimulate our imagination and invite our contemplation.

The Contemplative Spirit

IN PURSUING THIS GOAL, Balthasar offers us helpful guidance in developing a more contemplative spirit. His emphasis is on the nature and foundation of the contemplative spirit, as well as the attitudes needed to develop it.

Individuals with a naturally contemplative spirit are able to maintain a non-controlling openness to reality and its mysterious depths. Their reflective spirit enables them to appreciate beauty and to immerse themselves without reserve in aesthetic experiences. Drawing on their inner resources, they manifest a broad but integrated view of life while preserving an inner peace and an attentive gaze.

The contemplative spirit takes on a distinctive form when shaped by the Christian faith. Through the initiating power of grace, Christian contemplatives are drawn to gaze on the glory of the Father, to put on the mind and form of Christ, and to reflect the light of the Holy Spirit. This large trinitarian perspective helps Christians to locate themselves within the great drama of salvation. Enlightened by meditation on the Word made Flesh, believers are able to perceive the divine manifested in the human and the mystery revealed in the ordinary, without obliterating or questioning the value of the finite world. Guided by the Holy Spirit, Christians are attuned to the splendor of divine revelation and the beauty of the world. As contemplatives advance in the spiritual life, they gain a deeper understanding of what it means to perceive the divine beauty while experiencing the enrapturing power of the glory of the Lord. Balthasar's description of the contemplative life is not intended for an elite few but, rather, serves as a reminder that developing a contemplative spirit is the task of all Christians.

Authentic faith which gazes steadfastly on the form of Christ is the essential foundation for a genuine contemplative spirit. Guided by the gift of faith, believers entrust themselves to God, thereby gaining a deeper understanding of themselves, as well as the divine goodness, truth, and beauty. Human beings can be understood properly only from the perspective of faith because our nature is like clay in the hands of the divine potter. Thus, we are "hearers of the

---

"Our situation today shows that beauty demands for itself at least as much courage and decision as do truth and goodness, and she will not allow herself to be separated and banned from her two sisters without taking them along with herself in an act of mysterious vengence."
—The Glory of the Lord

Word" who can rise to our full dignity only by listening carefully and responding faithfully to the divine summons. We are made in the image of God and can only achieve our perfection by contemplating the divine splendor radiating in our minds and hearts. Since God has created us as partners in a dialogue, we can fulfill our purpose only by cooperating with divine grace in building and spreading the kingdom in the world.

The perspective of faith also reveals a loving God who takes the initiative in approaching us, while always remaining the transcendent one. Believers do not require proof of God's existence nor justifications for the divine plan. On the contrary, the divine splendor mediated by Christ provides its own proof and justification. Like a great work of art, the glory of the Lord cannot be controlled or categorized, but must be accepted on its own terms. Jesus Christ, "God's greatest work of art," is the primary manifestation of the always mysterious divine splendor. Therefore, if we are to develop a more contemplative spirit, we must be attuned through faith to the beauty of the form of Christ, manifested in his life and teaching and especially in his death and Resurrection.

As Balthasar makes clear in his classic work *Prayer* (Ignatius Press, 1986, new translation), contemplative prayer is the essential means for all Christians to be properly attuned to the splendor of the Lord. In prayer, Christians should first listen to God's word spoken through Christ and reflected in the Scriptures, and then respond as one would in a simple conversation. Influenced by the Ignatian method, Balthasar suggests that we place ourselves imaginatively in particular biblical scenes. In this way, we can have the same kind of "immediacy of communication" with Christ as did the disciples. Contemplation is not just hearing the Word, but also gazing on the splendor of God manifested in Christ. Mary, the Mother of Jesus, is the model for all Christian contemplatives, because her gaze was unswervingly directed to the Word, not as something external, but as the deepest mystery of her own being. She heard the Word and responded with total obedience. For us as well, the Word made Flesh is the access to the Father and, therefore, the key to the contemplative spirit.

Loving the World

JESUS CHRIST BRINGS THE RICHES OF HEAVEN down to earth so that we can come to God, not by devaluing the world, but by loving it properly. Balthasar maintains that the Eastern methods of meditation are essentially world-denying because they attempt to surmount all images and concepts in a search for the infinite. Christian meditation, on the contrary, is not abstract, but concrete. It approaches the infinite through the finite. It centers on the definitive form of Christ who reveals the unfathomable riches of the mysterious God. The purpose of Christian meditation is not only personal perfection, but also greater involvement in spreading the kingdom in the world. Finally, genuine Christian meditation is never merely an isolated activity, but is always a participation in the prayer of the whole church, which listens and responds to the Word.

For Balthasar, contemplation is the link between the worship of God in the church and the work of human beings to realize the kingdom on earth. We need a rich private prayer life which attunes us to the glory of the Lord in order to bring the proper reverence to the liturgy. Balthasar insists that the primary purpose of liturgy is not to build community or to gain personal benefit, but rather to contemplate and worship the transcendent God. If we have learned to pray constantly by cultivating a receptive spirit, then our liturgical participation will be more contemplative.

Our periods of private contemplative prayer also prepare us to participate in Christ's mission to redeem the world. When we truly perceive the glory of God, we recognize, at the same time, our call to be engaged in the cause of God. Commenting from another perspective, Balthasar asserts that "whoever desires greater action needs better contemplation." Christians imbued with the contemplative spirit are active in the world, but not totally absorbed by it. They do not renounce the things of this earth but, rather, struggle to love them properly, because in and through them God manifests his glory.

For Balthasar, love of the world and the search for its truth must be founded on an appreciation of its beauty. Contemplatives are able to see the divine splendor radiating in the harmony and symmetry of nature and the products of the human spirit. Formed by meditation and prayer, they are attuned to the eternal mystery, manifested in the tension and the power of earthly realities. Our contemplative spirit is nourished by encounters with beauty, which draw us out of ourselves and enable us to see reality, whole and integrated. Created beauty nourishes our spirit because it always reflects the glory of the Lord.

Meditative Pointers

IN OUR QUEST FOR A MORE CONTEMPLATIVE SPIRIT, Balthasar offers some practical and pointed advice. Cultivate the art of listening to the God who speaks to us through the Word which echoes in the church and the world. Use imaginative meditation techniques to get in touch with the Incarnate Christ as he appeared on this earth. Foster a contemplative spirit in liturgical celebrations. Be confident that God is attentive to prayers and responds to genuine needs. Do not get bogged down in systems and techniques, but keep a steady gaze on the glory of the Lord. Imitate the contemplative spirit of Mary. Do not simply contemplate the divine truth but live it out. Cultivate an attitude of habitual prayer by being alert in mind and heart to the presence of the Lord. Read the Scriptures with an open heart and not a critical mind. Be supple and pliable in the hands of God like clay in the hands of the potter. Consider contemplation as an end in itself and not as a means to even laudable goals.

Remember that God has already placed us in his presence even before we seek him. Do not seek new thoughts or emotional experiences in prayer, but simply rest in the presence of the Lord. Never aim at carrying out a prescribed program of prayer, nor rigidly adhere to a particular pattern. Expect dry periods and continue to pursue the life of prayer with serenity and joy. Finally, maintain a sense of awe and wonder before the glory of the triune God, revealed through Jesus Christ, the Word made Flesh.

Balthasar's vast and often original writings have provoked substantial criticism. Biblical scholars have chided him for his uncritical use of the Scriptures which ignores the results of modern biblical criticism. Some theologians have attacked his theology of grace, claiming that it still leaves a dichotomy between the natural and supernatural orders. Others have criticized him for failing to recognize the intrinsic value and abiding significance of the Eastern religious traditions. Liberals have expressed displeasure over his opposition to optional celibacy and the ordination of women as well as the influence he exerted on his friend Cardinal Ratzinger. Finally, critics have pointed out that his presuppositions prevented him from engaging many important questions of the day and blinded him to the valid insights found in contemporary schools of thought, both religious and secular.

Clearly, Balthasar's enduring legacy is found in his grand and original synthesis of Christian revelation. His theological aesthetics, which centers on the glory of God and the importance of contemplative prayer, functions as a great corrective to the fragmented and frenzied character of contemporary life. His vast writings are a rich resource for anyone interested in developing a more contemplative spirit. As his work becomes more accessible, Hans Urs von Balthasar will be increasingly recognized as a major figure in 20th-century theology.

Discussion Questions

1. What challenges do you face in trying to maintain a contemplative spirit?

2. Do you see connections between Balthasar's theology, his Ignatian retreat experience and his relationship with Adrienne von Speyr?

3. How would you describe the distinctive slant on Christian faith which flows from Balthasar's emphasis on the glory of the Lord manifested in Christ and the beauties of the world?

4. Which of Balthasar's practical suggestions would help you most in developing a deeper contemplative spirit?

Suggested Readings

Prayer (Ignatius Press, 1986). A readable classic work on prayer which draws on his major theological themes.

The Glory of the Lord: A Theological Aesthetics, three vol. (Ignatius Press, 1982-1986). The first volumes of his multivolume masterwork; often difficult reading but filled with stimulating inights suggested by his distinctive perspective.

Balthasar Reader, edited by Medard Kehl and Werner Löser (Crossroad, 1982). A fine selection of Balthasar's writings with a very helpful introduction to his thoughts by Medard Kehl.

The Analogy of Beauty, edited by John Riches (T & T Clark). A wide-ranging collection of essays by scholars who examine the meaning of Balthasar's major ideas.

CHAPTER 5

Edward Schillebeeckx
deepening our relationship with jesus

"WHO DO YOU SAY THAT I AM?" This question, originally posed by Jesus to his disciples, continues to challenge us today. It urges us toward a radical examination of the role Jesus Christ plays in our lives. Is our faith nourished by the stories of the historical Jesus recounted in the Gospels? Are we satisfied with the images of Christ which currently shape our religious sensibilities and guide our everyday behavior? Is our quest for meaning in life illuminated by the life and message of Jesus of Nazareth? Does our faith in Christ make us more open-minded or does it lead to exclusive attitudes? Is Jesus Christ a decisive influence on all aspects of our lives? To ponder these questions with openness and honesty is to recognize with greater clarity the need to deepen our relationship to Jesus Christ.

In his mature years as a theologian, Edward Schillebeeckx has written insightfully on these questions, including two massive volumes, *Jesus: An Experiment in Christology* (Seabury, 1979) and *Christ: The Experience of Jesus as Lord* (Seabury, 1980). He came to this task well-prepared by a life of Christian commitment and a distinguished career as a theologian.

Born in 1914 and nurtured in a large, stable Catholic family, Schillebeeckx joined the Dominican order and in 1941 was ordained a priest. His whole life as a priest has been devoted to serving God through his work as a theologian. After completing his doctoral studies on the sacraments under M.D. Chenu, a leading representative of the new theology, he occupied teaching posts at Louvain and at Nijmegan in Holland, where he taught from 1958 until his retirement in 1983. Along the way, he made important contributions to the work of the Second Vatican Council, lectured around the world, helped found the international theological journal *Concilium*, and survived three separate investigations of his theology by the Roman Curia. Despite health problems, he continues to address the controversial questions of the day and plans to write the third volume of his trilogy on Christology.

The writings of Schillebeeckx are diverse in subject matter and perspective. An early work, *Christ the Sacrament of the Encounter with God*, for example, uses both Thomistic and existential categories to place the sacraments in a personal context, while *God the Future of Man* employs modern sociological analyses to critique the secularization process in contemporary society. In general, his theology manifests the great interest in historical development which he learned from Chenu, as well as the passionate concern for relating the gospel to concrete human experience which has dominated his own personal life. He did not develop his own distinct philosophical system, but borrowed elements from Thomism, existentialism, linguistic analysis, and the Frankfurt school of social criticism in order to frame his theological responses to a complex and changing world. As his thought matured, he became more concerned with the institutional problems of injustice and oppression, and at the same time, more aware of the liberating power of Christian faith. The citation accompanying the prestigious Erasmus prize, which he received in 1982 for his contributions to European culture, termed his theology "transconfessional" in recognition of his ecumenical interests and his concern for the whole of the diverse Christian tradition.

His books on Christology, which manifest these concerns, were written so that people struggling with the problems of faith could better understand the meaning of commitment to Jesus Christ, who continues to liberate us today. From the great wealth of material in these books, let us explore three general ways that this outstanding Dominican theologian can help us deepen our relationship with Jesus Christ.

The Historical Jesus

SCHILLEBEECKX MAKES JESUS CHRIST more accessible to us today. Through prodigious research, he gathered and organized a truly amazing amount of biblical and theological scholarship which sheds light on the historical Jesus and his impact on the early Christian community. On the much-debated question of the relationship between the Jesus of history and the Christ of faith, Schillebeeckx avoids the extremes of both those who uncritically consider the Gospels to be objective biographies of Jesus and those who contend we can know practically nothing about the historical Jesus who stands behind the Gospels. He was convinced that contemporary exegesis could organically link the Christ proclaimed by the early Christians and the Jesus who inspired the proclamation.

Although the gospels were written by the second and third generation Christians who were neither eyewitnesses nor greatly concerned with objective reporting, they still provide us with a substantially correct picture of Jesus of Nazareth. Through studies of the intent of the gospel authors, the editorial process they used, the development of their material, and the consistency of the various

"Jesus' light burns in this world only with the oil of our lives, in quiet particular circumstances, in which we can emanate liberating life or dim or even quench this light, so that the world disappears in the clouds."

— Christ: The Experience of Jesus as Lord

traditions they employed, biblical scholars have recovered for us a faithful portrait of the life and message of Jesus. In order to trust persons as well as learn from them, we need substantial, though not exhaustive, information about them. Schillebeeckx helps give us confidence that in the Scriptures we have a solid basis for committing our lives to Jesus Christ, even though such personal dedication will always exceed the justification produced by logical arguments.

We know that Jesus was a Jew born into a nation suffering under Roman occupation. This oppressive condition produced various groups, including the Sadducees, who collaborated with the Romans, and the Zealots, who wanted to overthrow them by force. The occupation also fueled the expectation among many Jews that God would soon intervene decisively on their behalf, bringing history to a dramatic close.

After growing up in Nazareth, Jesus began his public life by participating in the baptism administered by John in the Jordan River. Through this symbolic act, which affirmed his identification with John's call for Israel to repent, Jesus launched his own mission. His preaching linked the call for repentance to the imminent coming of the kingdom or reign of God. Through his challenging parables, Jesus elucidated the meaning of the kingdom by suggesting radically new ways of living in accord with God's will and calling for a conversion of heart. The Beatitudes, proclaimed by Jesus, gave hope to the suffering and called for all to live out the ideals of the kingdom. The historical Jesus clearly taught the message of universal love and hope. The human quest for salvation is really God's cause as well.

Jesus not only proclaimed the kingdom, but he lived out its ideals in his own life. In him, it is clear that God is committed to the well-being of all people. Both friends and foes considered Jesus to be a miracle worker. Though he refused to work miracles for his own benefit, he did reach out and cure the sick, manifesting the presence of the saving power of God as well as his personal desire to alleviate suffering. He regularly associated with sinners and ate meals with outcasts, thus breaking down the barriers separating people and proclaiming, in practice, that God's love excludes no one. He gathered special followers, taught them the secrets of the kingdom, and sent them out to proclaim to others the coming of the reign of God.

FOR JESUS, THE JEWISH LAW was not an absolute in itself but a gift from God, which should lead people beyond legalistic observance to generous acts of love. His prophetic act of cleansing the temple in Jerusalem exemplified this general attitude and, in turn, produced both the admiration of the common people and the enmity of their religious leaders. Through his preaching, miracles, table fellowship, and attitude toward the law, Jesus acted as a liberator for people who suffered both from a lack of love and a restricted image of God.

The "Abba experience," according to Schillebeeckx, formed the core of Jesus' religious life. In other words, Jesus was sustained and nourished by an immediate and intense awareness of the presence of a loving and liberating God. This led him to address God in a totally unprecedented and very familiar fashion as "Abba," which best translates as "Papa" or "Daddy." This suggests that Jesus placed his center, not in himself, but in God, who paradoxically formed the very core of his being. In contrast to the exclusive tendencies in his culture, Jesus extended his intimate, familiar relationship with God to all people. The special prayer, which he taught to his disciples, not only reflects this outlook, but serves as a summary of his teachings.

Despite the increasing threat to his life from the religious and political establishment, Jesus decided, freely and with great trust, to go to Jerusalem. After his arrival he celebrated a last supper with his close friends. During this meal he spoke of his impending death as a self-giving which would bring salvation for others. In the story of the agony in the garden, we glimpse his great inner conflict, which was created by the realization that his mission to establish the kingdom would be cut short by his impending death. His perceptions were accurate. He was soon apprehended and brought before the Jewish Sanhedrin. Since they could not reach a verdict demanding the death sentence, they handed him over to the Roman authorities who crucified him as a political revolutionary.

His disciples, who failed to support him at this crucial time, were totally devastated by his death. Nevertheless, in a truly remarkable turnabout, they quickly regrouped and took up again the cause of Jesus. They located their new-found courage in Jesus himself, who had been raised to life by God and continued to support them as he had promised.

Although it is possible to dispute various elements of Schillebeeckx's detailed reconstruction of the life and teachings of Jesus, he has nonetheless done an amazing job of synthesizing the best of contemporary biblical scholarship and, in the process, has provided sincere searchers with a compelling and attractive portrayal of Jesus and his manner of life.

The Experience of Discipleship

SCHILLEBEECKX ALSO HELPS US appreciate the decisive impact which Jesus had on his disciples and can have on us today. Through a carefully calculated methodology, he relates the dynamics of our experience to that of the first disciples as interpreted by the New Testament. We can believe in Christ today only if the stories of faith in the New Testament resonate with our personal stories. We need to probe the experience of the first disciples in order to understand better our own relationship to Christ. In this way we may have our own limited version of the "Emmaus experience," which inflames the heart and reveals the risen Lord.

In the Gospels, we meet first-century Jewish people fascinated by an itinerant preacher from Nazareth who speaks with unusual authority. They stick with him and become his disciples. His message and way of life challenge their ordinary ways of thinking and eventually give new meaning to their lives. They become more confident, more convinced of God's love, and more compassionate toward others. They are liberated from their narrow notion of God and from their superficial approaches to life. None of this is merely their own doing.

It is a free gift. They feel as though they were reborn by the power of God and compelled by the Spirit to share this gift with others.

Jesus made a decisive impact on these people. He impressed them as a prophet and aroused their hopes that he might be the long-awaited final prophet. His precise identity was not entirely clear, but his wisdom and power were evident. After his death and resurrection, they came to believe firmly that he was, indeed, what he had claimed: the final prophet and the absolute savior. It was proper to describe him in images borrowed from the Hebrew scriptures as the Messenger of God, the Son of Man, the Son of David, the Kingly Lord, and the Son of God. This man was worthy of complete trust because he was from God and for all the people. Thus, the disciples were able to bet their lives on Jesus as the risen Lord.

Christians claim that Jesus Christ has universal significance. This individual, who transformed the lives of first-century Jews, can do the same for all people. This healer, who cured a few of the sick people in his own country, is the absolute savior of all human beings. This teacher, who never left his own land, has a universal message for all cultures. This man, who died on a cross as a criminal, empowers individuals and groups of all times and places to take hold of their own lives. Christians throughout the centuries have responded to the paradoxical claim that the universal love of the inexhaustible God has appeared definitively in a particular Jewish man. These believers also bet their lives on Jesus Christ, and thus come to know his saving power in a deeper way.

The Nature of the Christ

SOMETHING ABOUT THIS MAN from Nazareth prompts and justifies this amazing claim of universal salvific significance. Jesus Christ is the parable of God and the paradigm of humanity. In his story, we see the story of God's love for all people. He is the human face of God's mysterious care for us. He is God's unequivocal affirmation of all human beings. In him, we come to know that God is "mindful of humanity." Jesus is one with God in will and action. He identifies himself completely with God in his mission, message, and obedient death. In turn, God totally identifies himself with Jesus in his Resurrection.

Belief in Jesus is like a searchlight which illumines all aspects of human existence. He reminds us that we are all worthwhile and that our good efforts have ultimate meaning. In his life, we recognize the liberating power of love. He is the best that the human race has produced, and his words and deeds reveal to us something of our own untapped potential. He is like us in all things except sin, and so we can identify with him. In Jesus, we find a compelling example of obedient fidelity to God and committed service to others.

Throughout the centuries, Christians have struggled to articulate this mysterious uniqueness of Jesus. The Fathers of the church translated the functional explanations of Jesus in the New Testament into ontological explanations of his very being. He is true God and true man: one person with two natures, divine and human. The Council of Nicaea in 325 affirmed his co-essential being with the Father, and in 451 the Council of Chalcedon insisted on his

"True, well-meaning attempts are often made to explain Jesus as a good and perfect man—the 'second Adam'—but we shall never recognize him in his truly human identity if we eliminate from this life of Jesus his quite special, unique relationship to God which we find almost impossible to define. For it is precisely in this relationship that we have the origin, the meaning and the force of his message and his parables, his beatitudes and his liberating way of life."

— Christ: The Experience of Jesus as Lord

true humanity. After these councils, Christians tended to understand Christ primarily in terms of John's Gospel, which emphasized his divine kingship.

Today Schillebeeckx and other theologians are responding to contemporary experience by recovering alternative New Testament images of Christ. Although the dominant models are changing, the Christian community continues to find its enlightenment in the teachings of Jesus and its inner strength in the risen Christ. Christians of all times and places are obliged to define their lives and find their ultimate meaning in reference to Jesus, the Christ. Through his scholarly writings, Schillebeeckx has clarified for us the simple but decisive truth that God has saved us in and through Jesus Christ. In this brilliant reconstruction we can discern in a fresh way the continuing call to commit ourselves to Christ as did the early disciples.

Liberation and Salvation

FINALLY, SCHILLEBEECKX PROVIDES us with a contemporary reinterpretation of salvation that relates the liberating activity of Jesus Christ to our experience of suffering (cf. *Christ* pp. 646-893). With a deep compassion for personal suffering and penetrating insights into societal oppression, he reconstructs the gospel picture of Jesus into a contemporary model of Christ the liberator. In the story of Jesus, it is clear that God is on our side in the struggle against human misery. The spirit of the risen Christ empowers us today to challenge and overcome the structures which oppress individuals and groups.

Suffering is a constant in human history; so is the struggle to overcome it. At the personal level, we must contend with disappointments in love, deterioration of health, guilt because of sin, and anxiety over death. Our very finitude as creatures brings us pain, since our deepest longings always exceed our actual capabilities. Such deep "contrast experiences" are encountered whenever we sense the gap between our perceived ideals and the harsh realities of life. Societal oppression and cultural deprivation also produce suffering. Wars, exploitation, discrimination, illiteracy, and a host of other social ills multiply the inevitable misery built into human existence.

History has always been written from the viewpoint of the powerful and the successful. Borrowing insights from Jürgen Habermas and other members of the Frankfurt school of social criticism, Schillebeeckx became convinced of the importance of taking seriously the stories of those in history who suffered from oppression and lived on the margins. In order to gain a more accurate picture of the human condition, it is vital to keep alive the memory of the oppressed.

Some suffering enriches humanity and brings greater maturity and wisdom to individuals. A man who has suffered through the pain of guilt for his sins, for example, may become less self-righteous and more tolerant of the weaknesses of others. Individuals who dedicate themselves to a cause or work diligently in the service of others often experience suffering as a by-product of their commitments. On the other hand, human beings also experience an excess of suffering which does not enhance life but diminishes it. The Holocaust and massive starvation in Africa are examples of monstrous evils which defy rational explanations and tidy theories of evil. Such suffering is absurd and remains mysterious to us. The proper human response is to offer resistance and to stave off any future occurrences. We must steadfastly refuse to grant such evil the right to exist on an equal basis with the good.

Christianity teaches that the human effort to overcome suffering in our world is absolutely necessary, but that success will always remain partial and incomplete. The gospel calls us to work passionately for human liberation while remembering that total and universal salvation is a gift from God which transcends our history.

"His message and his public claim, finally his person itself, were indeed rejected by our world. According to all the rules prevailing at the time, he was executed. Nevertheless, even in his dying Jesus was not desperately concerned with his own identity and thus with self-survival."
— Christ: The Experience of Jesus as Lord

The persistence of human misery despite our best efforts raises the question of ultimate meaning. Given the fact of suffering and death, can we still believe that life is trustworthy and that God does not abandon us? Today our greater awareness of both the scope and the intractability of human misery has directed our longing for salvation toward health, wholeness and liberation.

With this analysis in mind, we can examine the way Schillebeeckx interprets the life, death, and Resurrection of Jesus. During his public ministry, Jesus went about doing good, especially by curing the sick and casting out demons. In this way, he provided concrete examples of the nature and the meaning of the reign of God. By his limited response to the suffering in his immediate surroundings, Jesus anticipated the complete and universal salvation which God would accomplish in the future. Jesus moved beyond the traditional assumptions of his time when he refused to link specific suffering with particular sins. The illness of the man born blind, for example, could not be blamed on his sins or those of his parents (John 9:3). Even though Jesus offers no satisfactory theoretical explanation, his cure of the blind man proclaims that God can overcome the limitations built into human creaturehood.

Power and Hope for All

AS WE HAVE SEEN, Jesus had an astonishingly positive impact on many people he encountered. They were transformed, liberated, and made whole. On the other hand, his good works drew the wrath of those who felt threatened by him and his message. His easy association with outcasts and his authoritative teaching challenged the position and style of the established leaders.

Thus we see that his death was not an accident or even a tragic mistake, but the predictable result of his provocative lifestyle. In other words, he died because he was absolutely faithful to the cause of liberation which he championed. Jesus did not seek death, though he died freely. Because he set no limits on his care for others and his resistance to suffering, he became for the powerful a stumbling block which had to be eliminated. Schillebeeckx insists that we can understand the saving significance of the death of Jesus only if we link the cross with his public ministry, which was devoted to liberating people from all kinds of suffering.

Though executed as a criminal, and apparently deprived of his opportunity to establish the kingdom, Jesus was raised to life by the Father whom he trusted even in the darkest moments. The Resurrection is an endorsement of his person, his liberating message, and his practical efforts on behalf of the kingdom. It confirms that God never abandoned Jesus, but remained with him throughout his whole life. Through the Resurrection, Jesus became life-giving Spirit, present as a power and hope for all people.

Moreover, the Resurrection reveals God as the "champion of the good," the loving warrior who fights against evil on our behalf. The great God transforms all the suffering in the world and brings history to a successful conclusion. God does not permit evil as a test, nor does he will the death of sinners. The mystery addressed by Jesus as "Abba" is totally trustworthy and diametrically opposed to all suffering. The Resurrection of Jesus is the promise that, at the end of time, human misery will be abolished and we will all share in the final victory.

The good news is that the risen Christ has the power to liberate us in the midst of suffering from undue anxiety and to strengthen us for the inevitable struggles. Faith in Christ brings a sense of personal integration and reconciles us with God and others. We can be people of hope because we share in Christ's victory. In him we know that suffering does not have the final word. Salvation has been achieved, and God's gift of universal healing and integration will triumph.

The Resurrection of Christ empowers us to liberate others and transform suffering. We are called to struggle intelligently and cooperatively against oppressive structures and unjust institutions. Our task is not to assign blame,

---

"Has something happened with him of such a kind that—as a result—something special can happen to us too? Only if something like this does in fact happen to us, so many years after Jesus' departure, can we make clear anything of the identity of Jesus to the world."

— Christ: The Experience of Jesus as Lord

---

but to be as compassionate as Jesus, who befriended the outcasts and healed the sick. Salvation as liberation and healing is always a gift from God which will be totally realized only beyond human history. This truth, far from discouraging us, frees us to cooperate with God in the task of liberation without resentment or despair. God's love not only triumphs in the long run, but also sustains us now.

Critics have attacked various elements of Schillebeeckx's Christology (for example his use of conversion language to interpret the reality of the Resurrection), and many details in his massive volumes are open to debate. On the whole, however, exegetes and theologians have reviewed his books favorably, marvelling at the scope and depth of his work.

Edward Schillebeeckx has performed an extremely valuable service by presenting a credible and attractive image of Jesus Christ the compassionate liberator, an image which enables us to relate the message of salvation to our real longing for integration and justice. Thus, he invites us to ponder anew the crucial question 'Who do you say that I am?' and in the process to deepen our relationship with Jesus Christ.

Discussion Questions

1. What role does Jesus Christ play in your life today?

2. Do you detect ways in which the scholarly life pursued so diligently by Schillebeeckx is related to his understanding of Christ?

3. What distinctive perspectives on Jesus and his significance emerge from the writings of Schillebeeckx?

4. How can the Christology of Schillebeeckx help deepen your own relationship to Jesus Christ?

Suggested Readings

The Schillebeeckx Reader, edited by Robert Schreiter (Crossroad, 1984). An excellent way to begin studying Schillebeeckx because it contains a broad sampling of his writings with a helpful introduction by the editor which traces the development of his thought.

Jesus: An Experiment in Christology (Seabury, 1979). A large, scholarly volume (767 pages) which examines the historical Jesus as seen through the witness of the early disciples.

Christ: The Experience of Jesus as Lord (Seabury, 1980). An even larger book (925 pages) which pulls together an immense amount of scholarship to elucidate the experience of saving grace in the New Testament and the practical meaning of salvation in today's world.

The Interim Report (Crossroad, 1980). A shorter, more readable summary of the presuppositions and major ideas of his two large books, *Jesus* and *Christ*, as well as his responses to the objections to his Christology.

CHAPTER 6

John Macquarrie
probing human existence

THE TRADITIONAL ADVICE "Know thyself" strikes a responsive chord in many of us today. We yearn for a deeper self-awareness and a better understanding of what makes us and others tick. The path to greater self-knowledge, however, is neither clear nor smooth. Human existence is complex and our perceptions can be distorted by illusions and rationalizations. Fundamental mistakes in method and approach can restrict our self-awareness and limit our understanding of human nature. Some religiously-oriented persons, for example, ignore helpful data supplied by common sense and the empirical sciences, thereby producing utopian interpretations of human existence. Others, captivated by the scientific method, discount personal experience and religious wisdom, thereby reducing human beings to objects or sophisticated machines. Furthermore, in our culture, the quest for self-knowledge often becomes a private search for self-fulfillment, which ignores both the communal dimension of human existence and traditional teachings about human nature. Without guidance, self-understanding is prone to distortions and illusions. Without dialogue, it is difficult to discern the general characteristic of human nature and the recurring patterns in human existence. In short, we treasure self-knowledge, but it remains elusive and difficult to attain.

In my own efforts to probe the mystery dimension of human existence, I was fortunate to encounter a magnificent teacher, who by virtue of temperament and scholarship, provided a sharp contrast to the narrow superficiality which often threatens the quest for self-knowledge today. I first met the highly respected Anglican theologian John Macquarrie, in 1967 when he taught a course on existentialist thinkers at Union Theological Seminary in New York. Professor Macquarrie's vast knowledge of the Western intellectual tradition, especially the modern period, impressed me immediately, as did his ability to discern the strengths and weaknesses of individual thinkers. His book *Twentieth Century Religious Thought* (Harper & Row, 1963), which summarizes the essential thoughts of a vast array of theologians and philosophers, soon became an important resource for me in exploring the major trends in contemporary theology as well as the contributions of individual authors.

"A Theological Pilgrimage"

IN 1975, WHEN I DECIDED to do a doctoral dissertation on the thought of the German Jesuit Karl Rahner, I turned to John Macquarrie as the best possible person to supervise my project. By then he had moved from Union Theological Seminary, where he taught systematic theology from 1962 to 1970, to the University of Oxford, where he served as Lady Margaret Professor of Divinity, the prestigious post he held until his retirement in 1986. Working on my dissertation under Macquarrie's supervision gave me an appreciation of him as a person as well as an even greater respect for his scholarly contributions. His deep Christian faith, his great love for his wife Jenny and their three children, as well as his kindness and sensitivity, spoke to my heart. His profound grasp of contemporary philosophy and theology, which included a genuine appreciation for the contributions of Karl Rahner, helped me establish a broad context for my project. Most of all, he allowed me freedom to write my dissertation without imposing his structure on it—surely one of the best gifts a supervisor can offer.

Over the years, I have learned more about what Macquarrie calls his "theological pilgrimage." Some revealing personal conversations were especially helpful for understanding the way his faith journey has influenced his fundamental perceptions of human existence. Born in 1919 near Glasgow, Scotland, he grew up in a Presbyterian family (his father was an elder in the church) and was immersed in a Calvinistic environment with its moralistic atmosphere and pessimistic notions of human nature. Much of his early education reinforced these notions, including his theological studies (B.D., University of Glasgow, 1943), which included large doses of John Calvin and his twentieth-century kindred spirit Karl Barth. In sharp opposition to his Calvinistic upbringing, Macquarrie possessed a Celtic temperament which gave him a fundamental openness to the mystical side of religion (although he himself never claimed to be a mystic) and an abiding sense of the presence of God in the world, including all aspects of human existence. The need to deal with this fundamental tension, it seems to me, has supplied much of the motivation and energy for his life journey as well as his theological project.

Macquarrie's early philosophical studies (M.A., University of Glasgow, 1940) challenged elements of his Calvinistic training, providing him with a broader notion of God which corresponded to his innate sense of divine imminence. Strangely enough, his experience as a chaplain in the British army from 1945 to 1948 was especially important in his development of a more positive sense of human nature. The fundamental goodness of the ordinary soldiers, encouraging

"Belief stretches the human being beyond himself; it sets before him visions or speculations that do not let him settle down in the comfortable assurance of the familiar and the well known."

— In Search of Humanity

and helping each other in simple ways, made a deep impression on him, challenging once more the negative assumptions about human nature engendered by his Calvinistic training. While serving in North Africa, he encountered some friendly Berbers, members of an African tribe committed to Islam, who clearly found strength and enlightenment in their religious faith. The very existence of such good Muslims seemed to reinforce his intuitive sense that common grace was at work beyond the confines of Christianity. Thus, Macquarrie's experience as a chaplain opened him up to a larger world, setting the stage for his continuing efforts to fight religious exclusivism by discerning the presence of God in all aspects of human existence.

After the war, Macquarrie served from 1948 to 1953 as a minister in a Presbyterian parish in Northeast Scotland, an assignment which returned him to the more restricted Calvinistic world. During this time, he worked on a dissertation at the University of Glasgow exploring the influence of Martin Heidegger's philosophy on the theology of Rudolf Bultmann. His work earned him a Ph.D. in 1954 and was published as the first of his 20 books under the title *An Existentialist Theology* (Macmillan, 1955). Continuing his close connection with the University of Glasgow, he served as lecturer there from 1953 until 1962 when he accepted a position as professor of systematic theology at Union Theological Seminary in New York.

During his years in New York, he resolved part of his long-standing religious tension by joining the Anglican Communion and being ordained an Episcopal priest in 1965. Since the age of seventeen, his natural religious sensibilities had urged him toward fuller participation in the catholic tradition, but his sensitivity to his parents' feelings delayed the official move. For him, affiliation with Anglicanism was not really a rejection of his past, but rather a more integrated way of practicing his Christian faith. The broader catholic tradition, with its positive outlook on human nature, as well as its appreciation of mysticism, liturgical symbolism, and philosophical theology, was more in tune with his deep religious sensibilities.

Finding a home in the Anglican Communion seemed to spark a new creative phrase in his "theological pilgrimage." He soon published his excellent one-volume summary, *Principles of Christian Theology* (Scribners, 1966), which includes his most systematic treatment of human existence. Among his many other books, the most significant for our purposes is *In Search of Humanity* (Crossroad, 1983), which discusses in greater detail important aspects of human existence, such as freedom, conscience, love, and hope. Also of note is his *Theology, Church and Ministry* (Scribners, 1986) which contains his important essay on "The Anthropological Approach to Theology" with a response by Karl Rahner.

With some sense of Macquarrie's resolution of the fundamental tension of his faith journey, let us explore two ways in which he can guide our efforts to probe human existence.

The Role of Reason

JOHN MACQUARRIE PROVIDES US with a broad methodology for investigating human nature which refuses to rule out any possible sources of wisdom or insight. Thus, in opposition to rigid empiricists, he insists that we take seriously elements of our personal experience which cannot be quantified or measured. Countering the claims of secularists, he shows how we can draw on traditional Christian wisdom to deepen our perceptions of the human condition. Explicitly denying the exclusive Christian claims of Karl Barth and his followers, he gleans valuable insights from Eastern religions, Marxist thinkers, existentialist philosophers, and empirical scientists. Challenging the private pursuit of self-awareness, he demonstrates that great thinkers in the past and present have important things to say about the nature and purpose of human existence.

Macquarrie's openness is matched by his critical spirit. He responds to the total relativists who claim one interpretation of human life is as good as another by presenting forceful criticisms of both popular opinions and great thinkers.

"The human being is not just a microcosm but also the bearer of the image of God. He does not just reflect or sum up in himself the macrocosms, but has a creative share in shaping it. He is a bridge-being, finite and creaturely, yet creative and reflecting God. Herein lies the unique interest of humanity, though also its vulnerability."

— In Search of Humanity

His dialogue with theologians manifests this spirit. He is especially vigorous, for instance, in attacking the restrictive methodology of the great neo-orthodox theologian Karl Barth. He also offers telling criticisms of contemporary theologians who hold views close to his own. For example, while agreeing with much of Karl Rahner's theological anthropology, Macquarrie decries the arrogance he finds in Rahner's "anonymous Christian notion." With the same careful scrutiny, he examines the great theologians of the past, retrieving from them valuable insights while criticizing their weaknesses in the light of the whole Christian tradition. Thus, the pessimistic elements in Augustine's understanding of human nature are exposed and corrected.

A critical spirit also characterizes Macquarrie's treatment of philosophers past and present. The German existentialist Martin Heidegger, whose classic work *Being and Time* was translated by Macquarrie along with Edward Robinson, clearly exercised the greatest influence on Macquarrie's philosophical anthropology. Nevertheless, he did not hesitate to offer sharp criticisms of important elements in Heidegger's thought, including his excessive individualism. We find equally penetrating evaluations of philosophers ranging from Kant to Camus. For Macquarrie such negative criticism is actually an integral part of his whole positive effort to make available the best insights of great thinkers for the task of probing human existence in all of its complexity and depth.

Macquarrie's method is not only open but balanced. Following the traditional Anglican approach, he analyzes human existence in the light of scripture, tradition, and reason. He expounds and defends with special force the role of reason in probing human nature. Reason makes it possible to construct a philosophical anthropology which moves beyond mere storytelling and witnessing by discerning

"A human being can manifest the being of God only because God himself has descended into the created order. There can be a divinity in man only because there is already a humanity in God."

— Theology, Church and Ministry

recurring patterns and universal structures in human existence. In this way, reason prepares the way for a theological anthropology which makes use of revelation in analyzing human nature. Thus, Macquarrie's critical examination of a wide variety of sources, including personal experience, philosophical analyses, and scientific data, finally produces a Christian anthropology which understands scripture and tradition as the final norm for judging what is authentically human.

We can exemplify Macquarrie's methodology by noting the wide-ranging sources he employs in his treatment of the nature and function of conscience in human life (cf. *In Search of Humanity*, pp. 125-139). He sets a broad context for his discussion by: describing our common experience of alienation; recalling Aristotle's understanding of the relationship between habit and character; noting the etymology of the word "conscience"; relating our Western understanding of conscience to the classical Chinese notion of the Tao; and, finally, explaining and criticizing the theories of English philosophers, including John Stuart Mill.

In a typical move, he then turns to his philosophical mentor Martin Heidegger for a decisive insight into the nature of conscience as a personal call or summons to authentic humanity—a call often drowned out by the voices of "the crowd" which settles for a pedestrian conventional morality. Again, in typical fashion, he goes on to criticize his mentor for missing important insights found in the Christian tradition, including the impotence of conscience described by the apostle Paul and the bondage of the will noted by Martin Luther. In addition, using the traditional notion of natural law, he challenges the subjectivism and relativism found in many other existentialist thinkers. Finally, he states his own position, emphasizing the dialectical tension between two levels of conscience—one summoning us to authentic humanity as Heidegger insisted, the other calling us to be responsive to public values and positive laws. For Macquarrie, the Buddha, Confucius, and especially Jesus, "the image of the invisible God," serve as representative persons who have made creative advances in the search for authentic humanity by awakening the consciences of their followers.

Further explorations of his writings reveal Macquarrie's creative use of numerous other authors, including traditional theologians such as Augustine and Aquinas, psychologists such as Freud and Jung, neo-Marxists such as Bloch and Marcuse, contemporary theologians such as Tillich and Rahner and modern philosophers such as Wittgenstein and Sartre. Reading Macquarrie's penetrating analyses of human existence not only puts us in touch with traditional wisdom and great thinkers but also calls us to pursue our own search for authentic humanity with an open but critical spirit.

Self-Transcendence

TURNING FROM METHOD TO CONTENT, Macquarrie illumines our understanding of human existence especially through his insightful and wide-ranging analysis of self-transcendence. His examination of human transcendence, which is the crucial thread connecting the various elements of his anthropology, discloses to us the possibilities of personal existence, especially our openness to God, while respecting the realities of our essential finitude. The word "transcendence," which literally means "going beyond," suggests a dynamic understanding of human life whereby we are always called beyond any given stage toward possibilities as yet unrealized. As transcendent creatures, we are endowed with spirit, which enables us to rise above lower levels of life, to achieve self-awareness, and to act in creative and responsible ways. Conscious of our unfinished character as persons, we sense a call to move toward an authentic selfhood which is a deeper and fuller way of living.

Self-transcendence is rooted in freedom, which is our fundamental capacity to direct our own personal existence and to shape humanity itself. Since as human beings we are not entirely constrained by the determining forces of nature, we have the ability to affect our environment and to create a world for ourselves. For Macquarrie, human freedom is ultimately mysterious: "Freedom is the empty space, the room that is still left for maneuver and has not yet been filled up and determined. It cannot therefore be grasped by rational thought; it cannot be observed. We only know it through our own exercise of freedom" (*In Search of Humanity*, p. 13).

MACQUARRIE'S ANTHROPOLOGY is consistently dialectical, which means that he understands human existence in terms of polar opposites which must be kept in fruitful tension despite their tendency to become unbalanced. He calls us, for instance, to achieve an integrated synthesis of hope and anxiety without falling into either despair or utopian idealism. Following this general principle, it is obvious that human freedom is never pure openness and possibility but is always constrained by human finitude. Our freedom is limited by our current situation, which is produced by numerous factors such as our previous free decisions, our genetic makeup, our socioeconomic position, our time in history, and our sinful tendencies. This inevitable tension between freedom and finitude creates anxiety as we sense both the heavy responsibilities entailed in the call to actualize our potential and the essential limitations which constrain our ability to respond to this call. In the light of this analysis, we can understand the "flight from freedom" which chooses the familiar and the secure over the new and the risky. Nevertheless, freedom remains our great gift and opportunity. We are, indeed, made in the image of God, which suggests to Macquarrie that we are centers of freedom called to share in the divine work of creation.

This analysis of freedom leads us to a further exploration of human transcendence which always involves both potential and finitude. We are creatures blessed with self-awareness but we are, at the same time, subject to oversights and illusions. While it is true that the human race has the root capacity to develop qualitatively better forms of existence, automatic progress is not assured and regression is all too common. Transcendence does imply possibility and creativity but personal and societal limitations inevitably restrict our progress and our contributions. In short, self-transcendence is a magnificent gift, but one always limited by the realities of life.

For Macquarrie, self-transcendence is a dynamic force operative in all of our experiences and activities. Transcendence appears in all the essential characteristics of human nature. We use language, for example, not only as a means of communication but also as a creative way of opening up new areas of knowledge and experience. The language employed by the great poets, prophets, and scientists touches the imagination, revealing deeper levels and new possibilities of personal existence. Our experience of time likewise reveals a transcendent dimension. Although we are clearly time-bound in many ways, we also have the ability to transcend the present instant through our power to remember and to anticipate. We can place the individual segments of our lives into a larger framework of a whole lifetime, extending from birth to death. We have the lifelong task of using each moment well in order to become more fully human. An experience of transcendence is also involved in the demands of conscience, which prompt us to move beyond our actual self, with all of its limitations, toward our authentic self, with all of its high ideals.

Self-transcendence is manifested not only in our serious purposeful activities but also in the more spontaneous and freer aspects of life, such as play and art. Play, which springs from an "overplus of energy" and brings enjoyment for its own sake, reminds us that we are more than workers and that life has purposes that transcend economic goals. Creative artists enable us to perceive

"To know and accept finitude is perhaps the most important step toward personhood, but our delusions of grandeur are so strong and persistent that only the sufferings of failure, frustration and the like can bring us to a proper understanding."

— In Search of Humanity

hidden levels of reality and to experience aspects of our world with greater depth and intensity. Art has the power to reveal sublime spiritual truths which escape our ordinary perceptions and expressions.

For many persons, self-transcendence is most obviously revealed in personal relationships. To achieve our full humanity, we must break out of our isolation and commit ourselves to other human beings. Personal commitments, which direct our whole being and all our energies toward the good of others, enable us to transcend our selfishness and to experience the fulfillment connected with self-giving. In relationships characterized by genuine mutual love, we overcome the temptation to control and possess by actively enabling our beloved ones to actualize their own unique potentials. Moreover, Christian love calls us to transcend our natural tendency to exclusiveness by extending our care and compassion to others, even strangers and enemies.

"A Taste for the Infinite"

A MORE COMPLETE DISCUSSION of Macquarrie's treatment of self-transcendence would reveal his attention to the way our common experience is always colored by finitude. For him, however, even our experiences of limitation, including the final boundary of death, contain intimations of transcendence. The vanishing point of death, for example, not only gives structure and perspective to life, but also opens up the hope that human existence is not annihilated by death but is embraced within the divine life.

Macquarrie uses his analysis of human transcendence as a way of approaching divine transcendence. Human beings have a sense and a "taste for the infinite." The ultimate goal of self-transcendence is the inexhaustible mystery which we call "God." This suggests that ordinary human experience has a depth that can be called religious. Many aspects of our existence have a "transcendent reference" which provides direction and meaning.

In addition to these common experiences which have a religious dimension, Macquarrie insists that there are specifically religious moments when "there is concentrated at the center that awareness of the holy which ordinarily is there only on the periphery of experience" (*In Search of Humanity*, p. 211). These striking, explicit religious experiences make it possible to recognize the more subtle presence of the holy in everyday life.

Religious Experience

MACQUARRIE DISTINGUISHES two general types of religious experience which are complementary, though one or the other will predominate in a particular individual or historical period. The first type, characteristic of introspective persons and periods of social upheaval, involves strong negative experiences such as brokenness, guilt, and anxiety, which, in turn, foster a religious quest for healing and wholeness. When such moments of healing occur, religious persons attribute them not to their own power but to the grace of God. The second type of religious experience is less dramatic and more positive. The fragmentary character of human existence is experienced not so much as a threat but as a necessary stage along the path leading to greater fulfillment and ultimately to "deification," as the Greek fathers expressed it. Persons following this path experience certain spiritual delights and joys because they are more conscious of the presence of God than his absence.

While, according to Macquarrie, we cannot construct a totally convincing proof of God's existence, persons blessed with religious experiences do tend to attribute them to a power outside themselves which not only takes the initiative but also invites a wholehearted response. Thus, the human transcendance operative in religious experience suggests the transcendence of God who, far from being distant and aloof, is near and graciously present in the midst of human life. In his 1983 Gifford lectures, published as *In Search of Deity* (Crossroad, 1985), Macquarrie further developed his dynamic notion of a God who is both actively transcendent and graciously immanent. Along with other admirers of Macquarrie's work, I hope that he will have the time and energy to complete his next intended project, a book on the God-man which will extend and relate his previous work on humanity and deity.

As our brief survey indicates, the key to Macquarrie's anthropology is his notion of self-transcendence. Since we truly are "the meeting place of the finite and the infinite" an analysis of human transcendence forms an excellent foundation for further reflection, not only on God but also on all the essential Christian doctrines.

Some critics claim Macquarrie's penchant for balance has deprived him of passion, that his great clarity of expression has masked the complexity of important questions, and that his extensive dialogue with other thinkers has overshadowed his potential creative contributions. For me, on the contrary, Macquarrie has been a most valuable guide precisely because of his balance, clarity and respect for tradition. His creative work is solid because it is deeply rooted in a long and diverse tradition. His theology fosters dialogue today because it appropriates and shapes in a balanced way many ideas still operative in our culture. And his Christian anthropology strikes responsive chords because it clearly articulates our common experience of human transcendence. For these and other reasons, John Macquarrie remains a marvelous guide as we probe human existence searching for its deepest meaning and greatest possibilities.

Discussion Questions

1. How seriously do you take the quest for self-knowledge and how do you go about achieving it?

2. What do you think were the principal events in Macquarrie's "theological pilgrimmage" which influenced his outlook on human existence?

3. What does Macquarrie mean by self-transcendence and how is it manifested in human experience?

4. How could Macquarrie's analysis of human existence help you to know yourself better?

Suggested Readings

In Search of Humanity (Crossroad, 1983). A readable and insightful treatment of important aspects of human experience such as freedom, love and hope.

Principles of Christian Theology (revised edition, Scribner, 1977). An excellent one-volume summary of Christian theology which generally avoids technical jargon while relating traditional doctrines and contemporary experience.

Twentieth Century Religious Thought (Harper & Row, 1963). A great resource which provides clear summaries of major thinkers and their essential ideas.

In Search of Deity (Crossroad, 1984). Macquarrie's Gifford lectures which work out his contemporary understanding of God who is both transcendental and imminent.

Hans Kung
reforming the church

THE REFORM IN THE CATHOLIC CHURCH, unleashed by the Second Vatican Council, has produced a wide spectrum of responses. At the poles, reactionaries on the right keep fighting for a return to preconciliar days of rigid uniformity while revolutionaries on the left, disregarding tradition, want to dismantle the institution in order to meet the needs of the contemporary world.

Even within the broad middle range of general support for the conciliar reforms, diverse outlooks are obvious. Conservatives, for example, urge us to hold fast to the unifying power of the Catholic tradition while liberals call for greater fidelity to the transforming message of the gospel. Many of these liberal or progressive Catholics who developed high hopes for the continuing reform promised by the new council are now extremely frustrated by the current conservative trends in the church. This sense of frustration has helped swell the ranks of the selective or communal Catholics who have generally written off church leaders while continuing to draw selectively from the riches of the Catholic heritage.

Finally, an analysis of reform must recognize the generation of young people who did not directly experience the preconciliar church. Whether conservative or liberal, they view the church differently from the previous generation which lived through the transition. Liberal collegians, for example, are often mildly amused by stories of the "old

Church" and are generally bewildered by current examples of authoritarianism in the church. They live out a type of selective Catholicism without the perspective and sensitivity generated by years of struggle for reform.

Hans Küng, the well-known Swiss theologian, emerged as a spokesman for progressive reform within the church on the eve of the Second Vatican Council, and has continued to play that role ever since. His book *The Council: Reform and Reunion*, originally published in 1960, two years before the council began, alerted many Catholics to both the possibility and the need for reform. He did not hesitate to make concrete suggestions for change, such as limiting the power of the Roman Curia, which in the long run would facilitate the movement

"The Church, therefore, is the pilgrim community of believers, not of those who already see and know. The Church must ever and again wander through the desert, through the darkness of sin and error. For the Church can also err and for this reason must always be prepared to orientate itself anew, to renew itself. It must always be prepared to seek out a new path, a way that might be just as difficult to find as a desert track, or a path through darkness."

— The Church

toward Christian unity. In the spring of 1963, Küng undertook the first of his numerous lecture tours of the United States. Speaking to overflowing crowds across the country, this young, engaging, energetic theologian challenged his audiences with the vision of a reformed Catholic Church, celebrating religious liberty as well as the rights and responsibilities of its individual members.

During the Second Vatican Council, Küng fought for progressive causes, first as an adviser to Bishop Leiprecht and later as an official expert. Recognizing the great influence of the conservative Cardinal Ottavianni, he drafted a statement for one of the bishops suggesting a new doctrinal commission be elected with someone other than Ottavianni as president. When this maneuver failed, Küng, going against the advice of Karl Rahner, refused to take part in the work of this commission, which was drafting the document on the church. Instead he began to work out his own understanding of the nature of the church. This material, eventually published in 1967 under the title *The Church* (Sheed & Ward), encouraged Catholics to look honestly at the dark side of their graced but sinful church, always confident that God would remain faithful to his people.

The Need to Reform

RESPONDING TO ISSUES raised by the departure of English theologian Charles Davis from the Catholic Church in 1966, Küng wrote *Truthfulness: The Future of the Church* (Sheed and Ward, 1968), urging Catholics to stay in the church in order to work with all their strength for reform. While admitting the limitations and distortions in current church institutions, especially the Roman curial system, he argued that institutional reforms were both necessary and possible. He strengthened his case by recalling the surprising structural reforms periodically accomplished in the history of the church.

Küng, who did pastoral work in a large parish in Lucerne, Switzerland, for 18 months in the late 1950s, has always been attuned to the problems which ordinary, liberal Catholics experience with official church teachings and practices. Sensing the adverse effects of *Humanae vitae*, the 1968 encyclical issued by Pope Paul VI forbidding artificial contraception, Küng responded with his book *Infallible? An Inquiry* (Doubleday, 1971). He argued that an erroneous understanding of infallibility made such a restrictive statement on birth control seem necessary in order to preserve the papal teaching authority from the appearance of error.

The "candid preface" to this book, written on Pentecost, 1970, began with the forthright statement that the renewal of the Catholic Church had come to a standstill despite the magnificent success of the Second Vatican Council in opening so many doors. It went on to note the problems causing unrest among ordinary Catholics: birth control, mixed marriage laws, priestly celibacy, reform of the Curia, and the means of selecting suitable bishops. In all these problem areas, Küng saw a relapse into a preconciliar Roman authoritarianism and called for a new effort at reform.

Recognizing a pastoral need for a credible up-to-date summary of the Christian faith which would guide believers in a complex and changing world, Küng published *On Being a Christian* in 1974. Although this book drew critical responses from the German bishops and some theologians for its failure to affirm clearly enough the divine sonship of Jesus Christ, it struck responsive chords with many lay Christians. Küng's ability to address the concerns and to articulate the hopes of contemporary Christians was reflected in the popularity of this book, which was on the German best-seller lists for many months.

In 1979, Küng published an article assessing the first year of the pontificate of Pope John Paul II. He described him as "an impressive champion of peace, human rights and social justice," who appeals to the masses as a "morally trustwor-

"There is, however, one guiding light it [the Church] is never without, just as God's people in the desert always had a guide. God's world is always there to lead the Church. Through Jesus, the Christ, it has been definitively revealed to us. The word of Jesus Christ, as testified by the apostles, is the Church's guide. It is the world to which the Church appeals and according to which it must examine its activities in the confusion of this world."

— The Church

thy leader."   At the same time, through a series of rhetorical questions, he criticized the pope for an authoritarian style which failed to safeguard the rights of many people in the church, including women, married couples, priests, and theologians.

In December of that same year, Küng received an unexpected and devastating letter from the Sacred Congregation for the Doctrine of the Faith which declared that, because he "departs from the integral truth of the Catholic faith," he could not "be regarded as a Catholic theologian nor perform the task of teaching as one."

Liberal groups of Christians swiftly came to Küng's defense: two thousand students at Tübingen signed a petition on his behalf; his colleagues on the editorial board of *Concilium*, including Rahner, Metz, Congar, and Schillebeeckx, took issue with the condemnation; and theologians from around the world voiced their support. On the other hand, conservatives, including his former mentor, Hans Urs von Balthasar, supported the Vatican position. Küng himself, extremely worried about the ecumenical implications of the Vatican's action, vowed to fight his censure and to continue to articulate the concerns of reform-minded Catholics.

True to his intentions, Küng, on the eve of the November, 1985 synod of bishops, issued a scathing attack on the pontificate of Pope John Paul II, comparing him very unfavorably with the great reformer, Pope John XXIII. He accused the current pope of halting church reform, blocking ecumenical progress, and substituting unilateral preaching for serious dialogue with the modern world. According to Küng, all of this had been done without regard for the frustration and disappointment rampant among church members. Küng was especially intense in his criticism of the pope's treatment of women, insisting that "the women's question will increasingly become the test case of this pontificate." The article concluded with a ringing call for the bishops to act courageously against the reactionary forces in the Vatican and to speak out forthrightly for those experiencing alienation and oppression in the church.

Spokesman for Reform

THIS BRIEF SURVEY highlights the important role Küng has played in the past as a leader of the movement for progressive reform in the church and as a spokesperson for alienated liberal Catholics. To trace the highlights of Küng's story is to recall the spiritual journey of many progressive Catholics who have known both the hopes spawned by the Second Vatican Council and the disappointments which followed it.

The significance of Hans Küng, however, cannot be confined to liberal movements in the past. His scholarly and timely writings also contain enduring insights and helpful guidance for everyone interested in the continuing task of church reform. Among his many contributions, let us examine three in particular.

Küng provides us with important insights into the nature of the Christian community, insights which support and guide the conviction that the church must always be reforming itself. His book *The Church* encourages us to examine the church as it really is. The church, struggling to be faithful to Christ, inevitably manifests a dark side which results both from the sinfulness of its members and from its inevitable contact with the distortions and contradictions of society, such as sexism and racism.

Küng offers a particularly striking example of the sinful side of the church in his honest portrayal of the horrible history of anti-Semitism in the Christian world. Refusing any easy rationalizations of this demonic phenomenon, he clearly avows that "the weight of guilt is too heavy by far to be balanced by such self-justification. The church preached love while it sowed the seeds of murderous hatred; it proclaimed love, while it prepared the way for atrocities and death" (*The Church,* p. 137).

With equal candor, Küng uncovers many other examples of sinfulness in the church, including the abuse of power by leaders and the shameful treatment of women. His critique is a forceful reminder that a church aware of its propensity to sinfulness must always be reforming itself. Küng will not allow us to retreat from the consequences of this argument into a private world of personal conversion surrounded by unchangeable church structures. In Christ we are indeed new creatures already living out the gift of reconciliation with God (2 Corinthians 5:17-19). Our task, however, is to reappropriate this gift constantly, translating it into the life and structures of the community of faith. In this process, whatever forms human beings have instituted and constituted in the church are conditioned by human limitations and are, therefore, subject to reform. In other words, there are no irreformable areas in the church, because the essential nature of the church is always incarnated in historical forms. The church must always be reforming itself in order that its institutions and structures will more faithfully reflect the new being established by Christ.

For Küng, reform does not imply a revolution which would violently tear down the church structure. Nor does it suggest a mere restoration which would cover over its defects. Genuine reform remains faithful to tradition while searching for new and creative ways of responding to the needs of the contemporary world. Effective reform must strive for a renewal of both hearts and structures so that the church can be a more credible sign of the kingdom.

Basis for Reform in Scripture

WHAT CRITERIA OR NORMS ARE TO BE FOLLOWED in carrying out this reform? According to Küng, the church must always seek guidance from the example and message of Jesus Christ, as reflected in the Scriptures. Influenced by contemporary biblical scholars, especially Ernst Käsemann, Küng thinks that modern scholarship with its historical-critical method can provide this guidance by uncovering for us the essential characteristics and teachings of the historical Jesus. Jesus Christ, as revealed in this core message, is the norm for all church reform. With all of its limitations and errors, Scripture still provides us with criteria for judging the concrete life of the contemporary church.

As Küng states it: "The only measure for renewal in the church is the original gospel of Jesus Christ himself; the only concrete guide is the apostolic church" (*The Church*, p. 341). In the process of reform, we must continually ask whether particular developments in the church are in accord with the gospel or opposed to it. Those opposed must be challenged and rooted out so that the church better reflects her Lord. Thus the contemporary reform movement is not simply motivated by a desire to be modern but is primarily rooted in fidelity to Jesus Christ. It cannot be whimsical but must be guided by the scriptural norm.

"If the charisms of individual Christians were discovered and furthered and developed, what dynamic power, what life and movement there would be in such a community, such a Church."

— The Church

Not everyone agrees with Küng's criteria for reform. His emphasis on the historical Jesus as manifested in the Scriptures seems too narrow to those who would put more stress on the risen Lord and on the contemporary revelatory life of the church. His reliance on the work of contemporary biblical scholars to uncover the historical and normative Jesus strikes many critics as dangerous, especially considering the often shifting conclusions of biblical scholarship. Nevertheless, Küng's clear and consistent approach reminds all of us of the importance of turning to the Christ manifested in Scriptures as we contemplate church reform.

In further specifying the scriptural criteria for the continuing task of reform, Küng presents three models of the church: the People of God, the Body of Christ, and the Creation of the Spirit. His efforts to understand the church in relationship to the Holy Spirit are especially helpful to reform-minded Christians today. The Holy Spirit, spontaneously active in the whole history of the world as the source of energy and creativity, continues to grant us the gift of freedom today. The Spirit not only frees us from sin, law, and death, but also frees us for a life of love and service (Romans 8:2-11). We receive this gift through the church, which is the sign, witness, and temple of the Spirit. The Spirit takes the initiative in forming and building up the church, making it holy, and energizing its individual members. Despite this close relationship, the church remains sinful and cannot be identified with the Holy Spirit. The Spirit, which breathes where it will, is active not just in the church but in the whole world. We cannot control the Spirit, but must submit to it through a positive act of unconditional faith.

Küng puts great emphasis on the Spirit-filled experience of the community at Corinth as reflected in Paul's early letters. In his first letter to this community, Paul does not speak of elders or of bishops or of ordination; he stresses the charisms or free gifts of the Spirit bestowed on all baptized persons. These gifts, very diverse and often quite ordinary, enable individuals to affirm that Jesus is Lord and to utilize their talents on behalf of the community. The charism of leadership, for example, is intended for rendering service and not for gaining personal advantage. Proper use of individual charisms based on obedience to the Lord leads to unity and love, while avoiding both anarchy and a rigid uniformity.

Küng is convinced that current church reform must take into consideration the charismatic structure of the church which predominated in the early Pauline communities. A church which desires to be a genuine sacrament of the Spirit must celebrate the freedom of individual members as well as the servant role of the leaders. A church which recognizes itself as a creation of the Spirit will respond to the needs of the modern world, while remaining faithful to the traditional gospel. A church which hopes to be an effective instrument of the Spirit must always be reforming itself.

The Pursuit of Truthfulness

THROUGH BOTH WORD AND DEED, Hans Küng also reminds us of the need for truthfulness in the church as a basis for the project of continuing reform. My own sense of his passion for truthfulness goes back to 1968, when I attended his classes on ecumenical sacramentality at Union Theological Seminary in New York. As a result of this course, I came to appreciate his consistent methodology of rigorously judging the genuineness of all developments in the church according to the norm provided by the New Testament witness to Jesus

Christ. During that same term, Küng lectured one night a week to overflowing crowds in the large Riverside Church on the topic of truthfulness in the church. Whether he was analyzing developments in the church opposed to the Gospel, such as Roman authoritarianism, or calling for changes in official church teaching on pressing issues such as birth control and clerical celibacy, Küng's passion for truthfulness was both evident and electrifying. Many listeners, myself included, came away from these lectures with a renewed enthusiasm for church reform and a better understanding that it must be based on a genuine spirit of self-criticism and fidelity to the gospel.

Küng's book *Truthfulness: The Future of the Church* incorporates the material presented in these lectures. In the opening chapter, he defines truthfulness as "that basic attitude through which individuals or communities, in spite of difficulties, remain true to themselves without dissimulation and without losing their integrity; a genuine candor with oneself, with one's fellows and with God, a genuine candor in thought, word, and deed" (pp. 20-21).

By this standard, Küng finds a great disregard for truthfulness in the Catholic Church. This results from the defects of a traditional moral theology which neglected this virtue, as well as from a siege mentality in the church which precludes honest admission of sinfulness and errors. To overcome this dishonesty we should look to Jesus Christ, who called upon his followers to live in truth before God. The passionate protest of Jesus against the legalism and ritualism of his time challenges us to replace the hypocrisy and dishonesty in the church today with a healthy spirit of candor and truthfulness.

The message of Jesus had as its theme not the church but the kingdom or reign of God's truth and justice. Therefore, a church true to its own nature will not exalt itself but will function as a servant of the kingdom, a provisional and unassuming sign of God's decisive work in the world. A truthful church will strive to be obedient to God's will, ready to admit its guilt when it fails to respond to God's grace.

In John's Gospel, we find the basis for a deeper understanding of truthfulness. For John, Jesus himself is the truth (14:6) who came into the world to bear witness to the truth (18:37). His spirit will lead us into the truth (16:3), which is really a participation in the life of God (14:9-11). This is the truth that will set us free (8:32). Thus, the ethical demand for personal truthfulness flows from participation in God's truth. The genuine pursuit of truth, however, can never be merely a private quest, because this approach contains the seeds of fanaticism and doctrinal chaos. Truth is best pursued in the community of faith by individuals willing to learn from the traditional wisdom and to enter into dialogue with all people of good will. Church reform which reflects this scriptural understanding is really an act of fidelity to the God of truth revealed in Jesus Christ.

From this perspective, Küng vigorously attacks the falsehood and hypocrisy which he detects in the church, ranging from the authoritarianism manifested by the Roman Curia to the official, ideological teaching on birth control which has been maintained because of an unwillingness to admit errors in past church teaching. He is especially harsh on theologians who explain away obvious changes in church teaching by resorting to clever theories of doctrinal development rather than honestly admitting previous errors. Küng prefers candor, insisting that the church should not be embarrassed by having learned something new

---

"The Church which does not conceal her mistakes, but constructively comes to terms with them, is, because truthful, also credible. A more truthful and therefore more credible Church may expect and demand more understanding, more loyalty, more commitment, particularly in regard to her teaching, her creeds, declarations and definitions."

— Truthfulness: The Future of the Church

---

but should rejoice in the power of God, who leads it, despite its sins and errors, into a greater understanding of the truth. A candid church with a passion for truth will function as a more credible sign of the kingdom and a more insightful critic of the world. Thus, it will be better prepared both to detect and criticize various forms of deceit in our society and to celebrate and promote positive developments such as the current tendency toward honesty and authenticity in the arts and personal relationships.

Küng's plea for truthfulness in the church is clearly strengthened by his own willingness to speak out with courage and candor. Despite pressures, warnings and censures from church leaders, he has continued to carry on his theological work with a remarkable passion for the truth. His personal sincerity and deep faith are reflected in the closing words of his book *Truthfulness: The Future of the Church*: "The new truthfulness in the Church is a response to the deepest longings and strivings of the new age and a response to the message of Jesus Christ himself. What belongs both to the new age and to the gospel of Jesus

Christ in the Church will inevitably prevail against all contradictions and resistance, reversals and relapses, impediments and handicaps. The new truthfulness is the future of the Church. It must be grasped, not in fear, but with great gratitude" (p. 181).

Sensitivity and Ecumenism

FINALLY, KÜNG'S whole theological project is a striking reminder of the intimate relationship between the reform movement in the Catholic Church and the success of the ecumenical movement. Since the beginning of his academic career, Küng has been interested in overcoming the obstacles separating Protestants and Catholics. During his theological studies in Paris, he encountered the giant of Catholic ecumenical theology, Yves Congar, who taught him that real spiritual reform in the Catholic Church must include a reconciliation among all Christians. Moreover, Küng's doctoral dissertation on the notion of justification in the thought of the great Swiss Protestant theologian Karl Barth, made a major contribution toward reunion by demonstrating that agreement on the long-standing dispute over justification was possible.

Küng's sensitivity to Protestant objections to Catholicism was sharpened by his continuing relationship with Barth, whom he called his "fatherly friend and constant spiritual companion." This sensitivity was brought home to me while I was attending Küng's course on ecumenical sacramentology in 1968. We discussed the need for reform in Catholic sacramental understanding and practice, not only from the perspective of the modern secularization process, but also in the light of the classical objections formulated by Martin Luther. Any effective sacramental renewal must be in accord with God's word as witnessed in Scripture and should keep in mind the goal of Christian reunion. This material, not yet published, is an important element in Küng's overall theological project to solve the divisive disputes among Christians in order to pave the way for eventual reunion.

This motive was also operative in his book *Infallible? An Inquiry*, which began by noting that the ecumenical movement was at a standstill, in part because of the way papal authority is understood and practiced. Küng not only criticized the doctrine of infallibility proclaimed a century earlier at the First Vatican Council, but also offered a reinterpretation of the traditional notion of indefectibility, emphasizing that God does not abandon the church despite its sins and errors. Küng believes this interpretation is more faithful to the Scriptures and thus more appealing to the Protestant world.

Küng's subsequent books have expanded his ecumenical interests while retaining his fundamental concern for reconciliation. His popular summary of the Christian faith, *On Being a Christian*, had the explicit ecumenical purpose of presenting "what is decisive and distinctive about the Christian program and discovering what is common to the separated Christian Churches." In his long and comprehensive sequel, *Does God Exist?* (Doubleday, 1980), Küng entered into dialogue with the secular world, listening to the classic objections to theism and offering a straightforward explanation of the biblically-based Christian belief in God. The dialogue with the secular world was continued in his *Eternal Life?* (Doubleday, 1984), which examined the issue of coping with death in the light of a contemporary understanding of the scriptural witness to the resurrection of Jesus.

Noting that contemporary ecumenism must include the community of the great religions, Küng published a series of dialogues between himself and representatives of Islam, Hinduism, and Buddhism under the title *Christianity and the World Religions* (Doubleday, 1986). His aim was both to broaden our horizons of mutual understanding and to present Christianity in the light of the world religions. He was not interested in bringing about a unified world religion which would ultimately be founded on an irresponsible relativism, but rather in achieving a genuine state of peace among the great religious traditions based on a self-critical pursuit of truth.

Renewal as Basis for Reconciliation

SIMPLY MENTIONING THESE IMPORTANT BOOKS reminds us that throughout his stormy career as a theologian, Hans Küng has very systematically been about the business of church reform for the sake of reconciliation. With great courage, he has pressed for honest renewal within the Catholic Church so that it will be a genuine herald of the kingdom and an instrument of reconciliation in the world.

In this process, Küng has drawn strong criticism from many sources. Some have indulged in personal attacks, accusing him of being arrogant and disloyal. Serious theologians have questioned his methodology, challenged his functional Christology, and disputed his selective use of the Scriptures. His mentor, Yves Congar, once accused him of speaking like a revolutionary and not a reformer. Karl Rahner hurt Küng deeply when, in the course of his vigorous attack on the book *Infallible? An Inquiry*, he suggested that Küng should now be treated as a liberal Protestant. Fortunately, at Küng's initiative, the lingering rift with

Rahner was reconciled during a friendly luncheon meeting a few years before Rahner's death. Küng told me about that meeting right after delivering an impassioned lecture which combined a generally positive appraisal of Martin Luther with a scathing criticism of the Roman Catholic hierarchy for its ecumenical inertia.

For me, the lingering image of this stirring lecture combines with the story of his reconciliation meeting with Rahner to form a perception of Küng's enduring value. Through courageous actions and passionate words, Hans Küng forcefully reminds us that church reform based on truthfulness is our continuing responsibility and that all reform is for the sake of an ever-expanding circle of reconciliation.

Discussion Questions

1. Are you interested in church reform and how do you feel about the changes initiated by the Second Vatican Council?

2. How has the personal involvement of Küng in church reform affected his theology?

3. How does Küng understand church reform and what criteria and interests does he think should guide the process?

4. What practical approaches to reforming the church emerge from Küng's writings?

Suggested Readings

The Church (Sheed and Ward, 1967). A readable, comprehensive explanation of Küng's ecclesiology which includes an honest appraisal of the sinful side of the church combined with suggestions for reform.

On Being a Christian (Doubleday, 1976). A straightforward, popular summary of the Christian faith which reinterprets the major doctrines for the contemporary world.

Infallible? An Inquiry (Doubleday, 1971). A harsh and controversial critique of the standard teaching on infallibility and a reinterpretation of the traditional notion of indefectibility.

Theology for the Third Millenium: An Ecumenical View (Doubleday, 1988). Presents the presuppositions for a theology of the world which Küng continues to pursue.

Karl Barth
refining our image of god

THE DEEP SIGNIFICANCE of our image of God is often apparent to me in my work as a counselor and a spiritual director. I recall a striking example of a woman who is happy to share her story. Because of her rather strict Catholic upbringing, she had a heavy and repressive notion of God which helped produce neurotic guilt feelings and a rigid lifestyle. Shortly after getting married, she attended a weekend retreat which planted the seeds of a much more positive image of God, as the loving Father who desired her happiness and fulfillment. Gradually her confidence and self-esteem improved, leading to better personal relationships and increased involvement in the life of her parish. After many years, described as satisfying and rewarding, a series of tragedies struck her, including the breakup of her marriage. These events produced in her a deep rage against a God who had betrayed her. She quit going to mass and found it difficult to pray. The low-grade depression which pervaded her daily existence steadily eroded the self-esteem she had so carefully cultivated. She came to me seeking help to regain the warm and comforting relationship with God which provided her with such strength during the good years.

The story exemplifies not only the crucial role played by images of the deity in personal development, but also the close connection between our image of God and our self-image. My own sense was that the woman could not go back to her previous comforting but limited notion of God. Her tragic experiences had shattered that limited image. She needed a new and more comprehensive understanding of the divine-human relationship which would enable her to deal more effectively with the dark side of human existence.

In helping this woman discover a more balanced and effective image of God I drew on the thought of the great Swiss Reformed theologian Karl Barth (1886-1968). This and similar experiences have convinced me that we can all benefit from an encounter with the work of this giant of Protestant theology.

Both followers and critics of Barth (his name rhymes with dart) consider him to be among the most influential theologians of modern times. For instance, John Cobb, an important process theologian with serious reservations about Barth's work, calls him "the greatest theologian of our century" with "the greatest impact on the history of the discipline." Themes from Barth's thought have worked their way into Catholic theology, especially through Hans Küng, who wrote his doctoral dissertation on Barth's notion of justification, and the Swiss Catholic theologian Hans Urs von Balthasar, who wrote the outstanding commentary *Karl Barth: A Presentation and Interpretation of his Theology.*

The power of Barth's work is generated by his intense single-minded effort to place the transcendent God, triune and incarnate, in the center of Christian thinking. This effort, enriched by his thorough and creative reading of the Western theological tradition, as well as his penetrating insights into the self-destructive tendencies of modern culture, produced one of the most comprehensive theological statements of modern times.

While Reformed Protestants hear in Barth's theology many familiar themes and approaches, Catholics exposed to his thought, especially those of a more liberal bent, find themselves in a somewhat strange and often challenging world. Precisely because Karl Barth calls into question many of the assumptions of contemporary Christian theology, he has an important message for liberal Christians in their search for a refined image of God.

Accepting the Transcendent God

BARTH'S THEOLOGY challenges every tendency to identify God with our own personal desires, feelings, and thoughts. From the beginning of history, human beings have sought equality with God, often by reducing him to human proportions. The human heart knows the desire to manipulate *and* control the deity. Attempting to win divine favor by good works, or to stave off divine punishments by promises of improved behavior, is a recurring human temptation.

Prayer, so important to spiritual growth, can devolve into magical efforts to influence God. We can forget that our image of God inevitably reflects our own self-image with its limitations and distortions. Some individuals with low self-esteem, for instance, tend to view God as a heavy-handed ogre or an aloof judge. Others, like the woman in the opening example, construct a rosy image of God which effectively precludes facing the dark and tragic side of life. No doubt we can all find ways in which we tend to reduce the majestic God to our own finite proportions.

Modern times have produced no stronger challenge to this common human temptation than that found in the early writings of Karl Barth. His personal

"God's deity is thus no prison in which He can exist only in and for Himself. It is rather His freedom to be in and for Himself but also with and for us, to assert but also to sacrifice Himself, to be wholly exalted but also almighty mercy, not only Lord but also servant, not only judge but also Himself the judged, not only man's eternal king but also his brother in time."

— The Humanity of God

story is crucial to understanding the development of this trenchant criticism. Born May 10, 1886 in Basel, Switzerland, Karl was greatly influenced by his father, a Reformed pastor and university professor who guided his son's early theological education in conservative directions. From 1906-1909, Karl had the opportunity to study with the most eminent liberal theologians in Germany, including Adolf von Harnack and Wilhelm Hermann. These thinkers, heirs of Frederick Schleiermacher, who launched the liberal movement in 1799 with his famous book *On Religion: Speeches to Its Cultured Despisers*, spoke optimistically of the essential goodness of human beings and the inevitable progress of human history. They emphasized the fatherhood of God and the ethical imperative of love, while playing down the judgment of God, the miracles of Christ, and the reality of the Resurrection.

After completing these theological studies (it is ironic that this great theologian never did doctoral studies in theology), and being ordained in the Swiss Reformed

Church by his father, Karl eventually became a pastor. He served from 1909 to 1911 in Geneva and from 1911 to 1921 in Safenwil, a remote village in north-central Switzerland. In this small parish, he became known as "the Red Pastor" because of his active involvement in organizing a union for textile workers and his continuing efforts to secure improved conditions for workers.

"The well-known definitions of the essence of God and in particular of His freedom, containing such terms as 'wholly other,' 'transcendence,' or 'non-worldly,' stand in need of thorough clarification if fatal misconceptions of human freedom as well are to be avoided. . . . 'In his free grace, God is for man in every respect; He surrounds man from all sides. He is man's Lord who is before him, above him, after him, and thence also with him in history, the locus of man's existence.'"

— The Humanity of God

During this time, he became a member of the Social-Democratic party, a very radical move for a pastor in those days.

Barth's dominant interest, however, was preaching the Word to his congregation. In carrying out his ministry, he became increasingly dissatisfied with the approach he had learned from his liberal teachers. He later accused them of being too individualistic in their emphasis on personal experience and too relativistic in their denial of the absolute truths of revelation. His disillusionment with liberalism was intensified when, in 1914, ninety-three German intellectuals, including some of his former teachers, signed a manifesto supporting the Kaiser and his war policy. Furthermore, the experience of World War I shattered the general optimism about human progress which provided the psychological matrix for liberal theology.

Barth reacted to his doubts about the pastoral effectiveness of liberal theology by joining with a friend and neighboring pastor, Eduard Thurneysen, in a renewed study of scripture, especially Paul's Letter to the Romans. Barth's intense study led to the writing of his first book, a commentary on Romans, published in

1919. This work brought him instant fame as well as an invitation to become a professor of Reformed theology at the University of Göttingen. Barth himself, however, was dissatisfied with the book, and made a complete revision which was published in 1922.

This second edition of *The Epistle to the Romans* (Oxford University Press, 1968), in the words of Karl Adam, "fell like a bomb on the playground of the theologians." In this classic text of neo-orthodox theology, first translated into English in 1933, we hear Barth's most striking attacks on the cherished assumptions of liberal theology. All efforts to reduce or domesticate the great God are challenged by his interpretation of Paul's thought. While Barth later modified many of these views, even going so far as to say that he wished he had never seen the book, it is this volume with its intensely emotional message which shapes much of the popular understanding of the great Swiss theologian. It continues to serve today as the most powerful critique of any liberal tendency to reduce God to human proportions.

"Wholly Other"

INFLUENCED BY SÖREN KIERKEGAARD, Barth in his commentary insisted on the infinite qualitative difference between God and man. "The power of God can be detected neither in the world of nature nor in the souls of men" (p. 36). God is the "Wholly Other" and we all stand under the judgment of this God. "Men have imprisoned and encased the truth—the righteousness of God; they have trimmed it to their own measure and, thereby, robbed it both of its earnestness and its significance" (p.45). God's grace can never be earned, nor can we do anything on our own to escape the wrath of God. Even if we desire to cooperate with God in noble actions, we turn God into a mere notion, a projection of our own needs. "God alone is the merchant who can pay in the currency of eternity" (p. 62). Only when human beings discover that "all the world is guilty before God" will they be in a position to recognize God's faithfulness (p. 88).

As the apostle Paul made clear in a key passage, "God has shut up all unto disobedience that He might have mercy on all" (Romans 11:31-32). Barth insists that the true God "is distinguished qualitatively from men and from everything human, and must never be identified with anything which we name, or experience, or conceive, or worship, as God" (pp. 330-331). The living God "is never a known thing in the midst of other known things" (p. 331). Recognizing the limitations of our knowledge prepares us to receive the divine favor: "What is demanded of us here is that we should know we are understood by God—in our own lack of understanding" (p. 390). Despite the efforts of the false prophets to domesticate God, we still long for a genuine prophet who will honestly "set before us the complete strangeness of the Wholly Other" (p.446). Jesus Christ is that prophet "who exposes the gulf which separates God and man and by exposing it, bridges it" (p. 31).

In Barth's commentary, this message of ultimate hope for salvation, founded in the atoning death and resurrection of Jesus Christ, is never totally absent and is always presumed. The dominant refrain, however, is clearly the infinite gap between God and us and the impossibility of bridging it from our side. According to Barth, we cannot reach God by any human means; not through reason, with its natural theology and philosophical arguments; not through feelings or religious sentiments; not through experiences of nature or persons.

This theme, consistently argued and passionately proclaimed, continues to challenge Christians today, especially those whose image of God is formed by contemporary liberal theology. While Barth's critique obviously exposes the shallowness of any efforts to control God for selfish purposes, it also alerts us to our more subtle tendencies to confine the great God within our own images of the deity. The God we encounter in all aspects of our daily lives remains incomprehensible and beyond all words and images. Even our deepest religious experiences are only partial and incomplete pointers to the transcendent God. Self-experience, which is the vehicle of our experience of the deity, always remains ambiguous, pointing only indirectly to the transcendent One who infinitely exceeds our grasp. In the spiritual quest we must beware of cheap grace, naive optimism, and facile answers. In short, the early Barth continues to shout out his clear "no" to any liberal attempts to reduce the majestic Lord to human scale.

Cultural Expressions

BARTH NOT ONLY CHALLENGES our narrow personal conceptions of God, but also the temptation to identify God with cultural expressions and national purposes. It is common for nations to call upon the deity in support of their national policies, including their wars. In the United States, we have our own brand of civil religion, which does indeed verbally proclaim the sovereignty of God, but still tends to assume that God made us the new Chosen People, and the vehicle of his will in international relations. The power of the civil religion is so pervasive that dedicated Christians, often with little conscious awareness, can easily adopt the standards of the flag rather than the cross, especially in dealing with social questions and public policy issues.

Karl Barth in his life and his writings provided a powerful critique of the rampant nationalism fostered by Hitler in Germany. After his initial fame,

"(God) sanctifies us for eternal life as He sanctifies us for Himself. He wills the best for us as He seeks His own glory. He is Himself our hope as He is our Lord. He saves us from eternal death, and nourishes us to eternal life."
— Church Dogmatics: The Doctrine of God

occasioned by the publication of *The Epistle to the Romans*, Barth became a university professor, lecturing in theology at Gottingen, 1921-25; Münster, 1925-30; and Bonn, 1930-35. In 1933, shortly after Hitler's installation as chancellor of Germany, Barth founded a theological journal, using its pages to mount a vehement attack on Hitler as well as on church members who accepted an easy alliance between the gospel and the National Socialism espoused by Hitler.

Barth became a leader of the Confessing Church, a group of Christians who opposed Hitler's policies. When this group met at Barmen in 1934, Karl wrote the famous Barmen Confession, signed by two hundred leaders, which insisted on obedience to Jesus Christ as the only leader (Führer). Refusing to swear unconditional allegiance to Hitler or to begin his classes with the customary "Heil Hitler," Barth was dismissed from his teaching post at Bonn and expelled from Germany in 1935. Quickly assuming a theological chair at the University of Basel in his home town, he continued to attack the Nazi philosophy and constantly encouraged people in other countries to resist Hitler. Immediately after the war, Barth, faithful to his intuitive sense of God's mercy, called for a spirit of reconciliation which would lead to political freedom for Germany as soon as possible.

During the Nazi period, Barth continued to develop his theology. For him, Jesus Christ and no other is our victorious leader. Christ the Son of God bore the punishment of our sins, suffering on our behalf to meet the harsh demands of divine justice. Through the cross, divine love triumphs over the powers of darkness. Jesus Christ atoned for our sins, established the new order, and secured the grace of salvation.

Barth, in a theme which reminds us of contemporary liberation theology, insisted on the liberating power of the earthly Jesus. While Jesus did not identify himself with any particular group or champion any existing program, he did act with a remarkable personal freedom which called into question all existing programs and principles, thereby unsettling others, especially the authority figures. For Barth, ethics is always a part of dogmatics; moral imperatives flow from theological insights. Therefore, disciples of Christ must follow their Lord by saying a decisive "no" to all of the demonic forces in the world and to all the idols erected by human pride. In short, Jesus Christ is the victorious leader who gives us courage to deal with the dark forces of sin.

Barth's courageous actions and powerful writings challenge any lingering illusions that God can be enlisted on behalf of national self-interest. The struggle against the unspeakable cruelties of Naziism reminds us of the need to criticize the more subtle distortions of our civil religion, with its implicit assumption that God functions as an ally of the United States. Barth reminds us that, for Christians, Jesus Christ must remain the judge of all national policies and cultural expressions.

It is instructive for liberal Christians to remember that it was the Barthians, with their lofty image of the transcendent God revealed in Christ, who mounted the most concerted and sustained attack on Nazism. The natural tendency to identify God with cultural expressions and national aspirations is a continuing temptation even for committed Christians. Karl Barth not only forces us to face this dark inclination, but also provides the much-needed message of hope that God's cause, championed by Jesus Christ, will ultimately be victorious.

Divine-Human Relationship

BARTH'S LATER WRITINGS instruct us in the art of modifying and balancing our image of God. All of us are subject to limitations and distortions in our perceptions of the divine-human relationship. Our image of God is influenced not only by the ambiguities found in society, church and family, but also by the limitations built into our own self-image. Christians interested in self-growth, liberation of the spirit, and positive approaches to life have a tendency toward certain distortions in their image of God. We can, for example, be so caught up in the immanence of God that we forget the divine transcendence. Our sense of the mercy of God can be so strong that we neglect divine justice. We can be so dependent on a comforting sense of God's presence that any experience of divine absence becomes intolerable.

Karl Barth did not remain imprisoned by the notion of God he proclaimed so passionately in his early writings. During his years as a professor, he labored unceasingly to refine his understanding of God. Beginning in 1932, the fruits of his prodigious efforts were published as individual volumes under the general

"Who God is and what He is in His deity He proves and reveals not in a vacuum as a divine being-for-Himself, but precisely and authentically in the fact that He exists, speaks, and acts as the partner of man, though of course, as the absolutely superior partner."

— The Humanity of God

title *Church Dogmatics* (Edinburgh, T. & T. Clark). He planned to develop his ideas under five major topics: The word of God, God himself, creation, reconciliation and eschatology. By the time of his death on December 10, 1968, he had completed twelve massive volumes, getting as far as the last part of his treatment of the fourth of his five major topics, the doctrine of reconciliation.

For those not inclined to wade through these volumes, it is helpful to consult the comprehensive and clear summary produced by the outstanding Barthian scholar Geoffrey Bromiley, entitled *Introduction to the Theology of Karl Barth* (Eerdmans, 1979). In 1946, Barth himself produced a slim volume, *Dogmatics in Outline* (Harper & Row, 1958), which summarizes his intentions for his multivolume work.

Only an encounter with *Church Dogmatics* itself, however, provides a sense of Barth's amazing scholarship and creative reading of the Western theological tradition. When treating the doctrine of election or predestination, for example, he not only does a detailed exegesis of all the relevant scriptural passages, but also comments on numerous theologians, including major thinkers such as Augustine, Bonaventure, Aquinas, Zwingli, Luther, and especially Calvin. In this 500-page section, which is part of his much longer treatment of the doctrine of God, Barth demonstrates a truly awesome grasp of the historical tradition. Moreover, his radical departure from the traditional Calvinistic doctrine of a double predestination to heaven and hell in favor of a single predestination to heaven, clearly demonstrates his bold creativity.

In *Church Dogmatics*, Barth refines his major ideas on God as enunciated in his commentary on Romans by placing them in a larger theological context and by balancing them with other insights. His uncompromising insistence on the transcendence of God, for example, while not forsaken, is now balanced by his teaching on the immanence of God. He now clearly affirms that the majesty of God does not annihilate our humanity nor detract from our freedom. Through the Incarnation, we enjoy the honor of having Christ as our brother. The doctrine of reconciliation means that God is not only with us but personally identifies himself with us. From this perspective, we can no longer define God as "Wholly Other" but must recognize that we are exalted to fellowship with God precisely because of our solidarity with Christ.

Barth's earlier insistence on the transcendence of God the just judge is now balanced by his understanding of the God of mercy and love. This forms the basis for his extremely optimistic notion that we can hope for the salvation of all human beings. Thus, the dark foreboding mood of the early Barth is now replaced by an upbeat joyful confidence in the power of God to save every person who has ever lived. Moreover, Barth now speaks about a "primal revelation" through creation and even admits, though cautiously, that theologically significant insights can be gleaned from the world of philosophy and the secular sciences.

The more positive understanding of the divine-human relationship found in *Church Dogmatics* seems to correspond with Barth's own great zest for life. This hard-working, intense theologian also enjoyed travelling, meeting people, and reading all kinds of literature, including mystery stories. He had a great interest in the history of warfare, and visited the Civil War battlefields during his 1962 trip to the United States. He loved his wife, Nellie, and their four children. His eldest son, Markus, who became a highly respected biblical scholar, spoke of his father as his best friend, a close comrade who encouraged his children toward true freedom. Barth's passion for the music of Mozart was legendary. He said that when he went to heaven he would first inquire about Mozart and then about the theologians, such as Augustine and Calvin. Thus it seems fitting that the great Swiss theologian with his immense love for a wide range of human activities came to speak about the humanity of God, who produces in human culture "parables of his own eternal good will and actions," calling, in turn, for our "reverence, joy, and gratitude" (*The Humanity of God,* John Knox Press, 1982, p. 55).

The Great "Yes"

WITH ALL OF HIS STRIKING theological development, Barth still has serious limitations as a guide in our efforts to refine our image of God. He had, for instance, no sense of the power of mystical experience to reveal God, going so far as to call mysticism an "esoteric atheism." His vast writings on the nature of God demonstrated little appreciation of the revelatory power of the sacramental life of the church. He did not explore the insights of Eastern Orthodoxy or American theology.

A critic, Dietrich Ritschl, claimed that Barth never had a serious theological discussion with a communist, an atheist, a Muslim, or a Hindu. At times, he responded harshly to other theologians, failing to notice how they could have helped him refine his own notion of God. The prime example is the strident attack he mounted on his outstanding contemporary Emil Brunner for his openness to a limited form of natural theology. Even Barth's renowned ability to criticize pretensions to power which undercut the sovereignty of God had its limits, as he refused to condemn the Soviet invasion of Hungary in 1956—a failure which drew harsh criticism from the American theologian Reinhold Niebuhr.

Nevertheless, Karl Barth remains an extremely helpful, if limited guide in the process of deepening our perceptions of the deity. Through his classic work *The Epistle to the Romans*, he utters a clear and enduring warning against all temptations to make God in our own image. His courageous stand against Hitler can provide much-needed inspiration as we struggle against the idols and demonic forces in our own culture. His refusal to confine himself within his early thunderous assault on liberal theology is a graphic reminder that we must avoid fixations in our own notion of God, while always striving for a more adequate and integrated understanding of the deity.

Barth's comprehensive approach in *Church Dogmatics* to the doctrine of God, which is at once thoroughly trinitarian and consistently Christocentric, encourages us to stay in touch with the central doctrines of the Christian tradition as we probe the meaning of God's activity in the contemporary world. By treating ethical questions within the framework of his dogmatics, Barth reminds us that our image of God has ramifications for our everyday effort to live out the Christian message. Finally, Karl Barth's optimistic notion of a God who, despite our sinfulness and weakness, will ultimately accomplish the salvation of the whole human family, can offer hope to all of us increasingly aware of global threats, systematic evils, and personal tragedies. Such hope, as this great giant of 20th-century theology often insisted, is founded on the great "Yes" of God which shelters all of us, empowering us to offer "stout resistance" to evil. "By this great Yes and by it alone" we are summoned to advance in the freedom of the sons and daughters of God (Romans 8:21) and enabled to live with "maturity and soberness."

Discussion Questions

1. What is your dominant image of God and how does it affect your attitudes and behavior?

2. How did Barth's pastoral experience in Germany affect his understanding of God?

3. What does Barth's image of God as "Wholly Other" mean and how did it affect his major theological positions?

4. How does Barth's emphasis on divine transcendence challenge your own image of God as well as the claims of the American and civil religion?

Suggested Readings

Dogmatics in Outline (Harper & Row, 1958). A brief and readable summary of his major theological teachings.

Church Dogmatics, five vol. in thirteen parts (Edinburgh, T. & T. Clark). His massive masterwork which serves best as a comprehensive reference on particular topics.

The Epistle to the Romans (Oxford University Press, 1968). A classic text of neo-orthodox theology which gives the best feel for Barth's thunderous attack on liberal theology.

Introduction to the Theology of Karl Barth by Geoffrey Bromiley (Eerdmans, 1979). A faithful and clear summary of the *Dogmatics* by an outstanding Barthian scholar.

CHAPTER 9

Paul Tillich
relating religion and culture

WE LIVE IN A SECULARIZED CULTURE in which important areas of life are no longer subject to the authority of the church nor guided by explicit religious principles. Modern developments such as the industrial revolution, urbanization and the rise of capitalist economies, all supported by science and technology, have produced a culture which operates independently according to its own inner logic. Thus, philosophy functions independently of theology. Science operates by its own empirical method. Politics rests on the separation of church and state. Economics pursues its own goals without explicit consideration of religious values. Therapy, inspired by the Freudian revolution, reflects an anti-religion bias. And, public education does not take responsibility for passing on our religious heritage.

How are believers to understand and assess this tendency of our culture to push religion to the margins? What role should religion play in a secular culture? How can biblical religion and contemporary culture interact in a mutually beneficial way?

These were the problems which set the agenda for the man condidered by many to be the 20th century's finest theologian of culture, Paul Tillich (1886-1965). Born in Brandenberg, Germany, the oldest son of a Lutheran pastor, Tillich spent most of his adult life in the academic world. He received an excellent classical education, gaining advanced degrees in philosophy and theology. After completing his doc-

torate at the University of Berlin, he was ordained a Lutheran pastor in 1912.

Following World War I, he taught philosophy and theology at various German universities from 1919 to 1933, when he was dismissed from his position at the University of Frankfurt by the Hitler regime. After emigrating to the United States he held important professorships at Union Theological Seminary from 1933 to 1955, Harvard from 1955 to 1962, and the University of Chicago from 1962 to 1965, the year of his death.

Tillich's interests, however, always transcended the academic world. His experiences as a chaplain during World War I put him in touch with the thinking of ordinary young men as well as the tragic dimension of life. More than any other contemporary theologian, he entered into dialogue with the major spheres of modern culture, such as art, philosophy, science and psychotherapy. His vast writings are filled with references to contemporary cultural trends.

By his own account, Tillich lived on the boundary between church and society and between religion and culture, experiencing deep within himself the tensions of the age. Thus his whole theology, which is essentially a theology of culture, has an autobiographical flavor.

In examining ways in which Tillich continues to speak to us today, we can follow his threefold typology of the possible relationships between religion and culture. Adopting terminology found in Kant and others, Tillich distinguished heteronomy in which authoritarian religion dominates culture; autonomy in which culture is totally independent of religion; and theonomy in which the two interact harmoniously. While the terminology may be unfamiliar, the substance of Tillich's analysis contains helpful insights for us as we search for constructive ways of relating religion and culture.

"The Demonic Tendencies"

TILLICH'S PASSIONATE CRITIQUE of heteronomy alerts us to the continuing temptation of religion to dominate culture by undercutting its proper autonomy. Tillich's passion on this topic grew out of his family background. Paulus, as he was known to his friends, was raised by a mother who passed on to him an appreciation of democracy and a zest for life, and by a dominant father who, as a stern Lutheran pastor, imbued his son with the Prussian sense of authority, duty, and personal sin. At the age of 17, Paulus had to deal with the death of his mother, with whom he had an extremely close relationship. This event shattered his secure world, thrusting him into an early identity crisis as well as recurring periods of anxiety over the meaninglessness of life.

His ambivalent relationship with his father colored much of Tillich's own religious sensibilities. They enjoyed good times together, including nightly philosophical discussions which taught Paulus the essential compatibility between philosophy and revealed truth. He even followed in his father's footsteps by becoming a Lutheran pastor, although he remained highly critical of the church throughout his lifetime. On the other hand, Paulus felt a certain antipathy toward his father, accompanied by a strong need to gain independence from

"Religion opens up the depths of man's spiritual life which is usually covered by the dust of our daily life and the noise of our secular work. It gives us the experience of the Holy, of something which is untouchable, awe-inspiring, ultimate meaning, the source of ultimate courage."
— Theology of Culture

him. Often plagued by doubts and guilt feelings, he struggled all of his life against the dogmatic and moralizing form of religion preached by his father. His intense reaction against his father sharpened Tillich's distaste for religious authoritarianism of all kinds and fueled his efforts to expose the idols created by institutional religion.

He channeled this passion by refining and applying the "Protestant principle," which calls for vigorous protest against all distortions of the gospel message. By this principle he rejected every effort to assign absolute value to the church. He was especially attuned to what he called "the demonic tendencies" which draw on the positive energy of religion but produce destructive results. Thus he criticized the demonic temptation to use holy things like the sacraments as a means to manipulate God.

Tillich's criticism of religion was wide-ranging. He was harsh on both authoritarianism in the Catholic Church and the loss of a self-critical spirit in the Protestant churches. His reactions against distortions in Christianity—including anti-Semitism, the misuse of power, and failure to respond to the needs of the secular world—were pointed and intense. He chided the great Protestant theologian Karl Barth for his "supernaturalism," which refused to take modern culture seriously and criticized the psychotherapist Carl Jung for reducing religion to a private subjective realm. Late in his life, Tillich turned the Protestant principle on himself, admitting his own narrowness in failing to dialogue with world religions earlier in his theological career.

Tillich had a keen sense of the great damage done by the attempts of authoritarian religion to dominate the culture. A culture controlled by religion becomes stagnant, losing its creative energies. It degenerates into monolithic uniformity, because it is deprived of the dynamics and diversity provided by pluralism. Morality is reduced to a legalistic conformity, because it responds to external norms rather than flowing from an inner spirit. Philosophy is dominated by theology, while the arts are mere functions of the reigning ideology.

Tillich's critique deepens our perceptions of the current efforts to subordinate culture to religion. Thus, we recognize the clear dangers in the utopian dream of reactionary Christians who want to turn the United States into a "Christian nation" reflecting their particular brand of piety. We can also detect a more subtle threat posed by Christians who co-opt religious language by claiming that their political programs represent the will of God and are therefore the only truly moral option.

Furthermore, the criticism of religion advanced by Tillich calls into question the proposals of those who want to resurrect a traditional form of authoritarian religion in order to hold together a disintegrating culture. A religion which carried out this task by moderating pleasure-seeking and controlling liberation movements would end up stifling creative energies within the culture. Finally, Tillich helps us generate a critique of the so-called "American civil religion," that amalgam of Judeo-Christian religious themes and patriotic nationalism which functions as an ultimate concern for so many citizens in the United States. When the civil religion shapes fundamental attitudes, it is difficult for both biblical religion and countercultural forces to mount an effective attack on the demonic tendencies in the dominant culture.

A Spiritual Void

DRAWING ON HIS personal experience and utilizing his impressive analytical skills, Tillich also provides us with an in-depth theological analysis of the destructive tendencies built into our autonomous secular culture. Tillich knew firsthand the demonic forces unleashed by modern culture. While serving as a chaplain in World War I, he was deeply touched by his direct contact with the horrible carnage caused by weapons of destruction placed in the service of nationalistic purposes. After the war, Tillich became very aware of the split between an authoritarian church which had been withdrawn from modern culture and a

---

"The principle of evangelism must be to show to the people outside the Church that the symbols in which the life of the Church expresses itself are answers to the questions implied in their very existence as human beings."

— Theology of Culture

---

secularized society which had effectively rejected Christian teaching. Sensing a great moment of opportunity, he helped found the Kairos Circle, a movement which espoused religious socialism as the political vehicle for bridging the gap between religion and culture.

Unfortunately, these efforts could not gain the needed momentum; and Hitler, with his misleading promises of security, identity, and national pride, came forward to fill the spiritual void. As Hitler swept into power Tillich published his book *The Socialist Decision*, which pulled together his previous attacks on the Nazi ideology. As a consequence, Tillich was dismissed from his teaching post in 1933 at the University of Frankfurt along with many Jewish professors including Martin Buber. After verifying the horrible anti-Semitic intentions of the Hitler regime, he emigrated to the United States along with his wife Hannah, who remained a touchstone for him throughout his life.

The tragedies which Tillich witnessed in Germany, especially those perpetrated by the Nazis, provided an experiential base for his theoretical analysis of an autonomous culture. His experience convinced him that the problems of the contemporary world are ultimately religious. In the process of freeing itself from authoritarian religion, modern culture has created a spiritual vacuum enabling finite realities posing as absolutes to rush in and take over. Science and technology have helped create this problem by their amazing success in affording human beings greater control over nature and increased access to material goods. In the process, science became an idol, masquerading as an absolute value and creating a flase sense of self-sufficiency.

A self-sufficient culture inevitably becomes secularized because it ignores religion as unnecessary or banishes it as an obstacle to progress. When this occurs, the culture as a whole no longer provides a sense of depth nor an ultimate context of meaning. The great religious questions of identity and purpose are repressed, making the traditional wisdom of the past seem irrelevant. In short, an autonomous culture, according to Tillich, "has lost its ultimate reference, its center of meaning, its spiritual substance."

"The Christian message is the message of a new Reality in which we can participate and which gives us the power to take anxiety and despair upon ourselves."
— Theology of Culture

The spiritual void in a secularized culture intensifies the experience of anxiety which for Tillich is an "existential awareness of the threat of non-being." While anxiety over death always remains and anxiety about guilt is still a special problem for Americans influenced by Puritanism, people today are especially prone to the anxiety of emptiness and meaninglessness. The sense of emptiness is caused by traumas such as the breakdown of an important belief; while the loss of meaning flows inevitably from the superficiality of a culture void of a sustaining spiritual center.

Tillich's analysis warns us against superficial and misguided solutions to a deep cultural problem. We cannot, for example, overcome anxiety and transform our culture by mere conformity to social norms or by a private pursuit of our own good. Compulsive activity, repression of guilt, and denial of death only intensify anxiety. The common psychological ploy, often adopted unconsciously, of manufacturing manageable fears to replace anxiety does not deal with the real problem. Joining authoritarian religious groups is a short-term solution which fails in the long run. Turning to reactionary political leaders, a continuing temptation in an age of insecurity, will only intensify our societal problems.

With a clear awareness of the essential limitations of all these proposed solutions, Tillich claims that the only real answer is a religious courage which embraces anxiety while accepting the power of God to forgive and save us.

If we can accept the truth that God accepts us even when we are unacceptable, then we are freed to work together on the vital project of restoring the spiritual center to our culture. Anxiety remains a part of the human predicament but, as Tillich himself demonstrated, it can be transformed into energy for the struggle against the demonic forces which threaten our culture.

Religion of the Heart

IN ADDITION TO HIS CRITIQUE of religious heteronomy and cultural autonomy, Tillich presents the positive ideal of a "theonomous culture" in which religion and culture interact in a mutually beneficial way. Thus, he reminds us of the essential power of religion to transform culture and suggests ways to present the Christian message more effectively to achieve this goal.

As with many of his major insights, Tillich's notion of theonomy grew out of his own experience. During World War I, he suffered a breakdown as a result of the suffering and death he witnessed at the front. As part of his therapy, he visited art museums to experience the healing power of great paintings. In Berlin, he encountered a Botticelli painting of the Madonna which triggered in him an intuitive understanding of the way religious power can be revealed in and through particular culture forms. By his own account, this experience provided him with the essential notions for a theonomous culture. After the war, he continued his therapy for several months by visiting museums. In the process, he gained a great understanding and deep appreciation of the world of art, especially painting. In his lectures and articles on the relationship between religion and art he refined his original insight by showing how different artistic styles reflect diverse types of religious experiences. For him, the aesthetic experience had become a model for religious experience.

Drawing on his original insight, Tillich developed his general notion of a "theonomous culture" in which religion neither dominates culture nor withdraws from it, but plays the proper role of supplying "meaning, seriousness, and depth" to all cultural forms. He summarized his fundamental perception in the well-known epigram: "Religion is the substance of culture, and culture is the form of religion."

The key to understanding this relationship is found in Tillich's distinction between religion of the heart, which involves ultimate concern, and public religion, which includes institutional elements. The religion of the heart demands total involvement and wholehearted commitment. It is the state of being grasped by an ultimate concern, of being addressed by an unconditional demand, of being enlightened by an encounter with the holy. From this perspective, religion is not one aspect of life but "the substance, the ground and the depth" pervading the whole of life. The ultimate concern of religion appears in unconditional moral demands, in the passionate longing for truth, and in the infinite desire to express meaning.

Genuine religion of the heart recognizes that the only legitimate ultimate concern is the "God above God" who is beyond all images and cannot be controlled or manipulated. The true God is manifested in Jesus Christ who through his death and Resurrection brings the New Being, the divine power which overcomes all the conflicts and contradictions which threaten human existence. Those who are grasped by the power of the New Being form the Spiritual Community in which the proper relationship between religion and culture is recognized and established.

When Tillich states that religion is the substance of culture, he points to the essential power of religion as ultimate concern to supply meaning, to provide focus, to give direction to culture. To say that culture is the form of religion means that all cultural forms reveal the divine presence dwelling in the human spirit. In a theonomous culture the sharp distinction between the holy and the secular is overcome. Without being swallowed up or losing their independent existence, all secular forms of culture can manifest the Spirit. As Tillich states it: "The universe is God's sanctuary. Every work day is a day of the Lord, every supper a Lord's supper."

Tillich, of course, recognized that this essential power of the religion of the heart has to be lived out under the real conditions of existence with all of its ambiguities. Nevertheless, he was convinced that, despite human limitations and sinfulness, the power of religion can be unleashed for the well-being of the human community.

Tillich's treatment of religion as ultimate concern makes it clear that the relationship between religion and culture is broader than the relationship between church and culture. Persons outside the churches can be grasped by ultimate concern and can contribute to the project of humanizing culture. This suggests the need to form broadbased coalitions of individuals and groups committed to helping particular areas of culture achieve their proper goals. This occurs, for example, when lawyers of good will work together to make the legal system more open to poor people, or when parents work with professional educators to improve the quality of the school system. Church members must learn to speak the language of the world and to employ inclusive categories in order to draw more people of good will into the project of transforming culture.

From his own experience Tillich also came to understand that contemporary culture can speak a healing message to religious people. He gained insight and inspiration not only from art but also from other disciplines such as philosophy and psychology. According to his methodological theory, the culture cannot supply answers but can only raise questions for religion. However, his actual life and theological practice reflect the deeper theological notion that particular cultural forms can also manifest elements of the Spiritual Presence because they have been influenced by their encounters with revealed religion. Thus, Tillich instructs us, by his example more than his theory, to remain open to

"But the Divine Being is not a being beside others. It is the power of being conquering non-being. It is eternity conquering temporality. It is grace conquering sin. It is ultimate reality conquering doubt."

— Theology of Culture

the creative energies and constructive trends within culture.

For him, a theonomous culture can be created only through the energy and passion generated by the religion of the heart which draws its strength from the dynamism of the Power of Being, the omnipotent God. Creating such a culture is crucial to the preservation and well-being of the human family. The "struggle for humanity" according to Tillich can be successfully waged "only under the banner of theonomy."

Tillich was convinced that the Christian message has to be reformulated and refocused in order to be effective in creating a theonomous culture. His major contribution to this task is found in his three-volume *Systematic Theology*, produced during his years as a professor in the United States. This work employed his well-known "method of correlation" which insists that the contents of the Christian faith be formulated as answers to the questions posed by the culture. Theologians employing this method must first make sure they understand in depth the real concerns of people today as they are expressed in various cultural forms. Then they must present the Christian message as the answer to these existential concerns. If the culture, for example, is suffering from the anxiety of meaninglessness, then Christ must be presented as the bringer of the New Being which gives ultimate meaning to life.

This method, which is really an explicitation of a traditional method in theology, is valuable for all believers who wish to make a positive impact on contemporary culture. It warns us against presenting Christianity as an alien religion with answers to questions no one has. It also prevents us from reducing the Christian message to a mere echo of the answers already available in the culture.

"Estrangement"

IN HIS OWN RECONSTRUCTION of the Christian message, Tillich made a valuable contribution by switching the dominant metaphor from height to depth. Rather than speaking of God as the transcendent Lord ruling from the heights over human affairs, Tillich preferred to speak of God as the "ground of being," or the dynamic "power of being" which supports all human activity. Hence, God is found not by rising above the human but by descending to the true depths of human experience. Prayer is not so much raising our minds and hearts to God but being responsive to the Spirit who "intercedes with sighs too deep for words." The metaphor of depth encourages us to present religion not as an opiate which turns our eyes to the heavens but as the energy source which can bring unity and meaning to all cultural forms.

Tillich's sustained and productive dialogue with the existential movement, including the field of psychotherapy, provided him with important insights and fresh language for reformulating traditional Christian doctrines. The existential analysis of "estrangement," for instance, enabled him to reinterpret the traditional Christian notion of sin. As a result of the Fall we are estranged from the ground of our being, from other persons, and from ourselves. The term "estrangement" suggests the tragedy of the human predicament, because we are cut off from precisely those realities which alone can bring us integration and fulfillment. While Tillich often identifies human estrangement with sin, he also recognizes that the word "sin" with its distinctive meaning must be retained because it reminds us that we are not simply in a tragically flawed state of estrangement but that we can culpably turn away from God, others, and our true selves. From this viewpoint, individual sins appear not as violations of the law but as ratifications of our estranged condition. Sinful estrangement involves unbelief and pride, in which persons make themselves the center of their world, thereby losing their essential grounding in God.

Tillich's *Systematic Theology*, which can be read as a comprehensive theology of culture, contains many other valuable reformulations and insights. It would be especially helpful to examine the cultural implications of his dynamic notion of God, who is experienced both as ground and abyss (see *Systematic Theology*, Volume I, pp. 211-289).

Today, criticisms of Tillich are easy to find: his language is abstract, his method of correlation is flawed, his system is too tidy, his cultural analyses are dated, his ontology is questionable. It is certainly true that the liberation theologians have moved beyond him and that his categories and language have not carried the current debates. We should not forget, however, Tillich's passion for the project, his willingness to draw on personal experience, his courageous stance on the boundary, his example of productive dialogue, his warnings about the demonic forces, and his massive effort to make the Christian message meaningful for modern culture. Paul Tillich, theologian of culture, had the ear of many of his contemporaries and still deserves our attention today.

Discussion Questions

1. What do you think the proper role of religion is in our secular culture?

2. How did Tillich's particular experiences, including his war traumas, conflicts with the Nazis and life in the United States, affect his theology?

3. How does Tillich describe an ideal relationship between religion and culture and what is his criticism of secular culture?

4. How could we employ Tillich's theology to improve our contemporary culture?

Suggested Readings

Theology of Culture (Oxford University Press, 1959). A fine collection of clear, insightful essays on various topics such as psychoanalysis, art, existentialism and education.

Systematic Theology, three vol. in one (University of Chicago Press, 1967). A great summary work which consistently explains the Christian message as a response to real human concerns.

The Courage to Be (Yale University Press, 1952). A brilliant analysis of modern forms of anxiety and some creative Christian responses.

The New Being (Scribners, 1955). A fine collection of challenging sermons which provide a great entry into Tillich's thought.

CHAPTER 10

Reinhold Niebuhr
applying christian realism

TODAY, AS THROUGHOUT HISTORY, Christians struggle with the problem of relating their faith to the task of improving the social order. Some, of course, simply avoid public involvement, withdrawing into a private enclave dominated by personal and family concerns. Among those who choose to participate in the world of politics and economics, questionable approaches can be discerned. Enthusiastic believers, for example, sometimes claim to have a definitive blueprint inspired by Scripture for building a better society. Ordinary Christians often identify their faith with the American way of life, thereby precluding healthy social change. At times, idealistic Christians advocate policies which are so utopian that their recommendations are easily ignored. Some previously involved believers influenced by national traumas, such as Vietnam and Watergate, are now halfhearted participants, disillusioned with the political process. Obviously, the task of relating Christian faith to the social order is not only complicated but filled with pitfalls.

In sorting out these complex matters, it is helpful to consider the approach advocated by the outstanding teacher of social ethics, Reinhold Niebuhr (1892-1971), clearly the most influential theologian in the history of the United States. Niebuhr was not an abstract theoretician but, rather, a pragmatic activist whose energetic and sustained involvement in both the church and the political realm provided the experiential base for the approach which he named "Christian

realism." Let us examine some of the ways in which this biblically-based realism can speak to us today.

A Sense of Mission

REINHOLD NIEBUHR challenges Christians to participate wholeheartedly but without illusion in the political project of creating a better society. As Richard Fox, in his excellent book *Reinhold Niebuhr: A Biography* (Pantheon, 1985) makes clear, Niebuhr's personal involvement in the political world forms the basis for his realistic social ethics. Born June 21, 1892, in Wright City, Missouri, Niebuhr decided at an early age to follow in the footsteps of his beloved father, a minister in the Evangelical Church. When his father died in 1913, Reinhold, driven by a great sense of mission, was ordained and took over his father's pastorate. Shortly after, he decided to expand his very limited theological training by attending Yale Divinity School where he encountered the Social Gospel movement in vogue at the time among liberal Protestants. He received a master's degree from Yale, but never went on for a doctorate.

In 1915, Niebuhr became the pastor of Bethel Church in Detroit, a largely middle-class congregation which he served for 13 years. Attracted by his powerful preaching as well as his controversial lectures on current social questions, the congregation grew tremendously, drawing especially from the members of the new professional class. Niebuhr's interest quickly spread beyond the parish to the great social issues erupting in the Detroit area. He spoke out passionately against the pretensions of Henry Ford, accusing him of social irresponsibility for opposing much-needed worker benefits such as unemployment insurance and old-age pensions. With less passion, but considerable dedication, he also served for many years as a chairman of the mayor's Interracial Committee. During the 1920s, Niebuhr gained a national reputation through his provocative articles which appeared in important journals, including the *Christian Century*, which served as the voice of liberal Protestantism.

Due in part to his growing national reputation as a controversial writer and fiery lecturer, Niebuhr was offered the position of associate professor of Christian ethics at Union Theological Seminary in New York. He accepted and in 1928 began teaching at Union where he remained (despite extremely lucrative offers from Harvard and other institutions) until his retirement in 1960. During those years he not only continued to serve his Church, but also multiplied his efforts to influence public affairs. In 1930, for example, he ran a vigorous but losing race for state senator on the Socialist ticket. His marriage in 1931 to Ursula

Keppel-Compton, a graduate of Oxford who later taught theology at Barnard College, seemed to supply him with even greater motivation and energy for his social ministry. Just one year later, he published his extremely influential book *Moral Man and Immoral Society* (Scribners, 1960), which offered a striking analysis of the behavior of social groups.

From 1934 to the end of the decade, Niebuhr poured his energy into the Fellowship of Socialist Christians. As editor of the group's journal *Radical Religion*, he had an excellent platform for advocating Socialist principles. During

---

"Both the majesty and the tragedy of human life exceed the dimension within which modern culture seeks to comprehend modern existence. The human spirit cannot be held within the bounds of either natural necessity or rational prudence."

— The Nature and Destiny of Man (Volume I)

---

those years, he also managed to develop a solid basis for his social critique while writing his classic work, *The Nature and Destiny of Man* (two volumes; Scribners, 1941 and 1943). At the beginning of World War II, Niebuhr found himself moving away from the pacifism advocated by the Socialist Party toward the interventionist position adopted by President Roosevelt. To give voice to his own new Christian perspective on international relations, Niebuhr helped found the journal *Christianity in Crisis*, which first appeared in 1941. During World War II he worked furiously on many causes, including emigration of the Jews from Nazi Germany. After the war, he helped establish the liberal political group Americans for Democratic Action. Through all of this flurry of activity, he became the best-known and most influential churchman in the United States. This was symbolized by the decision of *Time* magazine to place him on the cover of their 25th anniversary issue, published March 8, 1948.

Worn out by his efforts, Niebuhr suffered a stroke in February of 1952 which impaired his speech and partially paralyzed his left side. Slowed down and often suffering from depression, he still continued with the help of his wife, Ursula, to publish books and articles on the vital issues of the times. This output included a small volume entitled *Man's Nature and His Communities*

(Scribners, 1965) in which he demonstrated his remarkable capacity for self-criticism by explicitly adopting a much more positive outlook on Catholicism and Judaism than he previously held. After retiring from Union in 1960, his health continued to deteriorate and he died on June 1, 1971, three weeks short of his seventy-ninth birthday.

As this brief biographical sketch suggests, Niebuhr was, indeed, a public theologian passionately involved in the great social questions of his time. He was a teacher of social ethics who was convinced that the Christian message, properly understood, would help prevent serious policy mistakes and support the proper course of action.

Christian Realism

WHILE HIS VIEWS on particular policy questions were generally unpredictable, he did develop a consistent approach to social ethics which is well-named "Christian realism." In general, this approach emphasizes the complexity of social problems as well as our limitations in solving them. All human realities possess a fundamental ambiguity. No economic or political system can be considered an absolute. We cannot expect to solve our social problems simply by using reason, education and moral persuasion because self-interest and power struggles are inevitably involved in social life. In the real world, Christians must adopt a pragmatic approach. This means making decisions on social questions based on careful calculations of which actions and policies will produce a net balance of good over evil.

As his thought developed, Niebuhr reinterpreted various Christian doctrines to support and clarify this pragmatic approach. Thus, he distinguished the ideal conditions of the future kingdom when God will bring the present chaos into final unity from the actual limitations of the kingdom as it exists in the real world filled with sin and ambiguity. While the kingdom ideals make decisive claims on us in every aspect of our lives both public and private, our concrete choices must also take into account the world's sinful tendencies and structures which make the attainment of the kingdom ideals virtually impossible. In addition, he employed the reformation notion of "justification by faith alone" to show that we must involve ourselves in the quest for justice even when the concrete situation is confused and tragic. By trusting in God's power to save us and our sinful world rather than in our own power to solve all human problems, we can overcome the temptation to withdraw from public life simply because moral choices are not clear and good results are not assured. In this regard, Niebuhr castigated the great neo-orthodox theologian Karl Barth for advocating a theology which leads to a withdrawal from the real world of power politics. He was especially incensed by Barth's refusal to condemn the 1956 Soviet invasion of Hungary, insisting that his silence on this crucial question manifested the weakness of his theology. Finally, Niebuhr insisted that the traditional "theology of the cross" can strengthen us to face the tragic dimension of life without falling into despair. The cross of Christ creates a framework of meaning which enables us to work realistically for a better world without expecting perfection.

Niebuhr's Christian realism also emphasizes the ambiguity of religion. On the positive side, religion variously described as biblical, profound and prophetic functions as a "citadel of hope" which enables us to deal with the tragic dimension of life. Through the use of symbols and myths, biblical religion points to a source of meaning beyond the empirical world. It provides the motivation to love others, checking in the process our temptation to selfishness and egoism. Profound religion contributes to the common good by challenging the tendency of privileged groups and nation-states to make an idol out of their own interests.

"The selfishness of human communities must be regarded as an inevitability. Where it is inordinate it can be checked only by competing assertions of interest; and these can be effective only if coercive methods are added to moral and rational persuasion."

— Moral Man and Immoral Society

It helps believers avoid cynicism by reminding them that the current contradictions in society are not normative or final and that history has "endless possibilities" for good which are yet untapped. By relativising worldly realities, prophetic religion reveals their true value in the divine plan. Religion provides us with transcendent principles by which we can evaluate the quality of social structures and the performance of political systems. Christianity is especially helpful in dealing with social problems because it reveals to us a God of judgment who condemns injustice, a God of mercy who frees us to work for a better world, and a God of hope who invests all our efforts with ultimate meaning.

Influenced by his younger brother Helmut (commonly known as H. Richard), an excellent theologian who taught at Yale, Reinhold also developed a negative critique of religion. Early in his career, he attacked liberal Protestantism for offering a doctrine of cheap grace, easy answers and automatic progress, which is not taken seriously in the real world of politics and economics. As reflected in his debates with Karl Barth, he charged that neo-orthodox Christianity makes God so transcendent and revelation so unique that Christianity no longer has any real connection with social life. Drawing on his profound understanding of American culture, he criticized Christianity in the United States for its tendency to identify itself with the American way of life, thus losing its power to criticize national pride and greed. Anticipating the contemporary feminist analysis, he noted that Christianity's emphasis on restraining pride and self-assertion can support social injustice by creating passive, dependent citizens. With special fervor, he attacked those believers who used religion to give ultimate meaning to finite political projects by identifying them with God's will. Responding to the Marxist critique of religion as an opiate, Niebuhr sought to unmask every utopian tendency in Christianity which could render Christians powerless in the real world.

Niebuhr's critique, formulated in an age of social optimism, hits hardest at Christians who proclaim simple answers to complicated questions, as well as those who use the gospel to baptize our American way of life. His Christian realism, however, also speaks a word of encouragement to those tempted to be pessimistic in a more cynical age. By word and example he urges us to remain in the political arena, pursuing limited goals intelligently and vigorously, always aware that the establishment of the kingdom is finally the work of the God of mercy and of hope.

Using Power for Justice

IN THE PURSUIT of social justice, Niebuhr offers us the specific admonition to use power realistically rather than to rely only on education and appeals to conscience. His failed confrontation with Henry Ford in the 1920s over workers' benefits taught him a hard lesson about both the enormous economic power of the wealthy and the great limits of rational argumentation and moral suasion. This experience caused him to question the fundamental principles of liberal philosophers such as John Dewey, who believed that education was the key to improving society. The liberalism spawned by the Enlightenment simply assumed that the human race, emancipated from authoritarianism and guided by reason, would continue along the path of inevitable progress. According to Niebuhr, secular liberals failed to understand both the inner dynamics of society and the ambivalence of human reason. His analysis is precise and penetrating. Society is composed of various groups or collectives, all seeking

---

> *"Special priveleges make all men dishonest. The purest conscience and the clearest mind is prostituted by the desire to prove them morally justified."*
> — Moral Man and Immoral Society

---

power. Imbalances in economic and political power produce injustices. Ruling groups in society will always seek special privileges, identifying their superior position with God's will. No group holding power ever voluntarily gives up its dominant position, but always attempts to keep the powerless in subjugation.

Moreover, collectives inevitably demonstrate more unrestrained egoism and destructive pride than individuals. The larger the group, the more likely it is to act according to momentary impulses and unexamined purposes. Nations, of course, are especially prone to pride because they are held together by emotion and always act out of self-interest. Nations tend to exploit other nations to protect their own economic interests. Paradoxically, the patriotism which prompts individuals to offer unselfish service to the nation can be easily turned to selfish nationalistic purposes. No transnational power block exists or can be realistically envisioned which will curb the power of individual nations. Nation-states tend to take on a sacred aura, hypocritically invoking God to support their own interests.

According to Niebuhr, reason cannot be counted on to check the pride of groups nor to restrain their will to power. On the contrary, reason is regularly employed by collectives to further their own aims and to preserve their privileged positions. Secular liberals fail to recognize that reason is a weak instrument, often enslaved by passion and distorted by social prejudice. Bound to their middle-class assumptions about the power of reason, liberal educators and social scientists cannot produce a better society because they fail to recognize the importance of power and the ambiguity of reason.

Niebuhr also directed his criticism at liberal Christians influenced by the Social Gospel. Unwittingly, they subvert the work of justice by emphasizing the establishment of the community of love. Their talk of love and moral values in the real world of power relationships sounds romantic and sentimental, thus dooming the gospel to impotency. It is not possible to oppose the Henry Fords of this world with moral idealism. Liberal Christians also tend to forget that the poor and oppressed are tempted to misuse their current limited power and that revolutions always bring new forms of oppression. Finally, abandoning his previous outlook, Niebuhr argued that Christian pacifism is an irresponsible position because it abandons any realistic chance of establishing justice and preserving peace.

Entering Power Politics

FOLLOWING OUT THE LOGIC of his analysis, Niebuhr insists that Christians must enter the real world of power politics. The educational approaches advocated by secular liberals must be joined to the proper use of power. Christians engaged in political life will necessarily be involved in the ambiguous business of making compromises and settling for the lesser of two evils. Drawing on our national experience of democratic pluralism, Niebuhr advocated extending the system of checks and balances so that all power groups would be restrained by other collectives with some measure of power. Decades before the civil rights movement of the 1960s, he maintained that black people must gain power in order to achieve their rights in relationship to the white majority. He also advocated nonviolence as a particularly valuable method for oppressed groups to employ in securing their rights. This tactic is effective because it robs the oppressor of moral conceit and increases the chances of creating harmonious relationships in the future. He admired Gandhi's successes with nonviolent tactics, judging him to be a shrewd political realist. Niebuhr himself, however, refused to rule out entirely the use of violence in securing justice, since force may be necessary as a last resort.

Niebuhr called upon liberal Christians to put a greater emphasis on establishing justice than on creating a community of love. While love is ethically purer than justice and better suited for personal relationships because it demands generosity, justice is more effective than love in creating a better society because it strives for equity and deals more effectively with power relationships. The religious spirit of love loses its effectiveness in proportion to the size of the community and the impersonal character of its relationships. Only romantic idealists believe that privileged groups and sovereign nations will be guided by the law of love taught by Christ. In the real world Christians must learn to work for "proximate justice." In other words, we cannot achieve total equality in society but we must take small steps to move in that direction. Concentrating on limited achievable goals helps us avoid disillusionment and cynicism. Even in working for proximate justice, we must be aware of the danger of creating new injustices and destroying the existing good.

Christian realism must not only counteract the negative aspects of power but must also use power for accomplishing good. Power is a necessary and valuable tool for establishing order, unity and justice in a community. Political power plays the essential role of curtailing the economic power which dominates in modern capitalistic countries. Christians must be involved in the various power groups which help formulate public policy in order to nudge society towards proximate justice. Believers should do so with a clear recognition that coercive power always ends up hurting innocent people. In this regard, Niebuhr liked to point out that even Gandhi's economic boycott of English goods in India, with all its aura of moral purity, still ended up hurting the children of the workers in Manchester, England, who lost their jobs as a result of the boycott. With this unflinching realism, Niebuhr wanted Christians to understand the moral ambiguities and the trade-offs involved in entering the arena of politics and economics. Still, for him such involvement is not only necessary but morally superior to withdrawal which simply perpetuates injustice.

In summary, Niebuhr challenges us to look realistically at the role of power in our society so that we can use it prudently to establish as much justice and equity as possible in any given situation.

Pride and Paradox

FINALLY, Niebuhr's Christian realism challenges us to take sin seriously as we work to improve the social order. Driven by his immense passion to establish a realistic social ethics, Niebuhr located the deepest roots of social conflict and injustice in human sinfulness. In his master work, *The Nature and Destiny of Man*, he drew on the Scriptures as well as the thought of Augustine and his followers to produce an ethically-oriented anthropology which remains one of the most insightful analyses of human sinfulness ever produced.

Niebuhr offers us a dialectical understanding of human existence filled with paradox. Human beings are immersed in nature as well as the historical process, but are also self-transcendent spiritual beings capable of acting freely. Our vitality flows from both our animal nature and our ability to see meaning in human existence. Made in the image of God, we have a yearning for the infinite but are tied to earthly realities. Because we are "both free and bound, both limited and limitless," we experience anxiety, a deep but vague fear with no apparent object. On the one hand, we feel anxious because we are limited and are painfully conscious of our limitations. We do not possess our own being and could cease to exist at any moment. On the other hand, anxiety

"Nations will always find it more difficult than individuals to behold the beam that is in their own eye while they observe the mote that is in their brother's eye; and individuals find it difficult enough."

— Moral Man and Immoral Society

occurs because we have unlimited possibilities which are never totally actualized. As free beings, we have so many options that we experience the "dizziness of freedom." Following fundamental scriptural insights reinterpreted by the existentialist philosopher Sören Kierkegaard, Niebuhr notes that finitude and anxiety are not sinful in themselves but are the "pre-condition of sin." In other words, the frightening experience of anxiety tempts us either to deny our creaturehood and mortality by sinful pride and excessive self-love or to escape from the dizziness of freedom in destructive sensuality. Thus, sinfulness arises not from ignorance or passion but from the culpable refusal to accept our essential creaturehood.

Although Niebuhr did recognize that self-abasement could perpetuate injustice, he concentrated on analyzing the sin of pride because of its obvious destructive consequences in the social order. He saw pride manifested in four different but related ways. Pride of power occurs when individuals feeling insecure grasp for power, status or possessions to ward off anxiety. Individuals are guilty of intellectual pride when they fail to recognize the limitations of their own perspectives or deny the "taint of self-interest" always involved in the pursuit and use of knowledge. Moral pride results when persons set up their own ethical standards according to which they judge themselves good and those who deviate from them bad. Given this outlook, sinners are no longer able to recognize themselves as sinners because God's standards have been disregarded. Under the sway of moral pride, even virtuous behavior becomes the vehicle of sin because it leads to self-righteousness. The arrogance engendered by moral pride is responsible for maintaining much of the cruelty and prejudice which exists in society.

Finally, spiritual pride occurs when individuals explicitly "boast before the Lord" by claiming divine sanctions for their own programs and policies. This leads to the worst forms of intolerance and domination because those suffering discrimination are treated as nonpersons outside the scope of God's care. Spiritual pride represents the essence and final expression of human sinfulness since it denies both the transcendence of God and the finitude of human existence. Anticipating the contemporary notion of social sin, Niebuhr insisted that sinfulness extends to the social realm. Original sin (the one empirically verifiable Christian doctrine, according to Niebuhr) is not a chronological event linked with the Fall, but a general condition of human existence which explains our propensity to sin. Our sinful actions, made possible by original sin, are inevitably translated into the social sphere where their destructive power is multiplied. Privileged classes, for example, intensify the evil of personal prejudice by using their power to dominate alienated groups.

Niebuhr castigated both secular and Christian liberals for failing to face the reality of sin. Without appreciating original sin, they are overly optimistic about achieving human progress through reason and love. Forgetting the propensity of individuals and groups to pride and arrogance, they propose utopian solutions which are not workable in the sinful world. In response, Christian realism insists on the power of sin to affect all things human and encourages individuals and groups to work effectively for proximate justice.

Critics of Niebuhr have exposed significant limitations in his theology. His Christology, for example, is clearly weak on the Resurrection and gives little prominence to Christ the liberator. He has emphasized human sinfulness so much that the power of grace is obscured. He failed to develop an ecclesiology and did not appreciate the social value of mysticism, liturgy, and spirituality. Feminists have correctly pointed out that his treatment of sin is one-sided because it emphasizes pride and self-assertion while neglecting the sin involved in excessive dependence and failure to achieve self-actualization.

It is possible to discern rejoinders to such criticisms within Niebuhr's own writings. In response to those who claim his theology obscures the power of grace, for instance, we find an impressive treatment of "original justice" which continues to echo in the call of conscience and a helpful discussion of the image of God which remains in human nature despite sin. The fluid and complex character of his thought allows for very different interpretations. This helps explain how both liberals and neoconservatives can claim him for their mentor and guide. However, as a giant of 20th-century theology, Niebuhr rises above his critics and transcends the debates among his followers. His Christian realism remains a powerful weapon against utopian thinking and naive solutions to complex problems. He continues to challenge all Christians to find effective means of relating the gospel to the real world where grace and sin always contend. In 1943, Niebuhr wrote a prayer which has become famous: "God give us the grace to accept with serenity the things that cannot be changed, courage to change the things that should be changed, and the wisdom to distinguish one from the other." Reinhold Niebuhr's active life and powerful teaching serve as a commentary on the prayer, reminding us to interpret it not as a justification for passivity but as a challenge to strive resolutely and prudently for greater justice and peace in our ambiguous and sinful world.

Discussion Questions

1. What role do you think Christianity should play in improving the social order?

2. How did Niebuhr's pastoral experience influence his social ethics?

3. What are the main characteristics of Niebuhr's Christian realism and how did he apply it to political strategies and public policy questions?

4. How does Niebuhr's life and theology challenge current Christian responses to social questions?

Suggested Readings

Moral Man and Immoral Society (Scribner, 1932). An extremely influential analysis of the dynamics of social groups.

Nature and Destiny of Man, two vol. (Scribner, 1941 and 1943). His masterwork, often underrated, which presents a Christian anthropology from the perspective of social ethics.

Man's Nature and His Communities (Scribner, 1965). A late work in which Niebuhr softened some of his harsh positions.

Reinhold Niebuhr: A Biography (Pantheon, 1985). A balanced presentation of the man and his life which has sparked renewed interest in his thought.

CHAPTER 11

John Courtney Murray
living as a christian in a pluralistic society

LIVING AS A COMMITTED CHRISTIAN in the United States, with its tradition of pluralism, is a complex project filled with opportunity and challenge. Believers from diverse religious traditions have flourished in this land of freedom maintaining their faith and making unique contributions to the common good of the country. On the other hand, the pluralism which enriches all aspects of our national life also creates its own set of vexing questions.

How, for example, can we maintain a sense of national identity and purpose in the absence of the traditional unifying symbols provided by a common religion? How can diverse interest groups engage in civil discourse and cooperative action while avoiding acrimonious confrontation and paralyzing factionalism? What public policies are we to adopt on divisive issues such as abortion and the teaching of religion in public schools?

John Courtney Murray, S.J. (1904-1967), the most influential theologian the Catholic Church in the United States has produced, devoted much of his life to exploring the relationship between religion and society. Throughout his distinguished career, which included three decades as professor of theology at Woodstock College in Maryland, he labored mightily to demonstrate that it is possible for Catholics to be both loyal members of their church and patriotic citizens of their country. In the process, this scholarly and urbane man won the respect of academics from various religious traditions and

helped to create the open climate which made possible the election of John F. Kennedy as the first Catholic president.

Murray, who wrote lucid and graceful prose, is best known as the architect of the Second Vatican Council's Declaration of Religious Liberty. Though silenced by the Vatican in 1955, he saw his views on religious liberty vindicated by the majority of bishops at the council. He facilitated this striking development of church doctrine by combining a brilliant historical analysis of the intent of official church teaching on the topic with an insightful examination of democratic structures in the United States. Through this scholarly effort he was instrumental not only in freeing Catholics from the suspicion of being unpatriotic, but also in bringing the American political experiment with religious liberty into the official consciousness of the whole Catholic Church.

As Murray, the sober realist, clearly recognized, however, this achievement simply brought the official church abreast of the sound instincts already shared by many in the contemporary world thereby paving the way for increased involvement of Catholics in society. Now we are faced with the continuing responsibility of relating our religion to the ever-evolving and always complex pluralism which constitutes life in the United States. Fortunately, we still find helpful guidance for this task in Murray's challenging writings—especially in his classic study of the American proposition, *We Hold These Truths* (America Press, 1985), originally published during the 1960 presidential campaign and reissued on the twenty-fifth anniversary of its publication.

The Public Discourse

MURRAY OFFERS US GENERAL GUIDANCE by emphasizing the importance of civil discourse and constructive dialogue as a means of living effectively in our pluralistic society. Building on a long tradition, he insisted that a political community is formed by persons "locked together in argument" and passionately engaged in reasonable discussion of significant issues. He well understood that citizens of the United States live in "emotional solidarity" because they inhabit a vast and rich land, share a common history of building a new nation, and are committed to a dream of the free pursuit of happiness. Nevertheless, Murray, ever the intellectual, insisted that constructive argument among responsible citizens is the great tool for deepening national self-understanding and creating a society of justice, peace, and unity. The health of the country depends on informed citizens debating the proper response of government to the problems of public order, as well as the best ways of achieving the broader societal goal of furthering the common good. Such conversations require not only mutual trust but also a common language, initial points of agreement, and a core of commonly-held truths. We can argue constructively only within a context of fundamental agreement.

Murray feared the "modern-day barbarians," who reject the role of reason in public affairs and who resort to the rule of force and fear. Barbarians replace

"The whole premise of the public argument, if it is to be civilized and civilizing, is that the consensus is real, that among the people everything is not in doubt, but that there is a core of agreement, accord, concurrence, acquiescence. We hold certain truths; therefore we can argue about them."

— We Hold These Truths

dialogue with monologue, reason with passion, and civility with harsh rhetoric. They think they have exclusive hold on the truth and are called to convert or coerce others to their way of thinking. Such barbarism, which tempts even good citizens, makes conversation impossible and deprives society of the necessary resources for achieving unity in the midst of diversity.

The problem of maintaining civil discourse in the United States is intensified by the existence of different world views and religious traditions. Murray had a profound appreciation of the comprehensive way in which individuals and communities are shaped by their world views. Catholics, Protestants, Jews, and secularists in the United States have distinctive sets of historical experiences, styles of thought, dominant categories, and spiritual sensibilities which combine to produce very diverse self-understandings. This concrete fact of religious and political existence in the United States creates interest groups which seek power and influence in order to determine the dominant ethos of the country. Thus, underneath the veneer of civility in our society there are what Murray calls "structures of passion and war," which include hidden resentments and profound distrust among the competing worldviews.

Murray's comments on civil discourse bring to mind the current political activities of the so-called new religious right. The problem posed for more liberal believers is not the actual participation of conservative Christians in the political process. That surely is their right as citizens and is in accord with the social dimension of the gospel. Difficulties arise when the style, language, and goals of the Christian right violate the norms for civil discourse which are necessary for a pluralistic society. Thus, when members of these groups speak as though their particular position on widely-disputed social and political issues is the only moral or genuinely Christian response, they make genuine conversation impossible. When they enlist God on their side and co-opt religious language for their own political purposes, they short-circuit our traditional political process of searching in common for wisdom and pragmatic solutions. Whenever extreme members of the religious right speak about establishing a Christian commonwealth or Christianizing our institutions, they undercut the very basis of our pluralistic society, which wisely forbids the establishment of any specific religion.

It is no wonder that many citizens who espouse the ideal of civil discourse find it so difficult to engage in constructive argument with the new religious right. Claims of divine assistance and moral superiority have a way of precluding rational debate and constructive conversation.

A Growing Edge

MURRAY OFFERS US NO EASY SOLUTIONS to this current problem. He does warn us against utopian dreams which envision perfect harmony and unanimous consensus, since these unrealistic expectations lead to frustration and political paralysis. His more realistic suggestion is to "limit the warfare" and "enlarge the dialogue." To do this requires, first of all, a conscious decision to move beyond the wounds and prejudices which have accumulated over the years among persons with competing worldviews and religious traditions. Furthermore, we must recognize that civil discourse is in the best interest of all citizens and that cooperative effort, based on mutual understanding and trust, is our best hope for improving our society. Dialogue must be enlarged because the great political and social questions have, in Murray's phrase, "a growing edge." This means that these questions are not solved once and for all by simplistic measures proposed by one of the competing interest groups; rather, they demand continuing dialogue among all segments of society in order to reach provisional solutions in changing circumstances.

Murray reminded a whole generation of Catholics in the United States that they could enter wholeheartedly into the political process of debate and compromise without denying the truth claims of their church. He has the same message for the new Christian right. The church does not need institutional privilege, and it should not assume a self-righteous posture in debate with others. The gospel thrives in an atmosphere of freedom, and Christians can make their best contribution to the common good by respecting the pluralism which freedom demands and enables.

Murray's life is a reminder that the high road of enlightened dialogue rooted in personal integrity can be surprisingly effective. Despite great provocation from doctrinaire secularists and reactionary Christians, he generally maintained a lofty standard of intelligent discourse and respectful dialogue as he argued his case. Confident of this style, he succeeded, as few others have done, in

> *"The American Catholic is on good ground when he refuses to make an ideological idol out of religious freedom and separation of church and state, when he refuses to 'believe' in them as articles of faith."*
>
> — We Hold These Truths

moving the whole church toward a constructive development of traditional teaching. Not only did he accept pluralism with a calm heart, but he approached the issues with a "cleansed imagination" so that the "structures of war" could be replaced by patterns of civil discourse. Murray thus remains today a valuable guide for all those who want to participate effectively in the great conversation which is crucial to the health of a pluralistic society.

"We Hold These Truths"

MURRAY HAS IMPORTANT things to say not only about method and style, but also about the substance of the public philosophy which is needed to hold our pluralistic society together. Traditionally, nation-states formed bonds of solidarity around a common religion. In the United States, however, national unity based on religion was impossible from the very beginning, because the colonists were drawn from many diverse religious traditions and included significant numbers of unchurched individuals. The Founding Fathers forged a solution to the problems created by religious pluralism by insisting on certain self-evident truths which could command the assent of reasonable people and bring a sense of common purpose to the nation.

These truths were founded on the conviction that God holds sovereign power over nations and individuals and has "endowed all persons with certain inalienable rights." Murray emphasized that this religious foundation of our public philosophy, or what he called "the American consensus," has been maintained

---

"On what grounds does the First Amendment command the common assent and consent of the whole citizenry? And how is it that this common assent and consent do not infringe upon the 'freedom of religion,' that is, the freedom of consciences to retain the full integrity of their convictions, and the freedom of the churches to maintain their own different identities, as defined by themselves. I take it that every church claims this freedom to define itself, and claims too the consequent right to reject definition at the hands of any secular authority. To resign this freedom or to abdicate this right would be at once the betrayal of religion and the corruption of politics."

— We Hold These Truths

---

throughout our history despite the dissent urged by the proponents of secularism. Thus, the Supreme Court, in the 1952 Zorach case, could state the principle often repeated by our presidents and other court decisions: "We are a religious people whose institutions presuppose a Supreme Being."

In addition to this foundational truth, the American consensus includes the notion that we are a free people under limited government. Through the British tradition we received the concept of government by law, not by human beings. We made our own contribution by enshrining this notion in a written constitution. The government would be limited, not only by law, but by the consent of the people it represents. Murray interpreted our consensus as reviving the ancient Christian distinction between state and society. The state or government submits itself to the larger truth of society, and thus must respect the freedom of societal institutions, such as the press, the university, and the church. The American consensus involves an act of faith in the power of the people to govern themselves, but it also recognizes that genuine freedom will be maintained only by persons who act with virtue and discipline because they accept their responsibility to a higher law.

According to Murray, elements of this consensus exist in the minds and hearts of average citizens, providing them with an almost intuitive capacity for eventually discerning serious distortions in government policy. The consensus exists in a more reflective and explicit fashion in the minds of scholars and experts, who through education and training are able to articulate the public philosophy and bring it to bear on changing circumstances and new issues. Since it has a personal and historic character, the public philosophy of the United States can continually evolve through public debate and reasonable argumentation.

Murray well understood the limitations of the public consensus as it has actually developed in our country. Some individuals, for example, have denied the existence of divinely sanctioned self-evident truths, while the society as a whole has systematically deprived certain groups of their God-given rights. Murray lamented any disintegration of the American consensus, insisting that we could insure the survival and well-being of the nation only by renewing it. We must gather around the public philosophy because it determines the broad purposes of the country, guides the formulation of policy, facilitates communication among the citizens, and makes reasonable dissent possible without leading to anarchy.

From Consensus to Legislation

THERE ARE ELEMENTS IN MURRAY'S ANALYSIS of the American consensus which even friendly critics would dispute, especially his contention that it is based on natural law theory and that Catholics are in a unique position to revivify it. Nevertheless, his explanations of the dynamics and content of the consensus offer us important insights for dealing with substantive issues of public policy in our pluralistic society.

To take just one example, his analysis suggests a way of understanding the position of individuals who abhor abortion but are convinced that a restrictive constitutional amendment will not work at this time. Their position rests on the recognition that in the United States today there is no consensus within general public opinion that fetal life should be accorded equal protection under the law. In this situation, legislation restricting abortion would only promote illegal acts and undercut respect for authority, much as the Prohibition laws did decades ago. Restrictive legislation would harden the position of pro-choice advocates and make genuine public debate on the question more difficult. Such legislation would repeat the mistake of the 1973 Supreme Court decision, which effectively established a pro-choice position before the society as a whole could even approach consensus on the matter.

"The entrenched segments of American pluralism claim influence on the course of events, on the content of the legal order, and on the quality of American society. To each group, of course, its influence seems salvific; to other groups it may seem merely imperialist. In any case, the forces at work are not simply intellectual; they are also passionate. There is not simply an exchange of arguments but of verbal blows. You do not have to probe deeply beneath the surface of civic amity to uncover the structure of passion and war."

— We Hold These Truths

Murray's analysis of the American consensus not only helps us understand the reluctance of some pro-life advocates to support a constitutional amendment, but it also suggests a positive course of action for all who favor a pro-life position. In other words, there is an alternative to the position espoused by those public figures who declare they are personally opposed to abortion but must simply obey the law of the land. The other option is to help shape the public consensus so that we can move toward general agreement in the country that fetal life possesses an inherent dignity and deserves protection under the law.

This effort should be directed especially toward those academic, political, cultural, and religious leaders who have the power to influence the public philosophy. These people are generally appalled by intemperate rhetoric, coercive activities, and acts of violence. Their natural tendency is to proceed by careful argumentation, patient dialogue, and reasonable compromise. Since they fear single-issue politics, they are more receptive to a pro-life ethic which consistently advocates peace, justice, and respect for life in all stages of its development.

The public consensus makes both constitutional and statutory legislation possible and effective. Prohibition did not work because there was no clear public philosophy supporting it. The civil rights legislation in the 1960s was more successful, because a favorable consensus had been reached among those who had the power to shape public opinion. Today, pro-life advocates have the opportunity to influence the public consensus through simple conversation, informed debate, and constructive action based on respect for all human life. Thus Murray's analysis of the American consensus suggests a viable alternative for those who recognize the inconsistency in a merely private opposition to abortion but are convinced that the time is not yet right for restrictive legislation.

And Liberty to Literacy

JOHN COURTNEY MURRAY has also written perceptively on the relationship between religion and education. For him, the problems involved are fundamental. A "religiously-informed citizenry" is crucial to the fate of free government and the well-being of society. Yet American students, and perhaps their professors as well, are like "untutored children" in religious and theological matters. A truly radical solution to this continuing problem of religious illiteracy should begin with the recognition that the "whole intent of the First Amendment was to protect, not to injure, the interest of religion in American society" (*We Hold These Truths*, p. 151).

The amendment is a pragmatic response to religious pluralism, not an ideological statement which makes secularism our official religion. The no-establishment clause, which exists for the sake of the loftier free-exercise clause, does not rule out cooperation between state and church, as is clear in the continuing practice of governmental support for chaplains in the armed forces. In the Zorach case, the Supreme Court summarized the best of our tradition when it spoke of a government which "respects the religious nature of the people and accommodates the public service to their spiritual needs."

This interpretation of the First Amendment opens up new possibilities for solving our problem of religious illiteracy. Murray roots his positive solution in the freedom of students to learn about their own religion. They need to explore with proper guidance the intellectual foundations of the faith which gives fundamental meaning and direction to their lives. Furthermore, it is in the best interest of society to respond to this aspect of religious liberty and to meet this need. Without religious knowledge, our society loses touch with the wellsprings of its freedom and is in danger of drifting toward totalitarianism. Since the state assumes responsibility for education in general, it cannot ignore the spiritual needs which arise in this area. If we had a genuine public commitment to pass along our religious heritage, we would find more effective ways of accomplishing this in our schools.

Murray emphasized the important role played by colleges and universities in this process. For him, "high talk about religion," as a body of self-validating knowledge, was possible and desirable within the Academy. Many students attending universities are religiously committed either as Protestants, Catholics, or Jews. While a university cannot judge the validity of these commitments, it should not deprive students of the opportunity to explore this vital dimension of their experience.

THE QUEST FOR RELIGIOUS KNOWLEDGE is best pursued according to rigorous academic standards. Professors who teach courses about religion should be especially careful to stress understanding and avoid evangelizing. These courses could legitimately treat the nature of religious faith as well as the content of the various systems of belief, both in their inner consistency and in their relationship to other areas of knowledge. While recognizing the practical problem of finding trained scholars for such courses, Murray insisted that persons teaching about a particular religious tradition should themselves be adherents of that belief system. He was convinced that a university does not have to worry about academic standards of objectivity if it simply turns its students loose to explore, under expert guidance, the world's great religious traditions.

Murray's thoughts on this topic deserve to be brought into the current debate on educational reform. We continue to suffer from religious illiteracy, even though collegians are demonstrating an increased interest in religious questions. Most of our colleges and universities do not have departments or programs of religious studies. Recent reports emanating from the academic world which offer so many helpful suggestions for reforming undergraduate education have totally ignored the vital question of religious studies. For instance, "Integrity in the College Curriculum: A Report to the Academic Community" (Association of American Colleges, 1985) discusses curricular reform without even mentioning the study of religion.

Given the dynamics of the current debate on higher education, Murray's line of argumentation is precisely on target. He unmasks the underlying assumption that religious courses in public universities and colleges necessarily involve proselytizing and are thus a violation of the First Amendment. His argument for promoting religious literacy is intelligible to various segments of our population because it is rooted in a respect for the freedom of students and a concern for the common good of the country. He understands that the task of education, including religious education, is not to reduce contemporary pluralism to unity, but the much more modest one of reducing it to intelligibility. Those who recognize the importance of overcoming religious illiteracy have a powerful ally in the Jesuit theologian who explored in such depth the societal implications of religious understanding.

A full analysis of John Courtney Murray's thought would explore his many limitations as a theologian, including his focus on a narrow range of topics, his failure to bring more biblical teaching to bear on the religious liberty question, his flawed efforts to achieve a better integration of the natural and supernatural orders, and his rather uncritical acceptance of the American way of life. On the other hand, a more complete treatment would also reveal the profundity of his thought and his important insights into many other contemporary topics, including the nature of freedom and the question of federal aid to private schools. Even our brief discussion, however, reveals John Courtney Murray as a Catholic theologian so immersed in the real experience of life in the United States that he remains for us today a valuable guide for living in our pluralistic society.

Discussion Questions

1. How does your faith influence your life in a pluralistic society?

2. How did Murray's experience as a citizen of the United States affect his position on religious liberty?

3. What did Murray mean by the "American consensus" and how was it to be achieved and applied to public policy questions?

4. How could Murray's style and insights enrich Christian participation in political life?

Suggested Readings

We Hold These Truths (America Press, 1985). A series of demanding, carefully reasoned essays exploring church-state questions and the meaning of the American proposition.

The Problem of God, Yesterday and Today (Yale University Press, 1964). A penetrating study of a crucial question from biblical, theological and contemporary perspectives.

Problems of Religious Freedom (Newman Press, 1965). A lucid summary of the two major views on religious freedom, their historical development and the issue as debated at the Second Vatican Council.

John Courtney Murray: Theologian in Conflict by Daniel Pelotte (Paulist Press, 1975). A study which provides helpful background information for understanding Murray's position on religious liberty.

CHAPTER 12

Johann Metz
overcoming individualism

SOCIAL CRITICS HAVE HEIGHTENED our awareness of the way individualism dominates our society. Powerful voices proclaim that persons should assert their individuality and "do their own thing." We have lived through the "me decade" of the seventies and have been bombarded with the "yuppie mentality" of the eighties. The common message is that the self-interest of individuals is more important than the good of society as a whole. Some persons pursue their own interests by striving for more possessions or greater socioeconomic success. Others, rejecting materialistic values, express their individuality by striving for self-improvement and greater self-actualization. Both styles are highly individualistic, demonstrating little regard for the public good.

Individualism has fostered an anti-institutional bias which is reflected in commonly voiced complaints. Young people grumble about the restrictive character of family life. Collegians decry the restrictions imposed by the bureaucratic structures of the university. Workers express frustration over the impersonal character of corporations and the ineffectiveness of unions. Politicians speak about getting government off our backs. Christians claim that the institutional church impedes their spiritual growth. The prevalence of such negative attitudes encourages persons to think of themselves as autonomous individuals who can best find fulfillment through emancipation from all types of institutions.

The German theologian Johann Baptist Metz has proposed a political theology designed precisely to challenge and overcome the individualistic bias built into modern Western culture. Metz, who began his career as a brilliant student of Karl Rahner, has gradually developed his own theological perspective which places his teacher's fundamental insights into a larger social and political context. Expanding Rahner's anthropology which defines human beings as infinite searchers for truth and goodness, Metz insists that we understand ourselves and others, especially those who are powerless, as social creatures heavily influenced by economic and political factors. Furthermore, he recognizes that the social context created by individualism suffers from essential contradictions which must be brought to light and surmounted. Finally, he proposes the development of a political Christianity which draws on the "dangerous memory of Jesus" to carry out this task of social transformation.

Suffering and Death

MAJOR THEMES IN METZ'S THEOLOGY can be traced to his traumatic experiences during World War II. Metz was born August 5, 1928, in a small Catholic village in Bavaria about 30 miles from Flossenburg, the site of an infamous concentration camp where the Nazis imprisoned thousands of Jews on their way to the death camps and where theologian Dietrich Bonhoeffer was executed. At the age of 16, Metz was taken out of school and pressed into military service. With almost no training, he was sent with a company of boys his age to the Western front to fight the rapidly advancing American army. One evening his company commander sent him back to the battalion headquarters to deliver a message. When Metz finally returned the next morning, he discovered all of his young comrades had been killed in an intense attack by planes and tanks. After gazing at the lifeless faces of his friends with whom he had once shared youthful laughter, he wandered through the forest for hours, emitting over and over again a "soundless cry" which has haunted him ever since. This horrible experience, which shattered his boyhood dreams, has forced him to wrestle with the question of what happens to those who suffer and die and what hope we can have for them.

This question is sharpened and expanded for Metz by what he calls the "Auschwitz challenge." The silence of the German people over the Holocaust also came to haunt his consciousness. In the village where he grew up, no one talked about the concentration camp thirty miles away. His mother always denied knowing anything about it. His great teacher and close personal friend,

Karl Rahner, never discussed the Holocaust in his theology. For Metz, Auschwitz raises again the meaning of the suffering of innocent victims. It also presents a profound indictment of both the culture which allowed such an unspeakable catastrophe to happen and the traditional form of Christianity which lacked the will and the power to stop it. Metz insists that the Holocaust must be remembered so that we can face the profound distortions embedded in contemporary society.

Near the end of the war, Metz was captured and taken to a POW camp in France before being sent to the United States. After the war, he returned to Germany, entered the seminary and eventually was ordained a priest for the Archdiocese of Munich. His training took him to the University of Innsbrook in Austria, where he studied under Karl Rahner and completed doctorates in both philosophy and theology. In 1963, he became Professor of Fundamental Theology in the Catholic faculty at the University of Münster. He was going to leave there in 1979 when the University of Munich offered him a teaching position, but an intervention by Cardinal Joseph Ratzinger, then Archbishop of Munich, helped to block this move. Rahner vigorously protested Ratzinger's action, testifying to "the Christian and ecclesial character" of his former student's

"We can pray after Auschwitz, because people prayed in Auschwitz."

— The Emergent Church

theology, even though it had taken a different turn from his own approach. Nevertheless Metz was denied the new position and remained at Münster where he has taught ever since.

Metz's political theology reflects a variety of influences beyond his original association with Rahner and his doctoral study of the existentialist philosopher Martin Heidegger. For instance, Metz's dialogue partners include Ernst Bloch, the Marxist philosopher who emphasizes hope and the newness of the future; Walter Benjamin, the social critic, who insists that we read history from the viewpoint of the oppressed and the forgotten; and Jurgen Habermas, a leader of the Frankfurt School, who offers telling criticisms of modern Western consciousness. Furthermore, the experience of the Latin American base communities as articulated by the liberation theologians has given Metz a concrete sense of how a political Christianity can function in practice.

Metz's mature theological perspectives have been developed gradually through several stages. It is as though he has gradually refined his thought in order to respond to the questions raised by his painful experiences during the war. His major publications reflect this development: *Theology of the World* (Seabury, 1969), which offers a positive assessment of the secularization process; *Faith in History and Society* (Seabury, 1980), which is much more critical of the contradictions in modern society; and *The Emergent Church* (Crossroad, 1986), which argues for a church aligned with those who suffer from the injustices built into the contemporary world.

While Metz's theology reflects the European political situation and employs the language of German academic theology, it still contains a very pointed message for middle-class Christians in the United States.

The Effects of Privatism

METZ ILLUMINES for us the distortions in our culture as well as their root causes so that we can act more effectively to overcome them. According to Metz, the dominant trend in Western culture, since the Enlightenment in the 18th century, has been a continual flight from the public world into the private realm. This "privatizing tendency," which affects all aspects of contemporary life in the West, began with the Enlightenment insistence that reason rather than authority should guide the creation of a better world. As part of this project, the state had to be separated from the church and given autonomy in the political realm. This created two spheres of human concerns: the political, which was public, and the religious, which was private. With religion relegated to the realm of private morality, economic concerns and "the principle of exchange" became the basis for public life. Consequently, the possession of private property, and not religious values or moral worth, grounded and safeguarded the claim to self-determination and self-government. This created the bourgeoisie or what we call the middle class, which is socially conditioned by a market economy, political freedom, and particular cultural values such as hard work and competition. Metz harshly criticizes bourgeois priorities, which place economic advancement above compassion and personal status above the needs of the powerless.

The effects of the privatism spawned by the Enlightenment are extensive, touching all aspects of modern life. In the religious realm, for instance, the church becomes a captive of the middle class which uses it to legitimate bourgeois values. Theology stresses the personal word of the Lord addressed to individuals and neglects the social or prophetic word which calls for the transformation of society. Christian charity is directed toward alleviating the sufferings of individuals, but disregards the unjust structures which imprison whole groups

"When Christianity takes its place in the movement towards the development of world-wide community it will be able to express, in and for that great community, its understanding of a solidarity that is free from violence and hatred."
—Faith in History and Society

in poverty. Holiness is associated with a personal piety which easily ignores the social dimension of the gospel. Preaching and religious formation strive to inculcate private virtues without relating them to the common good. Christian eschatology focuses exclusively on the salvation of the individual to the neglect of the richer biblical tradition of the ultimate salvation of the whole world.

While privatism has had obvious effects on the religious sphere, it has also penetrated in more subtle ways the very foundations of contemporary life. Modern consciousness is shaped by "evolutionary logic" which has become a "pseudo-religious symbol" for a self-contained world with no need of divine grace. In other words, the modern mentality simply assumes that science and technology can guide us along a path of continual progress. In such a self-contained world, we experience time as an endless and ultimately boring continuum or as an "empty infinity" in which nothing significantly new or surprising can happen. Hence, our fear is not so much that the world will end in catastrophe, but that a "faceless evolution" will continue to roll over us, rendering us powerless and making genuine liberation impossible. This perception leads, in turn, to fatalistic apathy and, at times, to fanatical violence as victims sense that they are trapped with no way out.

Turning to the personal realm, Metz points out the strange paradox that our privatized culture, which ostensibly celebrates the individual, actually ends up devaluing persons by making them the object of uncontrollable societal forces.

In a world dominated by technology, human beings are in danger of being reduced to sophisticated machines. We become "faceless people" incapable of dreaming great dreams or imagining creative possibilities. Moreover, the cultural ethos diminishes both our desire to take responsibility for those in need and our ability to live in genuine solidarity with others. This occurs despite the great emphasis we place on improving personal relationships. Our efforts to experience authentic encounters, to improve communications, and to achieve intimacy will remain encased in the private sphere if we overlook the socio-political obstacles to achieving genuine community. Love in the family, for example, is difficult to maintain in a society dominated by superficiality and hardness of heart. Middle-class people cannot achieve genuine solidarity with the poor by giving them money, which serves as a substitute for compassion, while passively accepting the unjust structures which produce poverty. In our society, which celebrates affluence and uses money as a unifying symbol, solidarity is possible only among persons of relatively equal power and status. Unfortunately, these people often relate to one another on the basis of personal or mutual self-interest and not genuine care. Thus, our emphasis on interpersonal relationships does not help to overcome privatism because society prompts us to evaluate them in economic terms.

When individuals are dominated by their private interests, the world of politics inevitably suffers. Thus, citizens tend to forget those who died for the country and to overlook the traditions which molded the culture. The affluent and the middle class fail to see the sufferings of the poor and the powerless who are purposely kept out of sight. Politicians are unable to articulate a grand vision for a renewed society which expresses the public consensus of the people. In addition, the privatized language of personal encounter and intimate address which predominates in our culture is inadequate for dealing with the important political issues of the day. The mass media reenforces the privatization of politics by dealing with public policy questions in terms of individual personalities.

Metz believes that we are at the end of the historical period initiated by the Enlightenment and dominated by the bourgeoisie. The bankruptcy of our privatized culture has opened up a critical period during which we are threatened by a "collective darkness" that could rob us of the positive gains of freedom and justice made possible by the Enlightenment. People today seem to be "voyeurs of their own downfall" as they fall into apathy over such great societal problems as the nuclear threat, the arms race, the destruction of the environment, and the exploitation of the South by Northern countries. Given the magnitude of the problems, indifference and passivity are indefensible. For Metz, it is not enough to contemplate the evils afflicting humankind or to analyze the world's "psychosocial pathologies." The important thing is to work together to resist the darkness by transforming ourselves and our world.

Anthropological Revolution

IN ORDER TO EFFECT this transformation, Metz calls for an "anthropological revolution" in which middle-class people free themselves from the clutches of their privatized lifestyle with its tendency toward consumption and domination. Positively, we must begin to live "in solidarity with the living and the dead," which suggests special care for the victims of history as well as those currently suffering from oppression. We need a revolution in consciousness which will enable us not only to understand ourselves as social and political beings but also to react resolutely on behalf of the poor and the oppressed. This revolution demands both a radical conversion of heart which refuses to accept the world as it is with its patterns of injustice and also a fundamental reorientation of our lives so that we can relate to nature and other people on the basis of care rather than domination.

This anthropological revolution is difficult to achieve because the opposing tendencies and values of our privatized culture are so pervasive and powerful. Our success ethic blinds us to the noncompetitive values found among oppressed people and less affluent cultures. Our ability to control nature through scientific knowledge tempts us to extend this dominating mode to all aspects of life, including our interpersonal relationships. The tendency to equate full personhood with the power to control and subjugate others reenforces an egoistic and isolated understanding of human nature which undercuts the possibility of mutual relationships. In addition, our contemporary "evolutionary consciousness" with its optimistic appraisal of human progress makes it more difficult to achieve solidarity with those who suffer. When we forget the dark side of human nature and the tragic sufferings built into history, we lose our capacity to mourn and grieve as well as to comfort and console. Finally, the problem is compounded by the tendency of our privatized society to produce human robots with an "ant mentality" who are incapable of resisting the dominant trends of society. We are tempted to settle into a permanent fatalistic resignation, all the while excusing ourselves for remaining passive spectators in a world threatened by catastrophe. In short, the dominant presuppositions in our culture make it difficult to establish solidarity with the living and the dead.

In order to overcome these cultural distortions, Metz calls us to understand ourselves as essentially social beings. This self-understanding is rooted in the religious conviction that all human beings stand as subjects before God. To be a subject means not only that we are answerable to God, but also that we are responsible for ourselves and our world. Together with all other subjects, we form the one human family. We are interdependent beings who must learn to see ourselves as integral parts of a single history and a unified world.

In order to appreciate our interdependence, we must gain a proper understanding of freedom. The best of our experience suggests that genuine freedom is found within community and not in isolation. Freedom is not achieved by distancing ourselves from others or by rejecting all forms of institutional life. In the Hebrew Scriptures, individuals become free by participating in the life of a whole people liberated by God. In the Gospels, Jesus creates a new people called to live the life of freedom in the power of the Spirit. Today, in small Christian communities around the world, people are rediscovering this biblical notion that true freedom is achieved in solidarity by praying and working together for justice.

The social anthropology proposed by Metz calls us to a radical conversion. By actively seeking solidarity with the oppressed and by working together for justice, we will come to recognize the essential truth that we are, indeed, social creatures responsible before God for the task of transforming the world.

Reinterpreting Faith

IN ORDER TO OVERCOME privatism, Metz also challenges us to live as authentic disciples of Jesus who himself worked for the cause of God in the midst of the contradictions of his world. To move us in this direction, Metz proposes a refocusing of Christian teaching, placing the emphasis on its practical political power to create a more humane society. Metz is convinced that a revitalized Christian faith can play a major role in forming a new post-bourgeois society which preserves the positive accomplishments of the Enlightenment, while moving beyond the individualism it fostered.

His reinterpretation includes a negative critique of the privatized version of Christianity commonly practiced in middle-class society today. Bourgeois Christianity has lost the social dimension of the teaching of Jesus by retreating into the private world of interior piety. One clear manifestation of this is the tendency to interpret the Sermon on the Mount exclusively in terms of internal attitudes, while ignoring its prescriptions for life in the world. Such a privatized

Christianity fails to carry out its proper task of criticizing the presuppositions and practices of the economic and political order. Through its presumed "political

"Yet the most important question of all is whether the 'Church for the people' can become a 'Church of the people.'"

—Faith in History and Society

innocence" it actually legitimates existing societal institutions and middle-class values.

According to Metz, most believers suffering from a crisis of faith are not questioning the truth of particular doctrines, but are disturbed by the failure of individual Christians and the church as a whole to live up to the social demands of the gospel. Many Christians today are living out a destructive dualism which assumes that grace is operative in their private lives but absent from their public activities. Discipleship is weakened when we merely "believe in faith rather than living the faith" with all of its transformative power. The Marxist critique of religion as an opiate and an ideology buttressing the status quo, properly applies to such a privatized form of Christianity which has become a mere object of belief.

The Dangerous Memory of Jesus

TO UNLEASH the transformative and liberating power of authentic Christianity, Metz urges us to reappropriate "the dangerous memory of Jesus." This striking and innovative theme which is the key to Metz's political theology reminds us that the Christian life consists primarily in a faith-filled, action-oriented remembrance of Christ's love as manifested in his Passion, death and Resurrection. Christianity cannot be reduced to an intellectual assent to particular dogmas. Christians, rather, are formed, maintained and motivated by the stories of Jesus preserved in the Scriptures and passed on by tradition. The New Testament stories preserve the memory of Jesus in a concrete and practical way. Each generation of Christians has the responsibility to retell the stories of faith, thereby unleashing anew their liberating power. Metz has proposed a narrative theology which will encourage all Christians, including the powerless, to tell their own stories of faith. This common effort will reveal the societal obstacles to belief, promote solidarity among believers, and release new power to challenge injustice.

We remember Jesus as one who stood on the side of the oppressed and rejected, demonstrating the liberating power of unconditional love. Because he was faithful to God's cause in the world, he was considered a traitor to traditional values by the religious authorities, called a fool by Herod, and executed as a rebel by Pilate. The story does not end there, however, but includes the joyful report of his Resurrection. Thus, the Christian memory is filled with hope that the salvation promised by Jesus will indeed be accomplished.

Remembering Jesus is not a disinterested recollection of past events nor a nostalgic recall of an especially holy period. It is a committed personal remembrance which makes Jesus really present again for us as a liberating power. This memory does not constitute an abstract philosophy with a vague content. It is, rather, focused on the concrete story of the historical figure Jesus of Nazareth, who had to deal with his cultural and historical situation as do we. The memory of Jesus creates our very identity as Christians, enabling us to live an authentic life of discipleship.

The memory of Jesus is dangerous because it contains an invitation to follow a homeless leader who suffered many trials and was executed as a rebel. The active practice of discipleship, which is the only way to come to a genuine understanding of Christ and his message, necessarily involves suffering and persecution as Jesus warned and history attests. The danger of following Christ is evident today in repressive societies which cannot tolerate the liberating truth of the gospel. Christians in democratic societies who take the subversive memory of the compassionate Jesus seriously will also find themselves in conflict with sinful patterns of competitive domination and with those who benefit from them.

Recalling the sufferings of Jesus can remind us of all those who have suffered throughout history. No happiness and no amount of social progress that we enjoy today can make up for the pain and injustice suffered by the deceased victims. This sobering thought should not lead us into a false sense of collective guilt or reduce us to a paralyzing self-hatred. It should move us, instead, to a "healthy grieving" for those who have been crushed by the historical process. We should learn to read history from the viewpoint of these victims and to challenge the type of social mechanisms which repressed them. The Christian memory does not contain a theoretical explanation for innocent suffering, but it does include the hopeful story of Jesus who died for all, descended into hell in solidarity with the deceased victims, and rose triumphantly as the first born of all the dead. A shared memory of suffering, informed by Christian faith, can draw us together in the common task of "interrupting the systems"

"In itself, the Christian idea of God is a practical idea. God cannot be thought of at all unless this idea irritates and encroaches on the immediate interests of the person who is trying to think of it."

—Faith in History and Society

---

which continue to oppress people today. It stimulates us to imagine new possibilities and more creative ways of reducing suffering without falling into the utopian dream of creating a perfect world.

Christian memory necessarily involves discipleship. It is only by following Christ that we recognize the deepest meaning of the stories preserved in the Christian tradition. The gospel stories themselves are a summons to conversion and discipleship. Only by trying to imitate Jesus can we come to know him and the power of his message. True discipleship always involves both putting on the mind of Christ and working to spread the kingdom in the world. In other words, we are called to be persons of prayer who, by coming closer to the Lord, learn to accept responsibility for humanizing society. Discipleship demands that we cultivate the virtues of selfless love and active compassion which, inevitably, bring us into conflict with those who place higher value on competition and success. The memory of Jesus actively embraced eventually proves to be inherently dangerous.

Thus, we see that political theology places great emphasis on the active practice of discipleship. In this regard, Metz speaks of the "primacy of praxis." This Greek term, which is also used by Marxist philosophers and liberation theologians, has a variety of complex meanings. In this context, it suggests that genuine Christian discipleship cannot be reduced to a merely verbal confession of faith. Discipleship is, first of all, a way of life which reflects the values exemplified in the story of Jesus and leads to a deeper understanding of the truth. Christian praxis involves both courageous suffering and virtuous activity which possesses intrinsic meaning. It is designed to spread the kingdom of love by interrupting and transforming structures which oppress people.

Discipleship inspired by the memory of Jesus reveals "the God of the living and the dead" who establishes universal justice for all. The Father addressed by Jesus is not a cruel tyrant but a compassionate Lord who opens up a better future for the suffering and extends forgiveness to the guilty. This God calls us to be responsible persons who will challenge existing patterns of domination, thereby enabling others to take charge of their own lives. As Metz points out, the biblical notion of God is extremely practical because it moves us to examine our priorities and to enter the struggle for justice.

A Counter-cultural Community

THE DANGEROUS MEMORY OF JESUS is kept alive by the church, a community of "social-critical freedom," which gives public witness to the liberating power of the gospel. As a large international institution organized into local parishes, the church inevitably wields political power. This power should be used to bring about a global reconciliation between rich and poor nations and to facilitate constructive social change at the local level. Rather than supporting bourgeois values and serving as an "opiate for intellectuals," the church must function as a counter-cultural community which offers a radical challenge to the false consciousness that puts a premium on consumption and domination.

Furthermore, the remembrance of Jesus provides the church with a proper orientation toward the future. The Christian community must witness to what Metz calls the "eschatological proviso," which means that God's promise of salvation will never be fully realized within history and that every human program and every institution is provisional and relative. Our hope must reside in "the God of the living and the dead" who alone can fulfill the promise of history. The apocalyptic imagery used by Jesus to describe the imminent coming of the kingdom challenges us to remain open to the divine initiative in history which can break up the existing patterns of injustice and create new and better possibilities. Strengthened by faith in this God of the future who fulfills history and gives it meaning, the church can preach a credible message of hope while, at the same time, criticizing the societal ambiguities which continue to cause human suffering.

Metz, who loves the church and wants to build it up, finds a great sign of this hope in the small Christian base communities springing up in the developing countries. By combining a deep spirituality or mysticism with local political involvement, these communities give a powerful witness to the memory of Jesus. Metz urges us to develop, in our own societal context, similar Christian communities which celebrate the dangerous memory of Jesus around the eucharistic table and promote individual and group responsibility for social transformation.

The theology of Metz is open to criticism from diverse perspectives. He has not produced a complete systematic political theology and his treatment of individual topics such as Christology remains sketchy. Rahner's defense against Metz's challenge to his fundamental approach seems to question some of the disciple's originality. Neoconservatives criticize Metz for failing to offer a comprehensive political analysis and practical proposals for improving international relationships. Critics on the left question whether his church-oriented proposals can really be effective in bringing about social change. Whatever judgment is made about the limitations of his political theology, there is no doubt that the major insights of Johann Baptist Metz function as a radical challenge to the individualism which dominates our culture.

Discussion Questions

1. How are you affected by individualism and privatism?

2. How would you describe the connections between Metz's wartime experience and his theology?

3. What are the fundamental principles of Metz's political theology and how does he use them to analyze societal contradictions and cultural distortions?

4. How can Metz's thought help us to overcome the individualism which is so prevalent in our culture?

Suggested Readings

The Emergent Church (Crossroad, 1986). A fairly readable collection of essays which contend that the church should be aligned with those suffering from injustice.

Faith in History and Society (Seabury, 1980). Very difficult reading (often attributed to a poor translation), but contains powerful criticisms of modern society and helpful suggestions for drawing on the "dangerous memory of Jesus."

Theology of the World (Seabury, 1969). An earlier work which takes a more positive view of secular society.

Poverty of Spirit (Newman Press, 1968). A good example of his spiritual writing which calls upon us to imitate the poverty of spirit practiced by Jesus.

CHAPTER 13

Gustavo Gutierrez

learning from liberation theology

DURING THE SUMMER OF 1982 IN LIMA, PERU, Henri Nouwen, the popular writer on spirituality, attended a course taught by the liberation theologian, Gustavo Gutierrez. These lectures, which drew approximately two thousand pastoral workers from around Latin America, profoundly influenced Nouwen. By his own account, he came to understand his North American-influenced spirituality as excessively spiritualized, individualistic, interior, elitist, and romantic. Struck by the commitment of Gutierrez to a life of solidarity with the oppressed, Nouwen was able to discern the limitations of his own way of living out and understanding the Christian faith. This experience, humbly reported by a man of great spiritual sensitivity, suggests the power of the message which Gustavo Gutierrez, the father of liberation theology, has for Christians in the United States.

As a result of personal conversation with Gutierrez, I came to understand more clearly the radical challenge inherent in the lifestyle and teachings of this soft-spoken Peruvian priest. He spoke passionately of the eight thousand people he serves in a parish in Lima, insisting that he is first of all a pastor and only secondarily a theologian. He reminded me that he has never been a full-time professor of theology in his own country. For him, the theological lectures and courses which take up a good part of his time are a faith-inspired effort to give voice to the experience of those struggling for liberation in Latin America. This brilliant thinker, whose seminal ideas have helped

spawn the whole movement known as liberation theology, truly finds his strength and inspiration in his solidarity with the poor and oppressed whom he serves.

Theology of Liberation

GUTIERREZ'S COMMITMENTS and theological reflections can be properly understood only in the context of his life story. He was born into a poor family (part Quechuan Indian) in Lima, Peru, on June 8, 1928. During his adolescence, he was bedridden for six years with a bone disease which left him with a permanent limp. After recovering, he attended San Marcos University where he took pre-med courses in preparation for a career as a psychiatrist. In the midst of his studies he changed his mind, deciding that he wanted to be a priest instead. Thus, he embarked on a new course of study which earned him a masters degree in philosophy and psychology from Louvain in Belgium and a degree in theology from the University of Lyon in France. During his European studies he encountered the "new theology," represented by Yves Congar among others. After being ordained to the priesthood in 1959, he did one semester of graduate studies in Rome before returning to Lima to do parish work as well as some teaching at the Catholic University in Lima. The responsibilities of his pastoral work brought him into contact with the poor and oppressed, placing him back into the social milieu of his youth. Viewing the situation with a more critical eye, he came to see that poverty is caused by unjust structures which affect a whole class of people. This meant that organized political action was absolutely crucial to helping oppressed people achieve a better way of living. At the same time, he realized that the new contemporary theology which he had learned in Europe was simply not adequate for guiding and inspiring an attack on the structural poverty embedded in South American society. At this point, Gutierrez began the long process of both reinterpreting and refocusing the Scriptures from the perspective of the poor. His desire was to articulate in the light of the Christian tradition the faith-filled experience of those struggling for liberation.

During the 1960s, through conferences with other theologians searching for an indigenous Latin American theology and through courses he taught at various universities, he gradually refined his ideas for a radically new approach to theology. At a conference in Chimbote, Peru, in 1968, he spoke for the first time of a "theology of liberation," presenting many of the main themes which have continued to shape the movement. This theology burst into public prominence at the famous conference of Latin American bishops held in Medellin, Colombia, during August and September of 1968. Among the 16 documents produced by the conference, Gutierrez wrote the one on "Peace," incorporating into it many of his seminal ideas. The major documents of Medellin recognized the structural causes of poverty and insisted that the poor must be involved in the political process of securing their own rights. The conference was thus a vindication of the methodology and the major themes being developed by Gutierrez.

He continued to refine his thinking, publishing three years later his classic work *A Theology of Liberation* (English translation, Orbis, 1973). This foun-

"Indeed, an awareness of the need for self-liberation is essential to a correct understanding of the liberation process. It is not a matter of 'struggling for others,' which suggests paternalistic and reformist objectives, but rather of becoming aware of oneself as not completely fulfilled and as living in an alienated society."

— A Theology of Liberation

dational book contained ideas and themes which have continued to influence the work of other liberation theologians such as Leonardo Boff and Juan Segundo.

In the years after Medellin, the so-called "base communities" flourished throughout Latin America. These small grassroots Christian communities are composed mostly of lower-class lay people who meet once or twice a week to read the Bible and apply it to their daily lives and to their social situations. Drawing on his pastoral experience with such groups, Gutierrez has continued his own efforts to articulate in lectures and articles the faith experience of the poor people he serves. Some of his most significant articles were collected under the title *The Power of the Poor in History* (Orbis, 1983). The theme of liberation spirituality, briefly treated in his earlier works, was more fully developed in his challenging *We Drink from Our Own Wells* (Orbis, 1984).

The whole liberation movement in Latin America has, of course, produced a backlash. When the Latin American bishops met again at Puebla, Mexico, in 1979, the conservative element tried to mute some of the liberation themes and practices espoused by Medellin. Although Gutierrez, like the other liberation theologians, was deliberately excluded from any official role at Puebla, he made important contributions from the sidelines, helping to defeat the conservative agenda. His most significant contribution was the background work he did on the document in which the bishops publicly affirmed the "preferential option for the poor."

As early as 1983, the work of Gutierrez was under suspicion in the Vatican. In 1984, the Congregation for the Doctrine of the Faith issued an "Instruction on Certain Aspects of the Theology of Liberation" which criticized those theologians who uncritically borrow from Marxism. Gutierrez adopted the position that this criticism did not apply to his own theology. Despite reported

---

"The Christian has not done enough in this area of conversion to the neighbor, to social justice, to history. He has not perceived clearly enough yet that to know God is to do justice."

— A Theology of Liberation

---

pressure from the Vatican, the Peruvian bishops have up to now refused to censure Gutierrez. Later Vatican documents such as the 1986 "Instruction on Christian Freedom and Liberation," while continuing to be critical of the use of Marxist concepts like the class struggle, have incorporated some of Gutierrez's major ideas, such as the importance of establishing a new social and political order.

Despite conservative opposition from Rome and Latin America, Gutierrez has continued his pastoral work as well as his teaching and writing. The publication of an updated and revised version of his *A Theology of Liberation* (Orbis, 1988) was an important tribute to the significance of his work. During the summer of 1988 many prominent theologians and other supporters gathered in Maryknoll, New York, to honor Gutierrez by discussing his work as well as the future directions of the movement he helped begin. The essays produced by these theologians including Schillebeeckx, Metz, Boff and Sohrino have been collected in *The Future of Liberation Theology* (Orbis, 1989), a volume which also includes some of Gutierrez's own articles and is appropriately dedicated to him.

Despite his pastoral duties, Gutierrez has been amazingly prolific, publishing numerous articles in various journals. Reading through a large stack of his published and unpublished material, I was struck by the amazing energy of this inspiring priest who combines so well pastoral and academic concerns.

Recalling the example of Henri Nouwen, let us now examine ways in which Gutierrez can deepen and expand our faith. We cannot simply import his thought as a whole into our societal context. We must, rather, examine both the method and the content of the liberation theology he represents, allowing ourselves to be challenged by its distinctive features.

"Liberating Praxis"

BY GIVING PRIMACY to liberating action in solidarity with the poor and oppressed, Gutierrez challenges every tendency to understand the Christian life in a detached and theoretical way. At the personal level, we all know the temptation to divorce our understanding of the gospel from the practical concerns of everyday life. The problem is intensified by popular preaching and teaching which fails to show the relevance of the Christian tradition for life in the world. Theologians who engage in abstract speculations, which are neither rooted in personal experience nor related to living the Christian life, also contribute to the problem. Even in the United States, with our strong pragmatic tradition, there is still a tendency to separate the social message of the gospel from the real life struggle for peace and justice in the world. Gutierrez offers a radical solution to this common temptation by insisting on the primacy of liberating activity in Christian life.

Gutierrez gained his major theological insights through his active involvement with the poor in his parish. This led him to the general principle that the truth of faith can be properly understood only from the life of charity. Gutierrez summarizes his insight: "We become Christians by acting like Christians." If we think of truth primarily as the conformity of our minds to the realities of the world, we will blunt our sense of the contradictions and distortions built into society. Truth results, rather, from participation in the struggle for societal justice and human liberation.

Gutierrez often speaks of "liberating praxis," by which he means concrete actions performed in solidarity with the poor and oppressed leading toward the creation of a transformed world and a new humanity. This activity always contains an implicit theoretical framework which guides the effort to create a better world. According to Gutierrez, liberating praxis must be at the center of the Christian life. From this perspective, the proper function of theology is reflection in and on such liberating praxis. Theology is always subordinate to the work for justice and the simple proclamation of the Word which accompanies it. Theologians have the important but secondary task of articulating the Christian message as it is actually lived out in communities of faith.

Modern liberation theology, which has its roots in the experience of the Latin American base communities, came to explicit expression around 1968, especially in connection with the Medellin conference. Although Gutierrez has insisted on the radically distinct character of liberation theology in relationship to other contemporary theologies, he has gradually become more interested in uncovering its connections with previous movements and earlier thinkers. For example, he has explored connections with the early Franciscans and has made a careful study of Bartolome de Las Casas, the 16th-century Latin American bishop who denounced the brutal exploitation of the Indians by his fellow Spaniards. While contemporary theology in Europe and the United States has taken as its primary dialogue partner the nonbelievers produced by modern secularization, liberation theology has entered into dialogue with the nonperson.

"But the process of liberation will not have conquered the very roots of oppression and the exploitation of man by man without the coming of the Kingdom. Moreover we can say that the historical, political liberating event is the growth of the Kingdom and is a salvific event; but it is not-the coming of the Kingdom, not all of salvation."

— A Theology of Liberation

In Latin America, the crucial question is not how can educated individuals believe in God after the scientific revolution but, rather, how can we speak in a credible way of a God who loves the poor living on the margins of society. The poor do not question the importance of religion but, rather, the inequities in their society. For theological reflection to be helpful and credible in this situation, it must flow from active involvement in the task of transforming society.

Gutierrez and other liberation theologians extend this fundamental insight by insisting on the primacy of orthopraxis over orthodoxy. While not denying the importance of genuine doctrinal orthodoxy as opposed to mere verbal assent to obsolete traditions, Gutierrez wants greater attention given to concrete charitable action in the world as a norm for judging the authentic Christian life. He recognizes common bonds among all oppressed people seeking a better life and calls for a greater dialogue among the theologians representing the poor in Asia and Africa, as well as black Americans and oppressed women around the world. This theology will not impose an orthodox theoretical structure on the experience of the people but will both reflect and correct their liberating praxis in the light of the Scriptures.

This theological method developed by Gutierrez can be employed in our situation as well. Rather than simply adopting and applying a particular theological system, we can learn to reflect on our common faith experience in the light of the Christian tradition. This approach will help to put greater emphasis on the active life of charity in a world filled with injustice. Dialogue with Gutierrez reminds us in a forceful way that we cannot simply talk in a detached way about the Christian life, but must commit ourselves to living it out in our concrete everyday existence.

Rereading the Scriptures

THE REINTERPRETATION and refocusing of the Scriptures accomplished by Gutierrez also challenges all tendencies to reduce Christianity to a private, spiritualized relationship with God. Unfortunately, pressures toward this kind of reductionism seem to be growing in our culture today. The traditional separation of church and state in the United States is interpreted by some to mean that religion should be banished from public life entirely. Evangelical movements stress the importance of a personal relationship to Christ often to the neglect of the social dimension of the gospel. Popular preaching in the mainline churches generally puts more emphasis on getting to heaven than on transforming this world. Many schools of theology, including the contemporary theology influenced by existentialism, have presented the great themes of grace, sin and salvation, primarily from the perspective of how they affect individual Christians.

By way of contrast, Gutierrez, in rereading the Scriptures from the viewpoint of his solidarity with the poor, rediscovered the social and public elements in the Judeo-Christian tradition. His reinterpretation of the notion of salvation in the Bible is the key to the content of his theology. While he affirms the advances made by contemporary theology in emphasizing the universality of

God's salvific will, Gutierrez is more interested in illuminating the meaning and quality of that salvation. For him, salvation is an inner-world power, definitively unleashed by Jesus Christ, which transforms and guides the whole unified historical process. Thus, Gutierrez rejects the notion that salvation is simply a matter of individuals saving their souls. In the Bible, creation and salvation

> *"The life and teaching of Jesus postulate the unceasing search for a new kind of man in a qualitatively different society. Although the Kingdom must not be confused with the establishment of a just society, this does not mean that it is indifferent to this society."*
>
> — A Theology of Liberation

are closely linked. The Lord of all initiates the history of salvation by creating the world and entrusts to human beings who are the summit of creation the task of helping to bring history to its fulfillment. From this perspective, there can be no separation between the natural world and the supernatural world of saving grace. We all participate in one integrated historical process, which always involves a conflict between the liberating power of grace and the enslaving tendencies of sin.

For Gutierrez and other liberation theologians, the Exodus exemplifies what biblical salvation is all about. God raised up Moses the liberator to lead his people out of their situation of slavery into the chosen land where they would enjoy social, political, and economic freedom. Liberation was hard won. The people at times preferred the security of slavery to the uncertainties of freedom. The Lord had to instruct them gradually so that they could come to understand the roots of their oppression as well as the joys and responsibilities of living in freedom. In the process of liberation, God made a covenant with the Israelites empowering them to be a light to the nations, a community dedicated to peace and justice. When Israel failed to live up to this covenant, God sent the prophets who called them back to the task of living out the liberation won in the Exodus.

The Exodus not only clarifies our understanding of biblical salvation but also illumines the current struggle to create a better world. From the perspective of the Exodus, salvation appears as a concrete historical reality which affects both the inner life of individuals and the public, social, and economic life of the community as a whole. History necessarily involves conflicts which must be faced and injustices which must be overcome. The oppressed today suffer from a false consciousness as did the Israelites of old. They need instruction and assistance so that they can become agents of their own destinies and take hold of the liberation process. The Exodus keeps us from "spiritualizing" the work of salvation by reducing it to an interior liberation of the soul. God's promise of salvation, enunciated in the covenant, affects all dimensions of human existence, including the physical and social as well as the spiritual and personal. This reminds us that the life of charity today cannot be confined to giving handouts to poor individuals, but must include the effort to liberate whole groups of people from unjust structures and oppressive systems.

Christ the Liberator

THE EXODUS, as Gutierrez has always recognized, must be understood in the light of the saving action of Jesus Christ. The Son of God became poor for us by being born into an oppressed and exploited people. Throughout his life Jesus identified himself with the poor of his time. In inaugurating his mission, he presented himself as the one sent by God to bring glad tidings to the poor and to proclaim liberty to the captives (Luke 4:18-19). As this itinerant preacher from Galilee moved about proclaiming the coming of the kingdom, he had, by his own account, no place to lay his head. Standing in the line of the prophets, he spoke in the name of the Lord but with a new and striking authority which unsettled the religious leaders. He proclaimed the good news that God's saving love extended to all humankind, especially the poor. He ate with outcasts and associated with sinners. His preaching was not directly political. Nevertheless, it aroused the hostility of the powerful because they sensed the challenge it presented to the established religious, social, and economic order.

For Gutierrez, the deepest meaning of the liberating message of Jesus is found in his parable of the last judgment in which he identifies himself with those in need (Matthew 25:31-46). The parable suggests a universal judgment of all people rendered according to their love of neighbor, especially the needy. It reminds us that true love is manifested in concrete action and that the deepest meaning of life is found by living in solidarity with others, especially the miserable and the wretched on this earth. Because of his actions and teachings which threatened the powerful, Jesus was executed before his time. God, however, raised him to life, thus vindicating his efforts to live in solidarity with the poor and oppressed.

For Gutierrez, the "poor Christ" is also the "liberating Christ." Through his saving death and resurrection, Jesus Christ has established a new creation and liberated us from sin with all of the injustice and exploitation it breeds. The God who led Israel from alienation to liberation made his salvation definitive in Jesus Christ. This salvation must still be worked out by transforming the historical process in all of its dimensions. In this way we prepare for the final and complete establishment of the kingdom of justice and peace for all people.

Thus we see that for Gutierrez, the inner-worldly character of salvation, so clearly manifested in the Exodus, is continued and fulfilled in the life and teaching of Jesus Christ. The theme of salvation which runs throughout the Scriptures can be reinterpreted as God's activity to liberate us in all aspects of our lives from everything that enslaves and oppresses us. We dare not, of course, identify any particular achievement of the liberation process with the kingdom of God. All partial triumphs over injustice are, however, signals of hope that God will one day complete his work of liberation.

Preferential Option for the Poor

THE SCRIPTURAL reinterpretation suggested by Gutierrez provides a foundation for the "preferential option for the poor." God, the vindicator of the exploited, loves the poor not because they are better but because they live in misery and oppression. As Mary's *Magnificat* (Luke 1:46-55) suggests, God will topple the mighty and raise up the lowly. In the Bible, material poverty is a subhuman condition, the fruit of injustice which must be overcome. Genuine evangelical poverty requires an attitude of total dependence on God, leading to a life of solidarity with the poor. The poor must be empowered to become agents of change so that they can fight injustice and transform society. The preferential option for the poor is not a Marxist idea leading to a welfare state. It is a biblically-based notion which recognizes that the poor have an important part in creating a better world. Those who join with the poor in the battle against oppressive structures not only help the needy, but also are enriched by the poor in what Gutierrez calls a "two-way evangelization." A church faithful to the example of Christ must, as liberation theologians insist, choose the side of the poor as they challenge the powerful. It is noteworthy that the bishops of the United States, in their economics pastoral, espoused this principle of the preferential option for the poor as it relates to our societal context.

Furthermore, Gutierrez challenges us to broaden our understanding of other important Christian doctrines. Jesus Christ, for example, is not only our personal savior but also the liberator of captives. The God revealed by Jesus is not only the transcendent Lord but also the defender of the poor who stands by them in the struggle for justice. Grace is not merely divine assistance to get to heaven but God's self-communication which transforms all dimensions of personal and social existence. Faith is not merely an intellectual assent to divine truths but an attitude of commitment and confidence, propelling us into the unknown world of solidarity with the exploited. Sin is not merely disobedience to God's law but a break with God that poisons human relationships and helps create unjust structures and oppressive systems. The Church is not merely a hierarchial institution but a community "born of the people under the action of the Spirit," functioning as a sacrament of divine liberation.

GUTIERREZ'S WORK OF REINTERPRETATION has borne special fruit in the area of spirituality (as is clear in his challenging and nourishing book *We Drink from Our Own Wells*). Reflecting on the experience of the poor in the light of the traditional biblical themes, he has developed a liberation spirituality which challenges the individualism and privatism so often evident in Christian life. Every authentic spirituality begins in an encounter with the Lord and leads to a life of discipleship. For liberation spirituality, this encounter is mediated by participation in the struggle for justice and leads to following in the footsteps of Jesus, who came to free us for a richer life.

Using another traditional biblical notion, Gutierrez understands the spiritual life as a journey in which we walk according to the Spirit (Romans 8). We make this spiritual journey, not as disembodied spirits but as flesh-and-blood creatures, located in a particular historical era and a specific social milieu. Living as a genuine disciple in the power of the Spirit requires a process of conversion. We must overcome our false consciousness and apathy by recognizing the pervasive power of social sin. Only then can we undertake effective action to create a society more responsive to human needs. Conversion to a life of solidarity with the oppressed calls for intelligent and wholehearted effort, but always with the realization that the whole project is totally dependent on God's free grace.

While Gutierrez is more aware than most of the misery accompanying poverty, he insists that the struggle for justice can bring an "Easter joy" which comes from the hope that God will ultimately triumph over all evil. Following the crucified Christ leaves no room for romanticizing the plight of the poor from a distance. We are called, rather, to share as much as possible in the life of the exploited with all of its hardships and ambiguities. Work on behalf of justice and peace often leads to intense experiences of solitude and loneliness in the midst of community life. This experience can deepen the hunger for a genuine faith community which provides guidance and inspiration. A church genuinely committed to the poor helps to meet this need for community. The Church offers support and hope to its members by celebrating the Eucharist as a memorial of the death and resurrection of Christ the liberator, and as a promise of the future kingdom of life in which all divisions and inequities will be overcome. It is this hope for communion with God and others which focuses the energy of those living out a liberation spirituality.

THIS LIBERATION SPIRITUALITY FUNCTIONS as a powerful corrective to other spiritualities which are excessively private, romantic, and other-worldly. Gutierrez reminds us that genuine religious experience is found not only in private meditation but also in the struggle for justice. The Spirit is at work not only in our souls, but also in the whole of our bodily social existence. Easter joy and Christian hope are found, not by denying the hardships of life and the conflicts of history, but by participating wholeheartedly in the struggle to create a better world and a transformed humanity. Most importantly, Gutierrez encourages us "to drink from our own wells," which means we must tap the living waters, the power of the Spirit flowing from our own experiences of living out the gospel in our cultural setting.

A theologian who attempts a radical reinterpretation of the Christian tradition is bound to stir up strong negative reactions. Thus, Gutierrez is accused of: using Marxism uncritically, failing to take seriously the specific differences among Latin American countries; reducing theology to politics, espousing the "theory of dependency" which blames the ills of the third world on international capitalism, advocating a brand of socialism which neglects land reform and democratic procedures, and engaging in a one-sided reading of the Christian tradition.

It would surely be enlightening to examine these objections in detail, but our methodology suggests we concentrate on a positive retrieval. It seems to me that we can profit from Gutierrez's radical refocusing of the Christian tradition even if we do not accept his social analysis or buy his total theological package. His challenge to all detached and private styles of Christian living and thinking is pointed and compelling. We indeed have much to learn from dialogue with Gutierrez and liberation theology.

Discussion Questions

1. How do we react to the plight of the poor and oppressed in the developing countries and in the United States?

2. How has Gutierrez's life among the poor affected his theology?

3. What are the main themes of liberation theology as articulated by Gutierrez and what impact do they have on spirituality?

4. What implications do the approach and the insights of Gutierrez have for our situation in the United States?

Suggested Readings

A Theology of Liberation (revised edition, Orbis, 1988). The seminal classic work by the father of liberation theology.

The Power of the Poor in History (Orbis, 1983). A collection of readable articles which develop major themes in liberation theology.

We Drink From Our Own Wells (Orbis, 1984). An inspiring book which explores crucial elements in a liberation spirituality.

The Future of Liberation Theology, edited by Marc Ellis and Otto Maduro (Orbis, 1989). A collection of essays in honor of Gutierrez by other theologians, including Schillebeeckx and Metz.

CHAPTER 14

Rosemary Ruether

overcoming sexism
through christian feminism

IN OUR CULTURE TODAY, we cannot avoid the questions posed by the contemporary feminist movement. What is the depth and the extent of the discrimination encountered by women in society and in the church and how can we raise consciousness on such issues? What are the root causes of sexist attitudes and how do we overcome them? What dynamics produced patriarchal societies and how can we create institutions that liberate rather than oppress women? Are there resources in the Catholic tradition which can be mobilized in this struggle for the emancipation of women? Can churches dominated by patriarchal structures be reformed so they can play a positive role in constructing a society based on equity and mutuality? In responding to these questions, the lead must, of course, be taken by oppressed women who understand them in ways that others cannot. Nevertheless, it is important for everyone to engage these issues, joining in the search for constructive solutions.

The leading feminist theologian, Rosemary Radford Ruether, continues to write with power and insight on these questions. With her keen sense of history and formidable analytical skills, she discloses the root causes and the oppressive power of patriarchal structures and sexist attitudes. Making use of a wide variety of resources, she not only criticizes the bias against women in the Judeo-Christian tradition, but also discovers and utilizes its liberating message and power. In her struggle against sexism, Ruether has constructed a radical feminist theology which challenges traditional notions

and opens up fruitful areas of inquiry. In short, Rosemary Ruether not only raises our consciousness on the problem of sexism, but also offers us helpful perspectives and approaches for achieving greater mutuality in society and the church.

As her revealing book *Disputed Questions: On Being a Christian* (Abingdon, 1982) makes clear, Ruether's approach to feminist consciousness raising is colored by her personal history. Rosemary Radford was born November 2, 1936, in Washington, D.C. Her father, an Anglican with very conservative political views,

---

"The Big Lie tells us that we are strangers and sojourners on this planet, that our flesh, our blood, our instincts for survival are our enemies. Originally we lived as disincarnate orbs of light in the heavenly light. We have fallen to this earth and into this clay through accident or sin. We must spend our lives suppressing our hungers and thirsts and shunning our fellow beings, so that we can dematerialize and fly away to our stars."
—Sexism and God-Talk

---

died when she was twelve, leaving very little lasting influence on his daughter. It was rather from her more liberal, Catholic mother that she acquired many of her enduring attitudes and characteristics: an independent spirit; an appreciation for the Catholic intellectual heritage combined with a critical attitude toward clericalism; and a solid sense of self-confidence which made her feel that she was equal to any other person and could accomplish any goal which she vigorously pursued. After her father's death in 1948, Rosemary lived with her mother and two sisters in the San Diego area. In addition to this exclusively feminine environment, she attended all-girl Catholic schools and spent time around the local Carmelite convent. This "cozy world" run by females in which she felt "like a favorite daughter" served as a "supportive matrix" preparing her for an active and constructive life.

In 1954, Rosemary entered Scripps College where she participated in an excellent interdisciplinary humanities program which taught her to understand the development of the Judeo-Christian tradition in relation to its historical and social context. It also provided her with the integrated methodology still evident in her theological work. During her junior year in college, she met Herman Ruether and, with a thoughtlessness that later astonished her, decided to marry him. Fortunately, her husband proved to be a very adaptable man, who supported her education and career, while sharing in the household and child-rearing duties. With his help, Ruether was able to complete, in a six-year period, from 1958 to 1964, a B.A. and M.A., as well as a Ph.D. from Claremont Graduate School. During this same period she gave birth to their three children. Although her truly amazing scholastic accomplishment brought her a great deal of personal satisfaction, the whole experience also sharpened her sense of injustice suffered by other women who attempt to excel in their careers while still meeting expectations at home.

After completing her doctorate, Ruether taught for two years at Immaculate Heart College, a private Catholic institution in Claremont, California. When her husband was offered the chance to teach political science at the American University in Washington, D.C., she went with him, eventually securing a position at the predominantly black institution, Howard University, where she taught for 10 years as an associate professor of historical theology. In 1976, she took a position which she still holds, as professor of theology at Garrett-Evangelical Theological Seminary in Evanston, Illinois. In addition to her teaching, Ruether has been a prolific writer, producing hundreds of articles and over 20 books, including her most important contribution to feminist theology, *Sexism and God-Talk* (Beacon Press, 1983). During these productive years, she has retained her "intense but non-exclusive" interest in the Catholic community. She attends mass regularly with her husband at the campus parish serving Northwestern University.

Defining Patriarchy

EVEN THOUGH HER OWN PERSONAL STORY is filled with positive reinforcement and significant achievements, Ruether has been able to identify with women who have been stifled by patriarchal structures and sexist attitudes. This sense of empathy, intensified by her own periodic brushes with sexist attitudes, has added passion to her insightful analysis of the deepest roots of patriarchy and sexism. According to Ruether, the whole history of Western civilization has been shaped by patriarchal social systems in which ruling-class males have set up patterns of domination which subjugate the lower classes, control women and exploit nature. The roots of patriarchy go back to tribal puberty rites which prepared young men for the important tasks of gathering and hunting. In the process they leave behind the female world of cooking and cleaning which is judged less important.

Thus, men, who define both the female and male worlds, are able to roam in the sphere of freedom, while women are confined to the realm of necessity and routine. Moreover, women internalize their inferior social status, falling into self-contempt and mistrust of other women. The experience of women is not valued and even their important contributions are erased from memory because the tradition is shaped and handed on by men. Women become objects, their bodies and their labor expropriated by men. The contemporary world offers many examples of these sexist attitudes; wife-battering, rape, job discrimination, and the fashion industry, which exercises a "sadistic tyranny" over the female body image.

Furthermore, it is difficult for women to rise above the constraints of patriarchy and to become true subjects of their own destiny. It is assumed that women attain status and find meaning through their relationships with men. Married women who do try to pursue an independent career are often handicapped because they are also expected to bear the primary responsibility for domestic and child-rearing duties.

RUETHER VIGOROUSLY DENIES THAT SEXISM with its "gender privilege" of males over females flows from any biological necessity or unconscious forces. It is, rather, a "massive historical crime," a culpable expression of "the will to power," exercised by the male ruling class. Women are the scapegoats bearing the repressed and negative aspects of the male psyche. In this situation, males are also diminished because they are blinded to the destructive elements in their own personality. It is frightening for both men and women to begin to unravel the tightly-woven fabric of sexism since such heightened awareness would demand totally new ways of relating on the basis of interdependence rather than domination.

Deepening her analysis, Ruether insists that patriarchy and sexism are rooted in dualistic thinking, which tends to understand reality in terms of polar opposites. In dualistic thinking, sharp dichotomies appear between spirit and matter, soul and body, male and female, human and non-human, grace and nature. The "first lie" or fundamental mistake is to declare one side of these paired opposites as good and the other bad, one superior and the other inferior, one dominant and the other subordinate. In patriarchal societies males are considered superior to women because they are fully human, endowed with the spiritual power of rationality. On the other hand, women are judged inferior, because they are identified with matter, body and nature.

"Thus the feminism we envision is one that is able constantly to build an integral vision of a new humanizing culture beyond patriarchy without becoming closed or sectarian toward any living cultural option or human community. It remains open to authentic spirit wherever it is found, and it extends to all the invitation to join a new dance of life without which life itself may not survive."
— Women-Church

Even worse, according to this sexist ideology, women, driven by their carnal nature and uncontrollable emotions, play the role of temptress, enticing men to abandon the life of grace and the spirit. Extending her fundamental insight, Ruether contends that dualistic thinking is also responsible for the deplorable patterns of domination found in racial, ethnic, religious, and environmental relationships.

Some persons, sensitive to the problems of dualistic sexism, propose that we all strive to become "androgynous" by incorporating both masculine and feminine characteristics into our psychic makeup. Thus men are encouraged to recognize and appropriate their latent "feminine" characteristics, such as compassion and intuition, while women are encouraged to develop "masculine" characteristics, such as logical thinking and aggressiveness. This apparently enlightened solution, often grounded in the theories of the renowned psychotherapist Carl Jung, draws special criticism from Ruether who considers it romantic and dangerous to the feminist cause. Arguing passionately against it and all approaches based on a supposed complementarity of the sexes, she insists that there is "no valid biological basis" for attributing certain capacities, such as reason, to men and others, such as intuition, to women. This approach is dangerous, because it reenforces sexism by perpetuating societal gender-stereotypes. Furthermore, it often forces individuals into behavior patterns which are not in accord with their natural tendencies. To complete the picture, we should note that Ruether does recognize that recent research on the brain suggests that men have a greater natural tendency, intensified by cultural factors, to identify their ego with left-brain rationality, while repressing their right-brain relational side. Even while admitting this difference, she insists that it does not justify different psychic profiles for men and women but, rather, shows "the capacity of both sexes for psychic wholeness." Ruether is passionate in her opposition to androgeny and all other theories of complementarity which stress male and female differences, because she is convinced that this approach will simply perpetuate sexist attitudes and patriarchal patterns.

Scriptural Sexism

IN ADDITION TO GATHERING AND FOCUSING the common feminist criticisms of our patriarchal society, Ruether has made an extremely important contribution by disclosing the sexism built into the normative Judeo-Christian tradition. The dominant assumption of this tradition is that patriarchy was the divinely-ordered pattern of creation and, therefore, functions as the norm for family life, political society, and even for the religious community. God the Supreme Lord set up a hierarchy of being and command, which extends through the descending order of angels, men, women, non-human nature, and matter. In other words, the Judeo-Christian tradition contains a patriarchal ideology, which sacralizes the existing societal patterns, legitimizing the oppressive social hierarchies of class, race, and gender as divinely established.

While the prophetic tradition in the Hebrew Scriptures sharply criticized the oppression of the poor, it not only remained silent about the oppression of women but offered justification for it. The Book of Genesis, for instance, helps to justify sexism by depicting Eve as the temptress who causes the fall of man and nature—a theme which became more explicit when the apostle Paul developed his notion of Christ as the second Adam. When Yahweh entered into covenant with his people at Sinai, the male interpreters of this paradigmatic event understood "the people" to mean the free, adult males. This either excluded women from the religious life of the people or forced them to relate to God through men. Unfortunately, this pattern is still operative today, especially in the dependence of women on male clergy. Despite the patriarchal structures among the Hebrews, women still played important roles in the drama of salvation.

The memory of their contributions, however, has often been erased from history, precisely because the biblical tradition was shaped and handed on by men.

A similar pattern of erasing women's experience occurs in the Christian Scriptures. For example, in listing the witnesses to the Resurrection, Paul makes no explicit mention of Mary Magdalene and the other women who play such an important role in the later Gospels as the first proclaimers of the Good News. In 1 Timothy 2:11-15, women's experience is again negated as they are enjoined to keep silence in church—a prohibition which indirectly suggests that women were speaking up and exercising leadership roles. The patriarchal assumption that women are subordinate and relate to God through men is repeated in Ephesians 5:22-23, where wives are told to be submissive to their husbands because "the husband is the head of the wife just as Christ is the head of his body the Church."

The sexism in the Christian Scriptures, always tempered by the genuine memory of the liberating teaching and practice of Jesus, becomes even more blatant in the history of Christian thought. In her book *Women—Church* (Harper &

"The Church is where the good news of liberation from sexism is preached . . . and where the community is spreading this vision and struggle to others."
— Sexism and God-Talk

Row, 1985), Ruether provides representative samplings of sexist attitudes among influential theologians. Tertullian, for example, called women "the devil's gateway"; Augustine claimed women possessed the image of God only when joined with a man; Aquinas assumed that women could not be leaders in society or church because they are "misbegotten males" destined for subjugation; Martin Luther taught that due to sin women are "far inferior creatures"; and Karl Barth, writing in our own century, repeated the fundamental basis for the whole patriarchal order by insisting that "just as God rules over creation. . . so man rules over woman."

According to Ruether, the history of Christianity manifests the continuing struggle between the historical institutional model of the church and the more charismatic model of the church as a Spirit-filled community. Although Christianity began as a charismatic movement within Judaism, it gradually took on the institutional contours of the patriarchal society in which it developed. Thus, bishops, patterned successively after Roman governors, feudal lords, and modern managers, functioned as the primary dispensers of God's grace to the people, undercutting in the process the more direct contact with Christ's spirit found in the charismatic community. In this process, the institutional model of the church, which fosters the subjugation of women, became dominant.

Throughout history, this dominance has been periodically challenged by Spirit-filled communities which tend to give women greater opportunities. For instance, the Quakers, founded in the 17th century enabled women to serve as preachers, evangelists, and administrators. Nevertheless, patriarchal structures and sexist attitudes have remained dominant to our own day, limiting the opportunities of women to develop their talents and to contribute to the well-being of the church.

Not only has the church appropriated the structures of patriarchy into its internal life, but it has, in turn, tended to legitimize the patterns of domination found in society. In the fourth century, for example, theologians began justifying the reign of the Christian Roman emperors by comparing it with the rule of the Son of God over the cosmos. By declaring the political and social order sacred, the church has made it more difficult to overcome all patterns of oppression, including sexism. Today, the institutional church is hard pressed to discern and to attack gender discrimination in society precisely because it has failed to achieve equality for women in its own life.

As this survey suggests, Rosemary Ruether's distinctive scholarly reading of Western history and the Judeo-Christian tradition challenges us to become more aware of the sexism built into our patriarchal institutions.

Built-in Discrimination

BUT RUETHER IS CONCERNED with more than consciousness-raising. According to her dialectical methodology, the negative critique of sexism serves the positive purpose of promoting greater integration and mutuality in human relationships. Far from dismissing the entire Judeo-Christian tradition as irretrievably patriarchal, she finds important resources in it for supporting feminist goals. In this regard it is important to understand her methodology. She begins her feminist theology with the critical principle that whatever promotes the full humanity of women is presumed to represent the authentic divine message, while anything that diminishes it is assumed to be opposed to God's will.

The emancipation of women, however, cannot be achieved at the expense of men, but must tend toward an as yet undetermined but inclusive understanding of humanity which liberates every individual of both genders and all social groupings. When Ruether re-examines the Bible and the whole of Christian

"Indeed, precisely as one takes seriously one's responsibility to transform the historical Church, it becomes essential to have a support community that really nurtures liberated ways of living together rather than remaining crabbed and frustrated by religious experiences of alienation and negation of this vision."

—Sexism and God-Talk

tradition in the light of this critical principle, she discerned not only the obvious sexism, but also a central prophetic tradition extremely useful for feminists. This tradition emphasizes God's defense of the oppressed, the need to criticize oppressive power structures in society, the importance of recognizing ideological elements in religion, and the coming of a New Age when injustice will be overcome. A comparison with Latin American liberation theology highlights the unique element in Ruether's approach. When theologians such as Gustavo Gutierrez examine the Scriptures in the light of the struggle of the poor for liberation, they find, from beginning to end, a God who continually demonstrates special care for the poor. By way of contrast, Ruether, in her rereading, finds no explicit critique of patriarchy or sexism, even in the prophetic tradition. Thus she is forced to search elsewhere for resources to support the feminist cause. She turns to the marginalized Christian traditions such as Gnosticism, which affirmed in principle the equality of women; classical theology which recognized the need for conversion from sinful existence to the life of the new redeemed humanity; pagan religions which included the cult of the goddess; and the modern movements such as liberalism which helped spawn contemporary feminism. This rich mix of resources gives Ruether's discussion of the traditional theological categories, such as God, Christ, and church, a fresh perspective and a distinctive content.

Language and God

IN HER TREATMENT of God Ruether insists that we need inclusive language grounded in the experiences and images of both women and men. Drawing on her positive experiences of her mother as an energizing and life-giving force, Ruether speaks easily of God as the "primal matrix" and "the great womb" within which all reality, human and non-human, matter and spirit, is generated. She links this notion with Paul Tillich's contemporary expression of God as "ground or power of being," an image which suggests that we are all encompassed by a vibrant source of renewed life.

From her studies of the religions of the ancient Near East, Ruether retrieves the idea that it is possible to image the divine without falling into a gender division which inevitably subordinates women. In these ancient religions, the earliest images of the divine were of the mother-goddess. And even when male gods first appear, they are "equivalent, not complementary images of the divine." In other words, the ancients saw divine sovereignty and power manifested in both male and female gods, suggesting that gender division is not yet the main way of thinking about life on this earth. Ruether finds in this ancient outlook the seeds of a contemporary image of the divine which transcends gender and thus challenges the sexist world view which flows from belief in a dominant, male God.

THE HEBREW SCRIPTURES, despite their patriarchal assumptions, remain a rich source of divine images with great liberating power. In the Exodus event, for example, Yahweh is portrayed as the God of liberated slaves who brings oppressed people to political and social freedom. The God who gave the Israelites their own land remains the champion of the oppressed, demanding that his people establish justice in their own society. Moreover, when the Hebrew Scriptures want to portray the unconditional love and immense compassion of Yahweh, they turn to maternal imagery. Thus, Isaiah pictures the Lord crying out like a woman in labor, while promising to lead the blind along the path of light (Isaiah 42:14-16). Female imagery is also used in describing Wisdom as an offspring of Yahweh, who cooperates in the work of creation and serves as the subtle representative of the divine presence in the world. The wise man takes Wisdom as his bride so she can instruct him in the mysteries of God's knowledge (Wisdom 8:2-4). Throughout her writings, Ruether employs this Hebrew imagery, describing God as the liberator who fights the injustices borne by women and others, the Mother who nurtures them to full personhood, and the Holy Wisdom who guides them to truth and meaning.

Turning to Christian sources, especially those outside the mainstream, Ruether extends her analysis by showing how feminine imagery has been applied to the Holy Spirit. The apocryphal Gospel of the Hebrews, for instance, speaks of "my mother the Holy Spirit." Similar attributions of female imagery to the Spirit are found in other early sources, such as the Acts of Thomas and the Gospel of Philip. Despite the dominance of male imagery in the mainstream Christian tradition, Ruether finds androgynous images of the Trinity, which combine the male Father and Son with the female Spirit, appearing periodically throughout history from the early Gnostics to the 18th-century Shakers.

WHILE RUETHER SEEMS TO CONSIDER the recovery of female imagery as helpful to the feminist project, she insists that it is not sufficient merely to add feminine imagery to a predominantly male God because this will simply perpetuate gender stereotyping, both in talk of God and in the treatment of women. Ruether constructs her own more radical solution from a number of sources. The Hebrew prohibition of idolatry suggests that no image of God, even verbal ones such as "Father," can be made into absolutes or applied literally. Classical theology, in its teaching on analogy, reenforces the point that our language and our images of God are more unlike than like the always mysterious divine reality.

Thus, while there is a divine source of both male and female existence, God is neither male nor female. This takes us back to Ruether's main point, that we need inclusive language and images for a God beyond gender which are rooted in the experience of both men and women. She finds this approach exemplified in the synoptic Gospels, which offer parallel stories incorporating the experience of both genders. In Luke's Gospel, for example, God's work of establishing the new dynamic kingdom is compared both to a farmer sowing seed and to a woman leavening bread (Luke 13:18-21). The life and teaching of Jesus is the obvious source of this striking use of inclusive imagery. He associated with women, broke the social taboos by speaking with them in public and, as appears in the Mary-Martha story (Luke 10:38-42), commended their participation in religious discussion. His teaching centered on the coming of the kingdom which would transform the prevalent mode of human relationships from domination to mutuality.

In encouraging his followers to think of God as *Abba*, a term which according to Ruether was used not only by children addressing their fathers, but also by adult males conveying respect for older men, Jesus suggests that a proper relationship to God undercuts the traditional patriarchal structure and sets up a new community of equals. Paul reflected this thrust toward equality in the teachings of the Master when he wrote that in Christ there is neither "Jew nor Greek, slave or free man, male or female" (Galatians 3:28). Ruether believes that this authentic memory of Jesus can be mobilized today to fight oppression of all types, including the domination of women perpetuated by patriarchy and sexism.

A Livable Cosmos

RUETHER ALSO CHALLENGES us to view other major areas of theological reflection from new perspectives. Thus a theology of creation should include a "new ecological ethic" which encourages us to create a livable cosmos for all by befriending rather than dominating non-human nature. A genuine anthropology must emphasize that all human beings possess a full and equivalent human nature and are called "to live relationally" on the basis of mutuality rather than manipulation or abnegation. Christology should not lose touch with the Jesus of the synoptic Gospels who challenged the existing patterns of domination and reached out to the most oppressed, including women. A full discussion of morality should stress the need for conversion from sexist attitudes, which would lead women to take responsibility for their own destiny and prompt men to enter into solidarity with women in the struggle for liberation.

Many of Ruether's practical suggestions for overcoming sexism appear in her treatment of the church. Although she recognizes the rage which moves women to repudiate totally the institutional church, she insists that the church will be renewed by a "creative dialectic" between feminist base communities and the institutional church. She expects women to find their spiritual nourishment and guidance from involvement in small feminist groups while still remaining in the Church. This enables them to use the institution creatively, while gradually transforming it into a genuine sign of liberated humanity and a useful instrument in the battle against all patriarchal institutions. The feminist base communities should combine a general concern for all forms of oppression in the world with specific efforts on issues where progress is possible. In this regard, Ruether is more interested in practical results than ideological purity.

Critics attack Ruether's feminist theology from both sides: radical feminists insist she is overly optimistic about the transformative power of the Judeo-Christian tradition, while moderates believe she is too harsh on the institutional church. Individuals have attacked her methodology, challenged her broad generalizations, questioned her Christology, and decried her lack of a consistent philosophical base.

Conscious of the limitations of her initial efforts, Ruether has welcomed other efforts and approaches to the ongoing task of constructing a viable feminist theology. For those currently struggling with the diverse questions surrounding the problem of sexism, Rosemary Ruether serves as an insightful and challenging guide.

Discussion Questions

1. How do you respond to sexism in our culture?

2. How has Ruether's personal experience influenced her theology?

3. What is Ruether's methodology and how does it influence her cultural analysis and her feminist reinterpretation of the Christian tradition?

4. What practical suggestions for overcoming sexism in our culture flow from Ruether's analysis?

Suggested Readings

Sexism and God-Talk (Beacon Press, 1983). An ambitious and provocative initial effort to redo Christian theology from a feminist perspective.

Women-Church (Harper & Row, 1985). A challenging examination of the relationship between separate feminist groupings and the institutional church.

Disputed Questions: On Being a Christian (Abingdon, 1982). Contains revealing autobiographical sections as well as explanations of her methodology and its consequences.

The Radical Kingdom (Harper & Row, 1970). An early example of her radical critique.

CHAPTER 15

Martin Luther King
struggling for freedom

THE THIRST FOR FREEDOM ARISES from deep within the human heart. But the life of genuine freedom is not easily won. Personally, we must struggle against the enslaving power of sin and come to terms with our limitations. Our pursuit of freedom can become selfish and excessively individualistic. We must overcome the temptation to escape from the burden of freedom and responsibility. The struggle for freedom also has a social dimension. Political coercion and economic deprivation threaten to crush the life of freedom for many of our brothers and sisters. Freedom is diminished for those who have few viable options. The most deprived must put all of their energy into mere survival. The struggle for freedom demands a wholehearted and intelligent effort to overcome the injustice built into institutions and social systems.

In this continuing effort, we are blessed with the guidance of the great contemporary apostle of freedom, Martin Luther King, Jr. (1929-1968). King, of course, is well known as the civil rights activist who helped desegregate the South. His significance, however, transcends even the amazing successes he achieved in desegregating the buses and opening up the voting booths for his people. As important authors, including the Lutheran historian Martin Marty and the black theologian James Cone, have insisted, King was an outstanding theologian with an important message for all of us. He was a public theologian who demonstrated great insight and un-

usual creativity in applying the Christian faith to public policy questions. He
was an activist theologian who developed his thinking through involvement
in the liberation struggles of his times, rather than through abstract speculation
on Christian doctrine. He was an American theologian, rooted in his black
Southern Baptist religious heritage, who was also able to speak a universal
message which continues to inspire people of all races and creeds.

In the dedicated life and inspiring teaching of Dr. King, we can discern
the attractive image of the life of genuine freedom. He challenges our narrow
notions of freedom by inspiring us to join the struggle for personal and societal
liberation. His understanding of freedom is rooted in the practice of the traditional
virtues. Thus, he remains a great apostle for freedom because he was a "drum
major for justice," a consistent proponent of loving nonviolence, and an eloquent
spokesman for the hope of universal liberation.

Encountering Cruelty

KING'S ORIGINAL THIRST for freedom flowed from his deep involvement
in the black church tradition. He was born January 15, 1929, the first son
of a Baptist preacher who had known his share of discrimination and was active
in working for the rights of black citizens in Atlanta. As a rather precocious
youngster, Martin easily committed to memory substantial biblical passages and
entire gospel hymns. By the age of 6, he had become an active member of
Ebenezer Baptist Church, singing hymns at church functions. While his middle-class status shielded Martin from many of the indignities heaped on less
fortunate black people, he did have his own striking encounters with the cruelties
of segregation. On one occasion, while traveling on a bus with his high school
debate team, he was forced to give up his seat to a white person. After being
cursed by the driver for moving too slowly, Martin had to stand for the entire
ninety-mile trip, while seething with a deep anger he would never forget.

For black people constantly exposed to such indignities, the church was a
place of refuge where they heard the biblical message of freedom and sang
the hymns promising the presence of the Lord in their struggles. Although,
as a teenager, Martin had trouble accepting some of the fundamentalist preaching
in his church and was uncomfortable with the unbridled emotionalism in the
services, he did assimilate the hopeful message and the passion for freedom
kept alive by the black church.

At the age of 15, King entered Morehouse College in Atlanta, where he learned the rudiments of modern biblical interpretation which enabled him to resolve some of his religious doubts. Thus, after two years of college, he was able to accept a call from his father's congregation, beginning his lifelong ministry as a Baptist preacher. Only in the light of this continuing relationship with the black church can we understand King's passion for freedom and his distinctive approach to human liberation.

King continued to develop and refine his deeply-ingrained religious sensibilities while studying at Crozier Seminary in Chester, Pennsylvania, from

"A third way is open to our quest for freedom, namely, nonviolent resistance, that combines tough-mindedness and tender-heartedness and avoids the complacency and do-nothingness of the soft-minded, and the violence and bitterness of the hardhearted."

— Strength to Love

1948 to 1951. During that time, he studied both the liberal Protestant theology associated with the Baptist Social Gospel advocate Walter Rauschenbusch, and the neo-orthodox theology espoused by the Christian realist Reinhold Niebuhr.

After graduating from Crozier, he entered Boston University where he earned a doctorate in theology, working out in the process his own synthesis which combined the liberal passion for social change with Niebuhr's sense of human limitation and sinfulness. Influenced by his reading of Gandhi and the existentialist philosophers, his theological synthesis emphasized both finite human freedom and nonviolent approaches to social change.

Rise to Prominence

ALTHOUGH KING POSSESSED a first-rate theological mind and could have pursued his interest in teaching theology, he made the fateful decision in May of 1954 to accept the position of pastor at the Dexter Avenue Baptist Church in Montgomery, Alabama. A little over a year later, he was thrust into national prominence when he was chosen by his peers to lead the bus boycott, occasioned by the arrest of Rosa Parks for refusing to give her seat on a bus to a white man. In his largely extemporaneous speech inaugurating the boycott, King enunciated many of the themes which would characterize his message for the rest of his life.

He began by noting that the large crowd of black people had gathered as American citizens "determined to acquire our citizenship to the fullest of its meaning." They did not intend to overthrow the political system but to

---

"I believe that unarmed truth and unconditional love will have the final word in reality. That is why right temporarily defeated is stronger than evil triumphant."

—Nobel Prize Acceptance Speech

---

demonstrate their belief that "democracy transformed from thin paper to thick action is the greatest form of government on earth." Referring to Rosa Parks, he gave expression to the frustration of his people who were "tired of being segregated and humiliated; tired of being kicked about by the brutal feet of oppression." They would settle for nothing less than "freedom and justice." With great wisdom, he linked the cause of his people with both the important institutions of the country and the enduring message of the Scriptures. If they were wrong in their cause, he insisted, then "the Constitution is wrong" and "Jesus of Nazareth was merely a Utopian dreamer."

Sensing the frenzied enthusiasm of his audience, King warned them to avoid threats and intimidation in seeking justice and freedom. Their actions were to be guided by Christian faith with love as their "regulating ideal." If they mounted their protests with such love and courage, then they would be judged favorably by history as a race of people who "injected a new meaning into the veins of history and civilization."

In this electrifying sixteen-minute speech, King not only moved his audience to support the bus boycott but also set the tone for the nonviolent movement he would lead. The bus boycott proved to be long and difficult. King was subjected to constant harassment, including arrest, frequent death threats to himself, his wife Coretta, and their baby daughter, and the fire-bombing of their home. One night, overwhelmed by the pressures and fears, he was close to resigning his leadership position. Alone in the kitchen of his home, he poured out his anguish to the Lord in prayer. And then, in one of the most important moments of his life, he heard an inner voice: "Martin Luther, stand up for righteousness. Stand up for justice. Stand up for truth. And, lo, I will be with you, even unto the end of the world." King understood this as "the voice of Jesus," assuring him that he would never abandon him in the struggle for freedom. Immediately, his trembling stopped and he experienced a deep inner calm and a renewed strength which did, indeed, sustain him in the darkest hours.

November 13, 1956, loomed as one of those dark days. It seemed as though the white leadership in Montgomery had found a way to break the bus boycott by declaring illegal the private carpools used by the black residents to get to work. On that very day, however, victory came to the protesters as the United States Supreme Court affirmed a District Court decision, declaring Alabama's bus segregation laws unconstitutional. King's response was magnanimous and conciliatory, as always. He advised his people to go back to the buses, not claiming a victory over the white people, but a victory for justice and democracy. The real goal was to overcome the "superior-inferior relationship" which preferential seating implied and to establish, instead, a sense of the unity and equality of all human beings.

Organized Nonviolence

THE SUCCESSFUL BUS BOYCOTT in Montgomery catapulted King into national prominence as a leader of the civil rights movement. Realizing the need for an organization to guide the struggle for freedom, he founded in 1957, with the assistance of his friend and adviser Bayard Rustin, the Southern Christian Leadership Conference (SCLC). During a trip to India in 1959, King enhanced his own leadership abilities by deepening his understanding of the spiritual aspects of the nonviolent strategies practiced by the late Mohandas Gandhi. Unfortunately, King's resolve to spend one day a week in fasting and meditation soon gave way to the press of events when he returned home. In order to devote full time to the SCLC, he resigned as pastor of the Dexter Avenue Church in January of 1960 and moved to Atlanta where he also served as co-pastor of his father's church. His farewell message to the black citizens of Montgomery was a challenging reminder that "freedom is never free" but is "always purchased with the high price of sacrifice and suffering."

King's own suffering for the cause of freedom took many forms. A deranged black woman stabbed him in a New York department store, almost killing him. Montgomery officials indicted him on trumped-up charges of falsifying his state tax return. Leaders in Albany, Georgia, refused to desegregate the city's public facilities, despite months of demonstrations led by the SCLC. J. Edgar Hoover,

---

"In a world whose cultural and spiritual power lags so far beyond her technological capabilities that we live each day on the verge of nuclear co-annihilation; in this world, nonviolence is no longer an option for intellectual analysis, it is an imperative for action."

— The Trumpet of Conscience

---

smarting from King's criticisms of the FBI's performance in Albany during the demonstrations, obtained and disseminated tapes of King's alleged sexual encounters with various women. Militant black leaders, disappointed with the results of King's nonviolent approach, attacked him for being too soft in confronting the white establishment.

Under Dr. King's leadership, the struggle for freedom also produced significant successes. In 1963, he took his campaign for civil rights to Birmingham, Alabama, a bastion of racial segregation. Through the skillful use of nonviolent strategies which exerted economic pressure and brought to national attention the vicious tactics of police commissioner Eugene "Bull" Connor, King was able to persuade business leaders to desegregate downtown stores and to hire black people in clerical and sales positions previously closed to them. King's success in Birmingham not only restored confidence in his leadership and his nonviolent strategies, but it also encouraged President Kennedy to submit civil rights legislation to Congress, outlawing segregation in interstate public accommodations and promoting integration in schools and federal programs.

Birmingham was also important because it provided the occasion for King's famous "Letter From Birmingham City Jail," in which he defended his effort to carry "the gospel of freedom" to the "most segregated city in the South." Accepting Reinhold Niebuhr's premise that groups are more immoral than individuals, King argued that nonviolent direct action was necessary to win civil rights because "freedom is never voluntarily given by the oppressor," but "must be demanded by the oppressed." In a brilliant section which cited Augustine and Aquinas, as well as Martin Buber and Paul Tillich, King went on to justify civil disobedience as a proper response to unjust segregation laws which violate the eternal law of God and which relegate "persons to the status of things." To break unjust laws "openly, lovingly and with a willingness to accept the penalty" demonstrates "the very highest respect for law." Those who engage in civil disobedience do not create tension, but bring to light "the hidden tension" lurking beneath the surface of every segregated society. Rejecting both the complacency of those "drained of self-respect" by long years of oppression and the hatred advocated by black nationalist groups, King insisted on "the most excellent way of love and nonviolent protest" in order to achieve freedom for his people. Charged with being an extremist, he found satisfaction in pondering the extremism of men like Amos, Paul, Martin Luther, Thomas Jefferson, Abraham Lincoln and Jesus Christ himself, who was "an extremist for love, truth and goodness."

After castigating church leaders for failing to join in the liberation struggle, King sounded again his fundamental message of hope, rooted in both the American dream and the Christian gospel: "We will win our freedom because the sacred heritage of our nation and the eternal will of God are embodied in our echoing demands."

"I Have a Dream"

LESS THAN SIX MONTHS after emerging from the solitude of the Birmingham jail, King stood before 250,000 demonstrators in the nation's capital and delivered his famous "I Have a Dream" speech. With electrifying eloquence, he wove together his familiar liberation themes into a grand vision which continues to inspire the struggle for freedom. The compelling cadence and striking imagery of this master orator built up to the powerful conclusion: "And when we allow freedom to ring . . . we will be able to speed up that day when all of God's children . . . will be able to join hands and to sing the words of the old Negro spiritual, 'Free at last, free at last; thank God Almighty, we are free at last.'"

The power of this great dream of freedom was evident in the following years. With amazing energy, King managed to publish some significant books, including a collection of sermons, *Strength of Love* (Fortress Press, 1963), which specified the religious content of the dream, and the story of Birmingham, *Why We Can't Wait* (Harper, 1964), which highlighted the power of nonviolence in the struggle for freedom. For all his efforts, he was honored by *Time* magazine as Man of the Year in 1963 and was awarded the Nobel Peace Prize in 1964. The same year, President Lyndon Johnson signed the Civil Rights Bill which desegregated public accommodations and reduced job discrimination. Another portion of the dream became a reality when the famous Selma-to-Montgomery march led to the Voting Rights Bill of 1965 which outlawed literacy tests and other restrictions used to keep black people from registering and voting.

But the dream of universal freedom, when taken seriously, can make extremely heavy moral demands and call for difficult decisions filled with dire consequences. Thus, it moved Martin Luther King to defy all the safe political advice by taking a strong position against the Vietnam War, which he saw as a tragic

---

"We are responsible human beings, not blind automatons; persons, not puppets. By endowing us with freedom, God relinquished a measure of his own sovereignty and imposed certain limitations upon himself."

— Strength to Love

---

conflict poisoning the soul of America and destroying the lives of innocent peasants abroad. This courageous moral stand helped plunge him into a nightmare. It cost him the support of his great ally, President Johnson, as well as important black leaders. Stokely Carmichael and other advocates of black power began to challenge his leadership in the civil rights movement. Further troubles ensued. An intensive campaign to gain better jobs for black people in Chicago achieved only minor results and was widely considered to be a failure. Riots broke out in major urban areas, such as Los Angeles and Detroit. Feeling alone and bearing the burden of failure, King fell into a serious depression. He responded by pouring his energy into planning a gigantic march on Washington to secure economic opportunities for all the nation's poor people. His public speeches took on a heavier tone, but always maintained a sense of ultimate hope.

He preached his final sermon on April 3, 1968, in Memphis, Tennessee, where he had gone to continue his efforts to secure justice for the city's sanitation workers. Returning to his familiar Exodus themes, he declared that he did not fear death because God had allowed him "to go up to the mountain" and to see the promised land. "I may not get there with you. But I want you to know tonight, that we, as a people, will get to the promised land." The next day, he was shot and killed by James Earl Ray. Despite their grief, his supporters from all over the country and the world vowed to keep alive his dream by continuing the struggle for freedom.

Martin Luther King's life is a magnificent commentary on the struggle for freedom which provides important insights and helpful guidance for all of us. Let us examine some of his major contributions.

Theology of Freedom

KING REMINDS US that freedom is God's great gift to us which demands that we take responsibility for ourselves and our actions. As his "kitchen experience" suggests, the struggle for freedom is a response to the call of God. When God speaks we must freely respond, confident that our loving Father will never abandon us. Through his redemptive sufferings, Christ has bestowed on us the gift of freedom and the power to use it wisely. We all possess the Spirit which moves us to take charge of our lives and to become our better selves.

This theology of freedom challenges B.F. Skinner and his followers, who claim that the common belief that we are free is a dangerous and destructive illusion. Denying human freedom, they concentrate on programming our environment in order to determine behavior in constructive directions. The successes of the civil rights movement suggest, on the contrary, that human beings can take hold of their lives and improve their lot precisely when they understand themselves as persons, not puppets. As King insisted, we are called to be faithful to "the drive for freedom" which moves us with a "cosmic urgency" to create a better world. While behavior is, indeed, determined in many ways by circumstances and structures, we do remain free to respond constructively and to take up a healthy attitude toward all the determining factors in our lives. This positive understanding of freedom as the root capacity to shape our lives was crucial in King's effective summons to the oppressed to rise above unjust systems and structures. It is also a striking challenge to all of us to act as authentic persons by taking full responsibility for ourselves and our actions. At times, we may experience our freedom as a burden, but we also know it as our great opportunity to shape our existence and to become what we will be forever.

Overcoming Oppression

THROUGH HIS ACTIVE INVOLVEMENT and his biblical preaching, Dr. King also challenges all individualistic notions of freedom by highlighting the social, economic, and political dimensions of the struggle for freedom. As we saw, King's own understanding of freedom was shaped in large part by the story of the Exodus, which he considered "the story of every people struggling for freedom." Human beings cannot in the long run be satisfied with Egypt. It is true that the pharoahs of this world cling to power because they do not understand that relationships of domination dehumanize both oppressors and oppressed and that cooperative relationships can enrich all. It is also true that some who are enslaved may prefer the "fleshpots of Egypt" to the novelty and demands of emancipation. Nevertheless, God has placed the longing for the promised land "deep down" in our souls, causing people eventually to "cry out for Canaan's land." They may have to walk painful miles through the wilderness to get there, but God will surely lead his people to the promised land.

Thus, King teaches us that dominant groups must be shown that sharing power is in their own best interest. Those suffering from a history of oppression must overcome their understandable fears and accept the challenges of a life of freedom. Those who enjoy freedom must remember that if some people are enslaved then the freedom of all is threatened.

King calls us to work together for mutual liberation because, by divine and natural law, all human beings are "caught in an inescapable network of mutuality, tied in a single garment of destiny." This unity of the human family is ultimately rooted in the love God lavishes on every individual person. Our task is to build a community of justice and love which reflects this reality.

The struggle for freedom demands that the systems of enslavement be transformed into liberating structures which enable people to achieve their full development. Social sin is a reality and must be countered by institutional reform. While some privileged individuals enjoy the luxury of many and varied options in life, the poor and oppressed live in a world of confinement without viable alternatives. Their struggle for freedom must include the battle to achieve economic opportunity and political power. Genuine freedom demands that individuals live in an environment which provides realistic opportunities to shape their own existence and to develop their own potential. In short, King's life demonstrates that the struggle for freedom is never merely a private affair but always has a social dimension.

The Beloved Community

THE ACCOMPLISHMENTS of Dr. King in the civil rights movement suggest the wisdom of combining a comprehensive religious vision with active nonviolent tactics in the struggle for freedom. King's great genius was to unite the biblical themes of the Exodus and the kingdom with elements of the American dream in an inspiring and illuminating synthesis which he called "the beloved community." In this ideal community, individuals sacrifice for the common good, schools provide quality education for all, churches function as the conscience of the nation, governments insure economic and political rights, and all institutions are fully integrated, providing "genuine interpersonal living." The beloved community strives to embody the charity taught by Jesus and to guarantee the rights proclaimed by the Founding Fathers. Rather than disparage the American civil religion, King utilized its best elements in constructing his inspiring dream for all citizens of the country. His dream was "deeply rooted in the American Dream, that one day this nation will rise up and live out the true meaning of its creed—we hold these truths to be self-evident, that all men are created equal." Thus, King provides us with a common vision which can still bring together people of diverse backgrounds and views in the struggle for freedom.

Furthermore, King's successes suggest that active nonviolence remains a fitting and effective tool in the work of liberation. Translating Gandhi's method into the American context, King demonstrated the power of meeting violence with nonviolence, hatred with love, injury with forgiveness. By publicly contrasting the brutality of the oppressors with the nonviolence of those protesting injustice, this method can raise consciousness and change public opinion. King also reminds us that active nonviolence embodies important Christian themes, such as the power of redemptive suffering and the admonition of Jesus to love our enemies. Nonviolent methods are well-suited to strengthen the moral resolve of the oppressed, to win over the hearts and minds of the dominant group, and to promote eventual reconciliation. King's steadfast refusal to turn to violence, even in the face of demeaning and lethal attacks on himself and his family, stands as a powerful contemporary witness to the ideal of forgiving love taught by Jesus Christ.

Finally, Dr. King gives us an indigenous liberation theology which can guide the continuing struggle to make full freedom available for all people in the United States. He helps us see the world and hear the Christian message from the viewpoint of sons and daughters of former slaves who have known the indignities of prejudice and continue to live on the margins of our affluent society. His insightful analyses have revealed the hardness of heart and the moral blindness of prejudiced people who project their own hidden fears and unresolved conflicts onto minority groups. His skillful use of nonviolent protests revealed to a whole nation the way oppressors are diminished and dehumanized by their domination of others. He moves us to look honestly at our national institutions, ready to unmask the social sin which produces racism and fosters the arms race while ignoring the real needs of the poor at home and in the third world countries. His message to us is that only active involvement in the struggle for freedom will reveal the true meaning of the Christian gospel.

Rejecting Marxist revolutionary approaches, King insists that our political institutions as well as our churches, for all their limitations, are still a valuable resource in striving for genuine liberation. Out of loyalty and love, we must criticize these institutions for not living up to their ideals. Nevertheless, we can still draw on their rich resources and inspiring symbols in order to further the cause of freedom. Thus, we see that King provides us with an indigenous liberation theology which does not depend on Latin American theologians, but rather remains faithful to our distinctive experience in the United States.

The importance and usefulness of King's contributions have been attacked from many angles: his theological writings are limited, lacking depth and sophistication; his nonviolent tactics often failed; his extramarital affairs undercut the moral power of his lofty message; and his trust in the power of love is utopian. Despite the criticisms, the life and teachings of Martin Luther King deserve more serious study and attention. His life illumines our longing for freedom. His theology of liberation is faithful both to the gospel and to the American experience. His dream, so elegantly expressed, maintains its power to inspire and guide the continuing struggle for freedom.

Discussion Questions

1. How do you experience the struggle for freedom in both the personal and social dimensions of life?

2. What influence did King's family, church and background have on his understanding of freedom?

3. What are the distinctive characteristics of King's theology of freedom and how did this inspire and guide his own work for justice?

4. How can the life and teaching of King guide us in the struggle for freedom for all?

Suggested Readings

Strength to Love (Fortress Press, 1981). A collection of inspiring sermons which provide the religious background, content and motivation of his dream of freedom.

Why We Can't Wait (Harper & Row, 1964). The story of the civil rights struggle in Birmingham which highlights the power of nonviolence in the struggle for freedom and contains his famous "Letter from Birmingham Jail."

Stride Toward Freedom (Harper & Row, 1958). Includes important autobiographical material and thoughts on nonviolence.

A Testament of Hope: The Essential Writings of Martin Luther King, Jr., edited by James Washington (Harper & Row, 1985). A fine collection of King's most important essays, sermons, interviews and book selections with an introduction by the editor.

CHAPTER 16

Alfred North Whitehead

reinterpreting theism in a dynamic world

WHEN THE HIGHLY RESPECTED THEOLOGIAN John Cobb was doing graduate studies at the University of Chicago in the 1950s, he experienced, by his own account, a serious crisis of faith. His courses, especially in philosophy and psychology, brought him into contact for the first time with modern currents of thought which "contained no place for God." This experience called into question his traditional Christian faith and set him drifting into a contemporary form of atheism.

The atheistic world view encountered by Cobb remains a familiar part of the intellectual landscape. It simply assumes that the God of classical theism is opposed to the concerns and sensibilities of educated people. According to this outlook, people aware of evolutionary theory must reject belief in the creator God of the Bible. Individuals interested in achieving personal development have to discard the moralistic God preached in the churches. Mature persons who have encountered human suffering can no longer believe in an all-powerful God who refuses to come to the aid of his suffering people. This brand of atheism does not concentrate on disproving God's existence, but simply assumes that theism is an outmoded superstition with no relevance for the modern scientific world.

In the midst of his personal crisis of faith—an experience which resonates with many contemporary believers—Cobb was introduced to the thought of the philosopher Alfred

North Whitehead (1861-1947), whose system merges theistic belief with a modern scientific view of the world. Whitehead's philosophy struck a responsive cord with Cobb, providing a framework within which his belief in God gradually came to life again. Cobb became convinced of the power of Whitehead's system, ranking him with Plato, Aristotle and Kant as "one of the greatest creative thinkers of all time." After solidly grounding himself in Whitehead's philosophy, Cobb went on to apply his seminal ideas to the specifically theological task of reinterpreting and applying Christian doctrines to the concerns of the contemporary world.

An Evolutionary View

THE EXPERIENCE OF JOHN COBB suggests the potential value of Whitehead's thought for those who are trying to maintain their theistic beliefs in a scientific age. Whitehead has worked out a comprehensive philosophical system which not only takes into account the evolutionary perspectives of modern science, but also demands the inclusion of a loving God as the foundation of the system. Some important American theologians, including Shubert Ogden, Daniel Day Williams, and Norman Pittenger, have joined John Cobb in adopting a Whiteheadian perspective in their work. Together, these "process theologians," as they are commonly called, have created a significant movement which deserves attention.

Strangely enough, the philosopher who has inspired this movement turned his professional attention to philosophical and religious matters only late in his life. Born February 6, 1861, in Ramsgate, England, Alfred was raised in a very religious family. His father, an Anglican clergyman, exercised great influence on his son, personally tutoring him in the classics until Alfred left home at the age of fourteen to attend public school in Sherborne. Excelling in mathematics, Alfred won a scholarship to the prestigious Trinity College, Cambridge, where he remained as a student and lecturer from 1880 to 1910. During those years he completed his doctoral degree, became a senior lecturer in mathematics, and collaborated with his friend and colleague Bertrand Russell in writing *Principia Mathematica*. In 1890, he married an Irish woman, Evelyn Wade, who helped him develop greater self-confidence as well as an increased interest in the beauty of the world beyond academia. They had three children, one of whom, Eric, was killed in action during World War I.

In the first volume of his proposed multivolume biography *Alfred North Whitehead: The Man and His Work* (Johns Hopkins University Press, 1985),

Victor Lowe suggested that for about seven years after his marriage Alfred was consumed with the question of religious commitment. As part of his quest, he visited the elderly Cardinal Newman in his oratory near Birmingham, evidently to discuss the question of becoming a Roman Catholic—an option he eventually rejected because of the authoritarian nature of the church. After reading a good deal of theological material and pondering the question privately, Whitehead was still unable to decide on a definitive religious commitment and thus adopted an agnostic position which lasted for a couple of decades. He simply could

"[God] is the lure for feeling, the eternal urge of desire. His particular relevance to each creative act, as it arises from its own conditional standpoint in the world, constitutes him the initial 'object of desire' establishing the initial phase of each subjective aim."

—Process and Reality

not find a theology which satisfied him intellectually, especially one in tune with the new scientific world view he had come to accept. Thus, Whitehead personally experienced the breakdown of both scientific and theological certitudes as well as the consequent struggle to maintain theistic beliefs in an evolving, interrelated world.

In 1911, Whitehead left Cambridge to continue his career as a mathematician at the University of London where he taught until 1924, when he accepted an invitation to come to the United States to serve as professor of philosophy at Harvard University. Thus, at the age of sixty-three, he left his homeland and his first love, mathematics, in order to begin a surprisingly brilliant career as a philosopher. He became very popular with the students at Harvard who appreciated his engaging charm and personal interest, as well as his profound knowledge and open mind. Energized by his new environment and his teaching responsibilities, he worked out a personally satisfying theistic system which impressed others as well.

The development of his ideas can be traced in his important books: *Science and the Modern World* (1925), which argued that reality could not be explained in totally materialistic terms; *Religion in the Making* (1926), which demonstrated the transcendent importance of religion in providing us with our deepest vision of reality; *Process and Reality* (1929), his masterwork which presented his key ideas on God in the framework of his comprehensive cosmology; *Adventures of Ideas* (1933), which included his ideas on the highest ideals of human existence; and finally, *Modes of Thought* (1938), which is a simpler, non-technical statement of his major ideas and, therefore, a good introduction to his thought.

After this great outpouring of stimulating material, Whitehead retired from his teaching position in 1937, retaining emeritus status until his death in 1947. He lived out his last years deeply saddened by the Second World War, but as Lucien Price suggests in his *Dialogues of Alfred North Whitehead* (Little, Brown, 1954), maintaining to the end a serene belief in the God who is in the world "creating continually in us and around us." It is precisely Whitehead's distinctive understanding of God which has inspired the work of the process theologians and can enrich our perceptions of the divine-human relationship.

A World in Process

CHALLENGING THE TRADITIONAL IMAGE of an unchanging God who governs a static world, Whitehead's theistic philosophy portrays an involved deity who changes along with the evolving world. Whitehead recognized that a credible cosmology could not be based on the outdated Newtonian physics which abstracted from time and duration. Thus, he developed his "philosophy of organism," which took seriously modern evolutionary theory. The world is best understood, not as a machine governed by fixed laws, but as an evolving process guided by creative energy.

According to Whitehead's cosmology, the world is made up of energy events or units of process, which he variously called "actual entities," "actual occasions," or "occasions of experience." Each actual entity is a product of the whole evolutionary process and all previous occasions of experience. In other words, an actual entity is a microcosm representing the whole universe. Actual entities exist only for an instant as they absorb and creatively organize past occasions. Influenced by the philosopher Leibniz, Whitehead coined the term "prehension" to describe the process whereby an actual entity is able to apprehend and absorb previous units of process. In this way, elements of the past influence the present, while current experience prepares for the future.

Thus, for Whitehead, the "really real" is never static but always in process. The building blocks of history are not fixed substances, but dynamic energy events. Becoming is a more concrete reality than being. A world in process cannot be explained by static categories and fixed systems. For Whitehead, to even hint at "dogmatic certainty" when analyzing an evolving world is an "exhibition of folly."

An Essential Unity

ACCORDING TO WHITEHEAD'S general philosophical principles, human existence must also be understood in process terms. Human beings are sophisticated actual entities or "complex societies" of energy events, bound together not by a traditional enduring soul, but by a "soul in process" or a "dominant occasion" which functions as a center of direction for the whole person. Thus, we humans do not have a fixed essence; each one of us is, rather, a living

> "[God] is the binding element in the world. The consciousness which is individual in us, is universal in him: the love which is partial in us is all-embracing in him."
> —Religion in the Making

process, an event of becoming, a sequence of moments. We know ourselves as an ever-changing series of experiences, each of which integrates elements of the past and prepares for the future. We have the capacity to fashion ourselves by selecting from the past actualities in order to create a better future.

Even as evolving occasions of experience, we possess an essential unity of emotional reactions to our environment. We shape our hopes and fears, our enjoyments and regrets into a consistent pattern of feelings. Our unity is not found in an enduring self but in our memory of the past, our enjoyment of the present, and our anticipation of the future. We apprehend previous experiences, absorbing them into the unity of a single experience. While Whitehead does not say much about personality and offers a limited examination of human existence (especially in comparison with Heidegger and other existentialists), he does make clear that we are beings in process who must take responsibility for our own development.

In Whitehead's philosophy, God is not an "exception to all metaphysical principles," but "their chief exemplification." If reality is essentially processive and evolving, then God must share in these characteristics. This principle calls into question the Aristotelian image of God as the unmoved Mover as well as deistic notions of a transcendent creator uninvolved with the world. Whitehead

"[God] does not create the world, he saves it; or more accurately, he is the poet of the world, with tender patience leading it by his own vision of truth, beauty, and goodness."
—Final Interpretation

was convinced that such outmoded images had "infused tragedy" into the history of the monotheistic religions and continued today to make theistic belief more difficult for individuals. As a corrective, Whitehead insisted that God himself is an actual entity who must be understood in the context of the cosmic process.

Thus, he included in his philosophical system a bipolar God who possesses both a "primordial" and a "consequent" nature. Through his primordial nature, the one God is the transcendent source of the created order, the "unconditioned actuality" at the base of reality, the unchanging "object of desire" for all actual entities, the summation of all ideals guiding the evolutionary process. As primordial, God is a non-temporal actual entity, possessing all the potential of the whole universe through what Whitehead calls "eternal objects" or "forms of definitiveness," capable of directing the development of every entity. In other words, the potential for growth enjoyed by every actual entity already exists in the primordial mind of God. While this terminology may be unfamiliar, Whitehead's descriptions clearly point to a transcendent, complete and eternal God similar to the Supreme Being portrayed by classical theism.

On the other hand, by virtue of his consequent nature, the one God is deeply involved in the "creative advance of the world." God not only guides the evolutionary process but also absorbs into himself all the experiences of every actual entity. He is not only transcendent but also immanent through total involvement in every aspect of the historical process. The God of Whitehead's cosmology changes along with the world by taking all actual experiences into "the immediacy of his own life." In his consequent nature, God is incomplete and "actually deficient," only gradually building himself up through his interactions with the world. Every positive development in the world brings newness to the divine nature, enabling God to surpass himself in a richer self-expression.

In summary, Whitehead offers a striking alternative to traditional notions of an unchanging deity in charge of a static world. While remaining a single unified entity, the God presented in the philosophy of organism functions as both a transcendent agent guiding the world's development and also as an engaged recipient fully responsive to the process.

Process theologians who have developed and refined Whitehead's seminal ideas are convinced that his image of a changing God is more intelligible and credible for individuals with a modern scientific mindset. Furthermore, process theism gives ultimate and everlasting significance to all temporal experience by insisting that it is absorbed into the divine nature. This is, indeed, good news for those troubled by the precarious and transitory character of a continuously evolving world in which the passing of time is a "perpetual perishing."

Overcoming Dualism

FURTHERMORE, WHITEHEAD'S THEISTIC cosmology offers a radical solution to the problem of dualistic thinking, which has produced a sense of isolation and fragmentation in the modern world. Whitehead himself believed that the problem of fragmentation was of even greater concern to his contemporaries than the problem of human finitude. At the beginning of the modern period, the philosopher Descartes (1596-1650) sharply distinguished physical and mental substances, thereby setting up unfortunate dichotomies between life and nature, body and soul, individual and society, world and God. In response to these dualisms, Whitehead's philosophy of organism presents a grand vision of an integrated cosmos in which all actual entities, including God, are essentially and necessarily interrelated. This interdependence exists as a relational reality even if it is ignored or denied.

Thus, we must learn to see the world whole by recognizing the fundamental connections in the composition of the "really real." The various forms of life, for example, cannot be understood in isolation from the physical world out of which they have emerged. In Whitehead's cosmology, every actual entity must be bipolar, possessing both a physical and mental pole. This does not mean that rocks have consciousness, but that every actual entity in the physical world absorbs past entities and, in some minimal fashion, shapes them. Unless the inanimate world possesses some "mental pole," we cannot account for the emergence of the higher forms of life in the evolutionary process.

According to Whitehead's distinctive form of "panpsychism," which insists that there is an element of spirit in all reality, we human beings are not only the products of the evolutionary process, but we continue to carry within us elements of the physical world out of which we emerge. We live within nature, dependent upon it for our very survival. While human beings do possess a unique worth and human history is the leading edge of the evolutionary process, the world of nature has its own intrinsic value and continues to support the process of history.

TO APPRECIATE OUR ORGANIC RELATIONSHIP with the world, Whitehead suggests we reflect on the way our personal experiences depend on our bodily condition. It is difficult, for instance, to feel exuberant while suffering from a severe headache. On the other hand, the pleasure of healthy exercise can lift our spirits. We do not live as disembodied souls detached from the physical world. We always experience ourselves as connected to the world through our bodies. Whitehead suggests that "in one sense the world is in the soul" because all the various moods and emotions which help constitute the soul are reactions to the experienced world. The whole history of the world conspires to provide the new occasion that we are. In short, a dualism which splits life from nature ignores our fundamental experiences of bodily immersion in the world.

This analysis also calls into question the Cartesian split between body and soul. We experience ourselves as unified persons and not as accidental mixtures of mental and physical elements. According to Whitehead, our practical lives are governed by a "basic persuasion" that there is "only one ego" which claims both the body and the stream of experience which constitute our existence. Body and soul form an essential unity, both possessing the "full reality of our immediate self." While the human soul has the capacity for "autonomous enjoyment" and plays a directive role in human existence, it never functions independently of the body. Thus, as thinking, feeling entities, we must "claim an identification with our bodies." A dualism which relates body and soul only accidentally fails to take into account the dominant influence of bodily feelings on the actual occasions of personal experience.

In addition, Whitehead's philosophy of organism provides a radical critique of the individualism which places personal growth in opposition to community participation. No actual entity can exist in isolation, but is always interrelated.

As sophisticated actual entities, human beings are essentially social and interdependent creatures. We first of all exist in community, only gradually establishing a relative independence within it. We achieve our individuality, not by autonomous activity, but by participating wholeheartedly in the life of the community. In this way, we both contribute to the well-being of the group and receive guidance and strength from it. The extreme individualism found in the modern world is finally unsatisfying and destructive because it denies an essential structure of human existence and, indeed, of all reality—the fundamental interdependence of all actual entities. In an interrelated world, we will find our deepest enjoyment in communion and not isolation.

Finally, the theistic philosophy of Whitehead challenges those who set up a sharp dichotomy between God and the world. As a non-temporal actual entity, God must be related to all other actual entities. Through his consequent nature, God is intimately involved in the world process, guiding its development and

"Neither God, nor the World, reaches static completion. Both are in the grip of the ultimate metaphysical ground, the creative advance into novelty. Either of them, God and the World, is the instrument of novelty for the other."

—God and the World

absorbing its progress. Thus, we enjoy an amazingly close relationship of mutuality with God because we both receive divine direction and contribute to the divine life. God, however, remains the transcendent one with a uniquely comprehensive and inclusive perspective. His experience encompasses all the enjoyment and suffering experienced by every actual entity. For Whitehead, the world finds its sustaining energy and its deepest significance through its intimate relationship with the immanent God.

Process theologians have effectively used Whitehead's organic philosophy in attacking the dualisms which have become part of modern consciousness. Shubert Ogden, for instance, has extended Whitehead's analysis of the unity of the human person by examining our experience of fundamental trust (cf. *The Reality of God*). Daniel Day Williams has challenged selfish individualism by showing that the immanent God "urges all things toward a society of real freedom in communion" (cf. *The Spirit and the Forms of Love*). Finally, John Cobb has effectively addressed the ecological crisis by drawing on Whitehead's integrated cosmology which roots human existence in the natural world (Cf. *Is It Too Late? A Theology of Ecology*).

Creative Purpose

FOR THOSE STRUGGLING with a sense of futility and estrangement, Whitehead's theistic philosophy offers hope by insisting that the world is filled with creative purpose and guided by a compassionate God who travels the path of life with us. In Whitehead's cosmology, creativity is built into the essential structures of the world. As we have seen, each actual entity not only apprehends past occasions, but also shapes them into a unified experience. Employing poetic language, Whitehead speaks of each new occasion of experience aiming at the "maximum enjoyment" of its creative moment of becoming. Entities

> *"What is done in the world is transformed into a reality in heaven, and the reality in heaven passes back into the world. By reason of this reciprocal relation, the love in the world passes into the love in heaven, and floods back again into the world. In this sense, God is the great companion—the fellow sufferer who understands."*
>
> —God and the World

absorb the past into a moment of "satisfaction" through a "process of feeling." This distinctive terminology, applied to all actual entities, suggests that the evolutionary process has direction and purpose. Furthermore, since all actual occasions possess the root capacity for self-creativity, they are able to further the constructive advance of the world and produce genuine innovations.

The creative aim of the universe is most clearly manifested in human existence which demonstrates a remarkable capacity for adaptation and innovation. In common with all actual entities, human beings are partly determined by past occasions of experience. The potentiality of every individual person at any moment is limited by many factors, including historical circumstances, physical capabilities, and previous decisions. At the same time, individuals retain a fundamental freedom to mold and integrate the past into a distinctly new event. Thus, we can consciously choose a "subjective aim" and then work intelligently to actualize it. Our freedom enables us to take on projects and see them through to completion. We can live life with spontaneity, freshness, zest, and intensity, creating in the process new forms of enjoyment for ourselves. In addition, our creativity enables us to make distinctive contributions to society as a whole and to bring new life to our world.

Whitehead also recognized the darker side of human freedom. We can make decisions which reduce the positive impact of the past and cut off constructive possibilities for future growth. Our project can be distorted and our ideals defaced. Even in our failures, however, we experience ourselves as related to an external standard and called by transcendent ideals.

For Whitehead, God is the ultimate source of these ideals as well as the creative energy luring us toward them. It is the divine function to supply importance and value for the human adventure. God is the "Eros of the Universe," providing it with energy and motivation so that the evolutionary process will seek out and actualize its best possibilities. In his primordial nature, God is "the entertainment of all ideals" and the "storehouse" of every possibility; while through his consequent nature, he knows the precise circumstances of every actual entity. Thus, in every concrete situation, God is able to offer to the world and to us the most appropriate possibilities for growth and development. God influences us by providing our initial aim or general direction as well as specific opportunities for actualizing our potential.

New Images of God

IMPRESSED WITH THE TENDER MESSAGE of Jesus the "gentle Galilean," Whitehead insisted that God deals with us through loving persuasion rather than coercive power. Traditional images of God as the transcendent creator, the divine law-giver, and the strict judge do not reflect the authentic teaching of Christ, but lead instead to a distorted sense of the deity as a repressive force, stifling human freedom and creativity. According to Whitehead's theism, God's inexhaustible love lures us into the adventure of creativity. We experience the divine summons gently calling us forward into a better future, a richer life, a deeper love and a heightened consciousness. While respecting our freedom, the deity, as the "Harmony of Harmonies," tenderly draws us toward "the experience of Peace." This increases our appreciation of beauty, expands our horizons, and preserves our energy, while decreasing our self-preoccupation, moderating our stress, and removing inhibitions. In guiding us to this high ideal, God refuses to use force, relying instead on persuasive power which expresses love and inspires worship.

In order to clarify his theistic position, Whitehead introduced new images of God rather than reinterpreting traditional biblical images. God, for example, is "the mirror which discloses to every creature its own greatness"; the "poet of the world who affirms the depths of reality and imagines what human existence can become"; and the "Fullness of Beauty" who moves us through attraction rather than constraint.

Of special note is Whitehead's famous description of God as "the great companion—the fellow sufferer who understands." This notion not only reminds us of the mutuality which prevails between God and human beings, but also highlights the suffering experienced by God in his consequent nature. For Christians, the cross is a symbol that God shares in our sufferings and, therefore, understands the struggles connected with the human condition. Furthermore, the cross which led Christ to a richer life suggests that the divine response to our life-denying sins is not harsh condemnation but a loving offer of new possibilities for a more abundant life. We can be people of hope because the divine companion is a compassionate, forgiving lover who not only preserves our past efforts but opens up the possibility of a better future.

PROCESS THEOLOGIANS POINT OUT that Whitehead's distinctive notion of a changing and compassionate deity is more in accord with both modern science and the biblical picture of God. The teaching of Jesus, for instance, surely supports the notion of a God who motivates us by loving persuasion rather than coercion. Some followers of Whitehead emphasize his rational system and others his empirical and experiential approach, but both groups find inspiration and direction in his brief but provocative discussion of the compassionate deity. Likewise, Whitehead's followers may argue about his position on personal immortality, but they are convinced that his theism offers a firm basis for hope and a powerful motive for sustained and constructive action in the world.

Other theologians less enamored with the whole philosophy of organism offer a variety of criticisms. Whitehead's theism, for example, is based on philosophical speculation and not on biblical revelation. His God is not really the transcendent Lord of the Bible but a limited agent of an impersonal creativity which functions as the real ultimate principle. His imagery for the deity is too bland, his system too speculative, his terminology too unfamiliar.

Nevertheless, even without accepting his total system we can gain a greater understanding and appreciation of the divine-human relationship from Alfred North Whitehead, who reminds us that the "Great Companion" brings unity, direction and purpose to our lives.

Discussion Questions

1. Do you experience any conflicts between religion and science?

2. How did Whitehead's training in mathematics and the sciences influence his theology?

3. What are the fundamental principles of Whitehead's philosophy and how did they influence his outlook on theism?

4. How could Whitehead's thought help deal with current conflicts between belief in God and the findings of science?

Suggested Readings

Modes of Thought (The Free Press, 1968). A non-technical treatment of his major ideas which serves as a helpful introduction to his thought.

Process and Reality (corrected edition, Macmillan, 1979). His masterwork, difficult but rewarding reading which presents his ideas on God in the framework of his philosophical system.

Religion in the Making (Macmillan, 1926). A consistently argued treatment of the importance of religion in developing a comprehensive vision of reality.

Adventures of Ideas (Macmillan, 1933). A readable and inspiring treatment of the highest ideals which should guide human life.

CHAPTER 17

Jacques Maritain
developing a christian humanism

THE WORD "HUMANISM" carries anti-religious connotations for many people. Atheistic humanists frequently condemn religion as an obstacle to full human growth because it makes believers dependent on authoritarian structures and prevents them from taking rational control of their lives. Christians typically associate humanism with its secular version, condemning it as a heresy which denies the proper role of God in human affairs. The net result of this presumed conflict between humanism and religion is that the vital tasks of human development, cultural enrichment, and social progress are handed over to nonbelievers while believers attend to the business of saving souls. In this situation, Christians with a broader understanding of their religion are put on the defensive, always forced to explain that they too are in favor of development and progress. Moreover, when Christians are absent from the project of improving human existence, the common good suffers and secular humanists are deprived of an important dialogue partner.

One way of overcoming the apparent opposition between humanism and religion is by developing an attractive and effective Christian humanism which promotes traditional humanistic goals in the context of faith. We will find a great deal of inspiration and enlightenment for this project in the life and thought of the Christian philosopher Jacques Maritain (1882-1973), for almost half a century the most celebrated intellectual in the Catholic world. His friends and col-

leagues generally agreed that they were even more impressed with the integrity of his character and the sanctity of his life than with the great cogency and power of his philosophy. Taking our cue from them, we will emphasize the way Maritain lived out the Christian humanism about which he wrote so extensively and incisively.

Search for Truth

BORN IN PARIS, November 18, 1882, Jacques received his early orientation from his mother, a free-spirited woman who helped him to develop a love of learning and an appreciation of the intellectual life. Although he was baptized by a Protestant minister and grew up in the general atmosphere of liberal Protestantism, he did not develop any serious religious convictions. As a teenager, Jacques experienced anxiety and frustration as he wrestled unsuccessfully with the great questions of meaning and purpose. His intellectual frustration increased when he went to the Sorbonne to continue his education. The University of Paris was at that time dominated by scientism—the notion spawned earlier in the century by August Comte that science should replace religion as a comprehensive world view. This restrictive approach to the deepest questions of life simply did not satisfy the young man's passion for truth.

In the midst of his search, Jacques met the woman who would become his wife, Raïssa Oumensoff, a bright and talented Jewish emigrant from Russia who shared his passion for the great questions of life. They read poetry together and discussed philosophy, all the while drifting further into skepticism. Depressed over their intellectual doubts, they made a sort of mutual suicide pact, giving themselves one year to "find meaning for the word *truth*." Fortunately, they found some "sense of the absolute" in the vitalistic philosophy of Henri Bergson, whose lectures they attended at the College de France.

Reacting against the dominant scientism, Bergson insisted that we could gain genuine knowledge of our evolving world, not through reason but through intuition, which establishes a "sympathetic communication" with living reality. Bergson's philosophy not only gave the young couple hope in their intellectual quest, but provided Jacques with the key notion of "intuition," which remained an important element in his mature thought. Bergson's philosophy as a whole, however, did not satisfy the young Maritain's thirst for a comprehensive system.

About a decade later, again with the help of Raïssa, he did find that more satisfying synthesis in the thought of Thomas Aquinas, the great medieval philosopher and theologian who had integrated Aristotle's philosophy into a Christian context. Convinced that Aquinas had given us a perennial philosophy containing the essential truth, Maritain became the leader of the movement known as neo-Thomism.

Throughout his life he labored unceasingly to bring Thomism into dialogue with the modern world, using the framework established by Aquinas to respond to a vast array of contemporary questions. In the process, he continued to refine his own understanding of "Thomistic realism," which insists on our ability

"It must be admitted that in general the youth of today, victims of the inhuman acceleration imposed on life, seem discouraged at the long preparations that intelligence requires. Nevertheless, to neglect the intelligence costs dearly. A reign of the heart which would not presuppose in the heart an absolute will to truth, a Christian renewal which would think it could do without wisdom and theology, would be suicide in the disguise of love. The age is swarming with fools who disparage reason."
— Art and Scholasticism

to apprehend the real world through the power of intelligence by abstracting from sense data and by making judgments about reality. In his master work on this topic, *Degrees of Knowledge*, Maritain distinguished three types of knowledge: scientific, which arises from empirical observation and apprehends things; metaphysical, which arises from analogical thinking and opens up the world of being and ultimacy; and supra-rational, which arises in mystical experience and leads to God. This philosophical analysis, which enabled Maritain to overcome both skepticism and scientism, provided the basis for his lifelong struggles against anti-intellectualism of all types.

A humanism which follows Maritain's example will be passionate about the truth. Reason is a great ally in this quest, enabling us to overcome skepticism while resisting the temptation to settle for easy answers. The anti-intellectualism which exists in both the secular and religious worlds must be unmasked as an escape from the responsibility to use intelligence in the service of human development. On the other hand, reason and logical analysis are not the only means of pursuing truth, nor can science provide an adequate world view. Our intellectual powers exceed what reason can achieve. Philosophy deals with questions beyond the scope of science. A genuine humanism fills out its understanding of the truth with all available resources, including the knowledge gained from philosophical reflection as well as the wisdom flowing from religious experiences. A contemporary humanism which learns from the open spirit of Maritain, rather than merely repeating his limited conclusions, will recognize diverse philosophical paths leading to the truth and not just one path marked out by Aquinas.

Catholic Inspiration

MARITAIN'S LIFE STORY includes the pursuit of a religious world view as well as philosophical truth. Shortly after getting married in 1904, Jacques and Raïssa encountered the novelist Leon Bloy, a devout Catholic who introduced them to the writings of the mystics and the saints. Bloy instilled in them his cherished conviction that the only true sadness in life is not to be a saint.

Greatly inspired by the way Catholicism provided Bloy with an integrated and serene outlook on life, the young married couple took instructions and were baptized into the Catholic Church in June of 1906. Catholicism became a total way of life for them, as it was for their friend Bloy. They attended daily mass, studied church doctrines, prayed the rosary, and practiced the church's teachings on charity and justice. Jacques tied his very identity to his religious conversion, describing himself as "a convert, a man God has turned inside out like a glove." For him, Catholicism provided an overarching world view and a comprehensive value system which guided and energized his long life of learning and service.

After his conversion, Maritain spent two years studying biology at Heidelberg and three more in the tedious but financially necessary task of editing a dictionary of practical life. He began his teaching career in 1912 at the College Stanislas and two years later was appointed to the chair of philosophy and modern history at the Institute Catholique in Paris, a position he held until 1939. During these years, he became famous as the leader of the Thomistic revival occurring in the Catholic world. At the request of the French bishops, he produced two textbooks on philosophy for Catholic collegians. Responding to increasing demands, Maritain gave numerous lectures and wrote many articles which were often collected into books. In 1936, he published his classic work, *Integral Humanism* (Scribner, 1968), which not only exposed the errors in the various forms of atheistic and agnostic humanism, but presented his own positive vision

"Wherever art—English, Greek or Chinese—has known a certain degree of grandeur and purity, it is already Christian, Christian in hope, because every spiritual radiance is a promise and a symbol of the divine harmonies of the Gospel."

— Art and Scholasticism

of a new Christian humanism. His fame also spread abroad, leading to many successful lecture tours in the United States and Canada.

In addition, Jacques refined and disseminated his ideas through the regular Sunday afternoon discussions which he and Raïssa hosted in their home during his tenure at the Institute Catholique. These gatherings, which developed into the famous Thomistic Studies group, regularly drew leading Catholic intellectuals from France and sometimes included visiting scholars from abroad. Typically, Jacques began these sessions with a formal exposition of some aspect of Thomistic thought which then served as a basis for informal discussion. Sometimes the group decided on some course of action such as issuing statements on particular justice and peace issues.

Art and Religion

THROUGHOUT THIS PERIOD, Maritain was especially interested in the world of the fine arts. Much of this interest was developed through his relationship with Raïssa, who was a fine poet with excellent artistic sensibilities. Together they formed lifelong friendships with many outstanding artists, including the painter George Rouault, the composer Igor Stravinsky, and the poet Paul Claudel.

Drawing on these contacts and experiences, Jacques wrote a number of books dealing with philosophical aspects of art, including his very influential *Art and*

Scholasticism (Notre Dame Press, 1974), first published in 1920, as well as his more comprehensive work, *Creative Intuition in Art and Poetry* (Pantheon Books, 1953).

According to Maritain, art opens up the transcendent dimension of human existence. Art is pursued for its own sake and has a spiritual value. Artists are required to quiet their senses and gather their spiritual forces so that their

---

"As regards the common task to be accomplished by the body politic, let us say . . . that for a Christian civilization which can no longer be naive, the common aim would no longer appear as a divine work to be brought about on earth by man but, rather, as a human work to be brought about on earth by the passing of something divine, namely, love, into human means and into human work itself."

— Integral Humanism

---

preconscious intuitions can be released into the artistic act. Beautiful art, which is known intuitively and brings delight, enables us to "glimpse the splendors beyond the grave" and to believe that the lost paradise which we seek is ultimately attainable. God is the supreme artist, the source of all beauty whose splendor radiates in the created world. Blessed with the ability to see deeply, artists are able to disclose "spiritual radiances" which others cannot readily discern. Thus, the task of the artist is to lead people to God by showing how the divine is manifest in the visible. Good art has the power to create a contemplative mood which not only delights the spirit, but also promotes noble and loving actions.

While it is not proper to speak of Catholic art, Maritain did believe that Catholicism orders the whole of life to divine truth and beauty, thus creating a healthy climate for artistic creativity. Maritain's deep appreciation of art, especially painting and poetry, not only nourished his soul but also provided him with a concrete model of the way religion and culture can form a fruitful synthesis.

Our analysis of this second aspect of Maritain's life and thought suggests that humanism and religion are not necessarily antithetical but can be mutually enriching. The humanist goals of personal development and cultural enhancement can be pursued in the context of a biblical faith. The God of the Bible grants to human beings responsibility for building the community of love and guarantees that this effort will find an ultimate fulfillment. Commitment to Christ demands that individuals develop their God-given gifts in order to serve better the common good. Christianity, far from impeding human growth, provides a broad vision and a context of meaning in which personal development can be pursued without falling into selfishness or tedium.

Furthermore, Christianity enriches the whole humanistic project by revealing the transcendent dimension present in all human existence. Human beings are made in the image of God and are, therefore, more precious than anything in the world. In striving for self-perfection, individuals open themselves to the divine spirit, thus preparing for their ultimate happiness when they will be totally possessed by God. When persons interact in a loving way, they bring to earth "the fire of eternal life." Cultural expressions which reflect the freedom of the human spirit direct our attention to the divine source of all human creativity. Biblical faith reveals the narrowness and superficiality of all self-contained humanisms which deny or neglect the ultimate source and goal of human progress. Moreover, Christian humanism furthers traditional humanistic goals by discerning the spirit of Jesus at work in all legitimate efforts to enhance human existence.

Politics and War

MARITAIN'S PERSONAL STORY also has a political phase or dimension. For about a 15-year period, he was associated with the right-wing anti-democratic movement known as "Action Francaise." When this organization was condemned by Pope Pius XI in 1926, Maritain severed all ties with it and its leader Charles Mourras. This long overdue, but still courageous action, earned him the bitter recriminations of his right-wing friends, including the novelist Georges Bernanos.

Maritain experienced a deep and enduring remorse over his unenlightened involvement with a political movement which was so counter to his natural instincts. Chastened, he determined to refine his political philosophy and to play a more active and prudent role in political affairs. During the Spanish Civil War, for example, he refused to join many of his Catholic friends in supporting General Franco, preferring instead to work for reconciliation both during and after the war.

When Germany overran France in 1940, Maritain was in North America on one of his frequent lecture tours. He and Raïssa were forced to stay in the United States for the duration of the war, taking up residence in the Greenwich Village section of New York City. During this time, he worked tirelessly on behalf of the Jews in occupied Europe. In his writings as well as his weekly radio addresses transmitted to France, he attacked the religious roots of anti-Semitism, insisting that the Jews were not collectively guilty for the death of Christ, and therefore should not be condemned by Christians for deicide.

Clearly influenced by his extremely close relationship with his Jewish wife Raïssa, Jacques demonstrated an unusual understanding and empathy for the Jewish people. This prompted the influential American theologian Reinhold Niebuhr to say of Maritain that no other Christian theologian spoke with such profundity and fervor about the plight of the Jews. Even more impressively, Maritain matched his words with vigorous and sustained action. Combining compassion with practical intelligence, he used personal influence and political contacts to help rescue individuals living under the Nazi threat. His lifelong efforts on behalf of the Jews were publicly recognized in 1961 when he was given the prestigious Edith Stein Guild Award for fostering cooperation between Christians and Jews.

From 1945 to 1948, Maritain served as French ambassador to the Vatican, a position he accepted very reluctantly after strong urging from General de Gaulle. As ambassador, he worked closely with Archbishop Roncalli, the future Pope John XXIII, who served as papal nuncio to France. He also exercised significant influence on Monsignor Montini, the future Pope Paul VI, who incorporated some of Maritain's fundamental principles into his social encyclicals.

Maritain's public service extended beyond church affairs to the secular world, especially through his involvement with the United Nations. In 1947, he was elected president of the second international conference of UNESCO and given the honor of delivering the opening address. Enunciating some of his favorite themes, he insisted that people from diverse cultures and spiritual traditions could still join together in common cause on the basis of a fundamental respect for human rights. Even if individuals have divergent views about the nature and origin of these rights, they can still live in harmony by accepting a common "civic faith" which seeks to preserve human dignity, freedom, and equality.

Based on this conviction, Maritain worked with others to produce the "United Nations Universal Declaration of the Rights of Man," which was unanimously adopted by the member nations in 1948. For him, the adoption of this declaration was of great historical significance because it laid the foundation for the pursuit of global peace and justice. Maritain was a true internationalist with a global vision. He understood the need for a world government, but also recognized the immense power of nationalism.

In many books, including *Scholasticism and Politics* (Image) and *Man and*

"Modern civilization is a worn-out garment. One cannot sew new pieces on it. It requires a total, and may I say, substantial recasting, a transvaluation of cultural principles: since it is a question of arriving at a vital primacy of quality over quantity, of work over money, of the human over the technological, of wisdom over science, of the common service of human persons over the individual covetousness of unlimited enrichment of the state's covetousness of unlimited power."

— Integral Humanism

State (University of Chicago Press), Maritain developed his notion of human rights as a firm foundation for a contemporary political philosophy. Rights belong to human beings not as isolated earthbound individuals, but as interdependent spiritual persons with transcendent goals. As communal creatures, persons are necessarily involved in society and the political realm. Their rights are best protected by a limited government which serves the best interest of the larger pluralistic society. Laws and authority are necessary but they should function as "a pedagogue of freedom." Through his very positive experience of living in the United States, Maritain came to see the value of democratic forms of government, which enable the citizens to participate in the political process.

Christian humanists who follow the example and teachings of Maritain cannot help but take seriously their responsibility to improve the social order. While the political realm must maintain its own proper autonomy, Christians have the responsibility to "transpenetrate" the social world, so that human beings can live in greater justice, harmony, and peace. Such a transformation can be accomplished primarily through lay Christians who bring moral values and ethical principles to bear on social questions and public policy issues.

According to Maritain, this involvement will require a new kind of lay spirituality which strives for a worldly sanctity. Recognizing the radical shift involved he stated his point sharply: "Thus a vitally Christian social renewal will be a work of sanctity or it will be nothing; a sanctity, that is, turned toward the temporal, the secular, the profane" (*Integral Humanism*, p. 122).

Christians must strive to create a new society which is both communal and personalistic. Such a society will promote the common good by enhancing the material well-being of individuals so that the spiritual freedom of all can flourish. The society envisioned by Maritain is neither the kingdom on earth nor a Marxist utopia. It is, rather, a vital political community inspired by gospel values in which human beings are free to strive for proximate justice and relative peace.

To move in this direction Christian humanists need a "prudential wisdom" and a feel for the concrete realities of the social order. They must have, in Maritain's well-known phrase, "tough minds and tender hearts." Their global vision should be matched by their care for particular individuals. Humanists supported and guided by their faith are free to work wholeheartedly for social progress and political reform even despite failures—precisely because they believe that the establishment of the kingdom is ultimately God's work.

After completing his assignment as ambassador to the Vatican in 1948, Maritain took a position as a professor of philosophy at Princeton University where he taught until 1960. During this time, he lectured widely around the United States, drawing large enthusiastic crowds and solidifying his reputation as the foremost Catholic intellectual of the 20th century. His aim was to make the perennial wisdom found in Thomism available to an expanding audience so that it would be utilized in dealing with contemporary problems.

He often returned to his favorite themes. Secular humanism, which replaced the gospel with reason, has robbed individuals of the ability to give themselves in loving relationships and has created a crisis of values in modern civilization. Marxism, which functions as a religion promising an inner worldly salvation, ends up sacrificing persons to the "blind god of history." Given these failures, the world desperately needs a new "theocentric humanism" which recognizes the "natural grandeur" of human beings "inhabited by God."

Such an integral humanism accepts both the irrational in human nature, in order to "tame it to reason," and the "supra-rational," in order to remain open to the "descent of the divine." A "humanism of the Incarnation" works to create a temporal order worthy of human beings and conducive to their material and spiritual well-being. To achieve this we need a "Christian-personalistic democracy" which guards against the individualism fostered by capitalism and the enslavement demanded by communist totalitarian regimes.

A New Christendom

RECALLING THE FRUITFUL SYNTHESIS of religion and culture in the medieval world, Maritain described his ideal society as "a new Christendom." He insisted that this did not mean a return to the past, but a renewed effort to humanize the properly autonomous social order through the power of gospel values. Employing his key "principle of analogy," he claimed we should neither imitate nor ignore the old Christendom. Instead we should take the timeless truths which successfully animated traditional society and apply them analogically to the very different conditions of the contemporary world. Thus, for example, we need a commonly held "civic faith" which unites and guides all citizens, just as in the medieval world the members of society were bound together by their Christian faith. The new Christendom will not destroy the progress of the past but will become more "truly human and progressive" by being open to the energizing power of the divine spirit.

Maritain gradually came to perceive a congruence between his notion of the new Christendom and "the direction of certain essential trends" existing in the United States. In his penetrating analysis *Reflections on America* (Gordian Press, 1975), he praised the way our sense of freedom tends to overcome a class mentality, making social mobility possible. He was likewise impressed with the way our principle of separation of church and state still permits a religious inspiration to penetrate secular life. While his treatment also brought out the flaws and limitations in American society, Maritain did believe that the United States of the 1950s embodied some of his important political ideals and provided fruitful ground for the development of a Christian humanism.

Today many find it difficult to be so optimistic about American society. Still, Christian humanists must continue the task of discerning the potential in contemporary society and of finding concrete ways to apply their religious traditions to the ever more complex problems of public life.

When Raïssa died in 1960, Jacques lost his loving partner and brilliant collaborator, the woman he called "half of his soul." Grieving but resigned, he left the United States to spend his remaining years in contemplation and writing at a monastery of the Little Brothers of Jesus in Toulouse. Late in 1965, Maritain, now a frail old man, journeyed to Rome to participate in the closing ceremonies of the Second Vatican Council. In an emotion-filled gesture which publicly recognized Maritain's immense contributions, Pope Paul VI solemnly placed in his hands the official text of the council's open and positive message to the intellectuals of the world.

Maritain applauded many of the accomplishments of the council, especially the important if limited progress made on the questions of religious liberty and the relationship between Christians and Jews. However, he feared the enthusiasm for novelty and disregard for tradition which he believed were fostered by certain conciliar trends. He registered his fears in his uncharacteristically harsh and strident book *The Peasant of the Garrone* (Macmillan, 1964), which made the best-seller lists in 1967. The appearance of this book signaled the already diminishing influence of Maritain in the Catholic world. The reform unleashed by the council found its intellectual energy and guidance not from Maritain and his fellow neo-Thomists but from the so-called "transcendental Thomists" such as Karl Rahner, who were more responsive to the dominant trends in modern philosophy and culture. By the time Maritain died on April 28, 1973, the torch of leadership among Catholic intellectuals had long since passed to others. Today virtual silence continues to surround the name and writings of Maritain, broken now and then by those who find guidance in his political philosophy or seek to dispute his economic theories. Even his beautiful ideal of Christian humanism is seldom discussed, at least in explicit terms.

Still, Christians cannot escape the responsibility of continuing Maritain's gospel-inspired efforts to enhance human life. We cannot leave this project to the secularists nor allow them to co-opt all the positive connotations suggested by the term "humanism." In responding to this continuing challenge, we should not neglect Maritain. Even those who do not find his neo-Thomistic philosophical system fully satisfying can still learn a great deal from the inspiring example and penetrating insights of this great man. He remains an impressive model for an integral humanism which embraces the best in the culture within a framework of gospel values. Jacques Maritain lived out an attractive Christian humanism which combined philosophical reflection with practical political action, personal development with concern for the common good, and the pursuit of knowledge with the warmth of love.

Discussion Questions

1. What does the word "humanism" suggest to you and does it have any anti-religious overtones?

2. How did Maritain's vast and varied life experiences affect his positions on philosophy, art, politics and religion?

3. What did Maritain mean by an "integral humanism" and how did the concept affect his outlook on society and culture?

4. How could Maritain's ideas help overcome the perceived split between Christianity and humanism?

Suggested Readings

Integral Humanism (Scribner, 1968). His classic work which exposes the errors in secular humanism and presents his positive vision of a Christian humanism.

Creative Intuition in Art and Poetry (Pantheon, 1953). His most comprehensive treatment of the philosophical aspects of the arts.

Man and State (University of Chicago Press, 1956). A clear statement of the foundations of his political philosophy.

Reflections on America (Gordian Press, 1975). A personal and insightful analysis of American society and culture.

CHAPTER 18

Pierre Teilhard de Chardin
developing a spirituality of work

WORK IS AN ESSENTIAL ELEMENT in authentic human existence. Unlike genuine leisure, which is aimless and spontaneous, work is planned, purposeful, and calculated to produce results. Unfortunately, it is not easy to achieve proper perspectives and healthy attitudes toward our work. Contradictions in our culture and perverted religious values, joined with our own destructive tendencies, can easily distort our approach to the planned and purposeful activities of life. Work, for example, can either be relegated to the status of an insignificant activity or exalted as an idol. Christians are often hard-pressed to relate their work to their faith in a consistent and meaningful way. In the face of these difficulties, we need a spirituality of work which will help us integrate our daily labor into a full human life.

The eminent Jesuit paleontologist and religious visionary, Pierre Teilhard de Chardin (1881-1955), wrote perceptively on these questions, especially in his classic work *The Divine Milieu* (Harper and Row, 1960), which offers a Christian framework and seminal ideas for developing an integrated spirituality of work.

The grand vision proclaimed in this book grew out of his deep religious experiences. Born in 1881, Teilhard at the age of 5 or 6 experienced tremendous anxiety over his mortality when he put a lock of hair close to a fire and it burned up instantly. His consequent drive to find something of permanent value eventually took him to ordination as a Jesuit priest in 1911 and a lifetime of intense work in building the imperishable kingdom. While he was serving as a non-combatant stretcher-bearer during World War I, a series of powerful, mystical experiences gave Teilhard a cosmic sense of the unity of the whole world, which informed his subsequent writings.

After the war, he returned to his doctoral studies in geology, completing his degree in 1922. This launched his scientific career, which included teaching at the Institute Catholique in Paris from 1920 to 1923, fieldwork in China from 1925 to 1946, and work as a research consultant in the United States from 1951 until his death on Easter Sunday, 1955. In addition to his numerous published scientific articles, Teilhard produced many other writings which articulated his religious vision of an integrated, evolving universe.

Unfortunately, Roman authorities, suspecting heresy in his thought, forbade him to publish his writings which dealt with theological issues. Thus his masterwork, *The Phenomenon of Man* (Harper & Row, 1959); his spiritual classic, *The Divine Milieu*; and eleven volumes of collected essays were published only after his death. His losing battle with Roman officials over the right to publish brought Teilhard untold anguish and deprived him of feedback from theologians and other scholars which would have helped him refine his thought.

Despite these restrictions during his lifetime, Teilhard's writings later became well known, influencing theologians, scientists, writers and politicians. Echoes of his thought resound in the Pastoral Constitution of the Second Vatican Council and in much of the postconciliar theology. Today Teilhard's influence has waned, as many people find his vision of the world overly optimistic and his synthesis of religion and science questionable. On the other hand, his suggestions for a contemporary spirituality which celebrates human effort in the world are still helpful and worth exploring. We will do so under two related headings: the search for objective significance in our work and the quest for personal meaning in all our labors.

Work and Worship

MANY PERSONS STRUGGLE with the apparent insignificance of their work. Individuals question whether anything is being accomplished in the great scheme of things by cooking another meal, making another sale, tightening another bolt, or teaching another class. Boring and repetitious acts often seem meaningless. Sometimes changing outlooks and attitudes intensify the problem. For example, a young man who became very concerned about social justice issues gave up a good job selling soap because that task now seemed unimportant to him. Even individuals with apparently challenging and exciting jobs sometimes wonder if all the extra energy and time they put into their work is really worthwhile.

Unfortunately, certain types of Christian piety intensify this problem by putting so much emphasis on the life of heaven that human activity on this earth is devalued. Teilhard thought that about 90 percent of the practicing Christians of his time looked upon their work as a "spiritual encumbrance" which took

"The deeper I look into myself the more clearly I become aware of this psychological truth: that no man would lift his little finger to attempt the smallest task unless he were spurred on by a more or less obscure conviction that in some infinitesimally tiny way he is contributing, at least indirectly, to the building up of something permanent—in other words, to your own work, Lord."

— Hymn of the Universe

them away from a close relationship to God. He sensed the great conflict in the hearts of many believers who live double lives because they cannot reconcile their faith in God with their care for the world. They are not able to find real organic connections between their worship on Sunday and their work during the week. In Teilhard's view the traditional solution of sanctifying one's daily efforts through prayer and good intention is helpful but incomplete, because it still considers daily work as insignificant in itself and detrimental to the spiritual life.

Teilhard experienced in his own heart the conflict between love of God and love for the world of human endeavor. By temperament, he was a son of the earth. As a child in Auvergne, France, he developed a great love of natural history and of the rocky countryside around his home. His father gave him an initial interest in the sciences, which he pursued throughout his formal education. By combining his scientific learning with his mystical intuitions, Teilhard came to a comprehensive vision of the world he loved so much. Throughout the evolutionary process, matter was gradually organized into increasingly complex structures. According to the law of complexity-consciousness formulated by Teilhard, the greater complexity matter possesses, the more consciousness it will exhibit.

Thus, for him, the world is a unified whole, moving irreversibly toward greater spiritualization and destined one day to reach its culmination in a personalized center of consciousness. This goal of the whole evolutionary process,

"As the years go by, Lord, I come to see more and more clearly, in myself and in those around me, that the greatest secret preoccupation of modern man is much less to battle for possession of the world than to find a means of escaping from it."

— Hymn of the Universe

which Teilhard called "Omega Point," has always been present in the world as the source of the love energy which fuels the process. A committed son of the earth, Teilhard believed in this evolving world and devoted himself to spreading his vision of its organic beauty.

Deeply influenced by his solidly Catholic family and the rich devotional life of his church, Teilhard was also a son of heaven. He had freely decided to become a Jesuit priest, and could not let his love for the world and his passion for science undermine his Christian faith. He needed a religious symbol system which would guide and enrich his faith in the evolving world and its personal center of universal convergence. His magnificent extended essay, *How I Believe* (Harper & Row, 1969), originally written in 1934, describes his struggle to achieve this integrated viewpoint.

At first he felt compelled to reject the traditional Catholicism taught in the schools and practiced by ordinary Christians. While the Christian teaching on heaven and a final personal union with God attracted him, the conventional piety, which devalued life in the material world and disdained human progress, was totally opposed to his own "sense of the earth." He could not reconcile himself and his deepest aspirations with that type of Christian spirituality.

Disappointed by traditional Catholicism, Teilhard extended his search for an integrating symbol system to the Eastern religions. The mystical sense of the ultimate unity of the universe, which predominates in the East, exercised a powerful initial attraction on him because it harmonized with his own cosmic sense. Upon further investigation, however, he recognized that he could never accept the Eastern teachings that the individual is ultimately swallowed up in the all, that matter is really illusory, and that human effort and progress are finally insignificant.

His search took him next to contemporary humanisms, including Marxism. He was attracted by their concern to build the earth through scientific research and to humanize the world by conquering time and space. On the other hand, he was disappointed by the refusal of humanists to accept the spiritual dimension of human existence, especially the drive for transcendence and personal immortality. He could never accept a world view which stifled the spirit and closed the human project in on itself.

Toward the Omega Point

THE ESSENTIAL LIMITATIONS of other world views took Teilhard back to his Christian roots and the great "eureka" moment of his life. In rereading the Scriptures from the viewpoint of his faith in the world, he discovered the great Pauline texts (Romans 8:19-23, Colossians 1:15-20, and Ephesians 1:9-23) which speak about the universal Christ who is the center of the universe, the goal of the dynamism of the material world and the personal reconciler of everything on earth and in the heavens. The cosmic Lord is present in the world, drawing it upward and forward toward final union with himself. The spirit of the risen Christ empowers us to share in the great task of building the earth and spreading the kingdom. There will, indeed, be a new heaven and new earth, established in and through the universal Christ.

In what Teilhard himself called "the major event" of his life, he came to understand that the cosmic Christ proclaimed by Christian faith could be identified with the Omega Point suggested by his analysis of the evolutionary process. The personalized center of the converging universe was, in deepest truth, Jesus Christ, the risen Lord. Teilhard's scientific vision of the world resonated with an authentic vision of Christ found in the New Testament. Thus, he could remain both a passionate son of the earth and a committed son of heaven. He had found the key to reconciling science and religion. A dynamic conception of a world evolving toward greater spiritualization could be integrated into belief in the risen Christ, who draws all things to himself.

After this great discovery, Teilhard spent the rest of his life refining, applying, and spreading his religious vision of the world. Within this framework, he articulated his positive notion of human endeavor in the world, including crucial ideas for a spirituality of work. Our daily labor is valuable and significant, not only by virtue of prayer and good intention, but also because it possesses an intrinsic worth. Through all of our good activities we become instruments and, indeed, living extensions of the creative power of God. Creation is not

"One cannot be but surprised (when one looks at it with a mind not dulled by habit) at the extraordinary care taken by Christ to urge upon men the importance of loving one another."

— Hymn of the Universe

an event accomplished once and for all by God alone, but an ongoing process in which we cooperate with God in bringing the world to its fulfillment. Hence, all legitimate work has intrinsic and everlasting significance because it partakes of God's creative activity.

Teilhard's understanding of the Incarnation also leads to a fuller appreciation of the intrinsic value of work. The presence of the Word made Flesh penetrates to the very core of the material world. As Teilhard insisted in his beautiful "Hymn to Matter," the material world is not a mass of brute forces, but a divine milieu, which is charged with a creative energy and "infused with life by the incarnate Word" (*Hymn of the Universe*, pp. 69-70). Thus our work in the world is not mere game-playing, but an effort to unleash matter's spiritual potential. The Incarnation will be complete only when all the creative power locked into matter is released and rejoined in the universal Christ. All of our activity, including the most humble work of our hands, contributes to the building up of the Body of Christ, which will reach its completion only at the end of time. An organic connection exists between our labor and the building of the kingdom, which the incarnate Word came to establish. In summary, Teilhard's theological interpretation of creation and incarnation highlights the essential goodness and ultimate value of all human effort.

Realizing the need to translate his religious vision into a practical spirituality, Teilhard concentrated on the intimate connection between liturgy and everyday life. Christians should leave church services convinced that life in the world offers continuing opportunities to be immersed in the divine presence. A healthy prayer life enables individuals to make explicit connections between their daily labor and the saving work of Christ. The sacramental life of the church, which divinizes the faithful, also sends them forth to divinize the world.

On one of his scientific expeditions, Teilhard found himself alone in the Ordo desert with no bread and wine to say mass. Extremely conscious of the presence of Christ throughout the universe, he offered a "mass on the world," in which the whole earth served as his altar and all the laboring and sufferings of people throughout the world constituted the consecrated bread and wine. Further applying this image, he advised all Christians to consecrate their work just as the priest consecrates the Host at mass. For him this intrinsic connection should shape our attitudes: "Right from the hands that knead the dough, to those that consecrate it, the great and universal Host should be prepared and handled in a spirit of adoration" (*The Divine Milieu*, p. 67).

While Teilhard recognized that unbelievers share in the preparation of the universal Host by their labors, he emphasized the contribution of Christians who explicitly appreciate the intrinsic value of their work and are committed to divinizing the world. These believers can demonstrate to others that "by virtue of the Creation and, still more, of the Incarnation, nothing here below is profane for those who know how to see" (*The Divine Milieu*, p. 66). In short, Teilhard's first contribution to a spirituality of work is an invitation to see with the eyes of faith the intrinsic significance of all human endeavor.

Work vs. Toil

HUMAN WORK CAN BE ANALYZED, not only from the viewpoint of its objective significance, but also from the perspective of its subjective meaning. A spirituality of work must be concerned with personal development as well as building the earth. In our culture, workers report a wide variety of responses to their daily tasks. A significant percentage describe their work as repetitive, boring, and confining. They dislike going to work, and they watch the clock until it is time to leave. Their jobs do not stimulate their imaginations, engage their emotions, or challenge their intelligence. They feel like impersonal cogs in a large industrial machine or like functionaries in a large bureaucracy. They live for the weekends as a time of escape, dreading the beginning of the work week which takes them back to their dull routines. For them, work is nothing more than burdensome toil devoid of personal satisfaction.

At the other end of the spectrum are those who enjoy their work and are absorbed by it. Their work is satisfying because it has a meaning beyond earning money and is linked with the goals of society as a whole. Their daily labor, which is often challenging and stimulating, serves as a catalyst for further development. For them, work is a vocation which requires a life of dedication. Some committed workers keep their jobs in a proper perspective and maintain healthy relationships with their families and friends. Others, the so-called "workaholics," become so compulsive about their jobs that they neglect other aspects of their lives including their personal relationships.

Between these extremes, many people find their work to be a mixture of burdensome toil and satisfying activities which engage their freedom, intelligence, and creativity. At times these workers are immersed in their tasks, while on other occasions they watch the clock, waiting for the day to end.

Individuals, as well as society, would benefit greatly if more oppressive toil could be transformed into satisfying work. Progress toward this goal demands both structural changes in society and the improvement of fundamental attitudes on the part of workers. While Teilhard has little practical advice on societal reform, he does offer helpful perspectives and insights for improving our attitudes toward our work.

We can find greater personal meaning in our work by becoming more conscious of God's presence in all of our activities. Teilhard's writings are especially helpful in sharpening our awareness of this divine presence. In his vision, God is not a remote architect of a static universe, but rather the immanent power which sustains and guides the evolving world. The universal Christ is not only the final goal of the converging cosmos, but also the ever-present energy which fuels the movement of history toward its ultimate end. Love is not an abstract ideal but a cosmic force which draws us into unity with the center of the universe. A divine fire burns at the center of the earth, uniting, illumining, and warming every aspect of human existence.

The Hymn of Gratitude

FROM THIS THEOLOGICAL PERSPECTIVE, it is clear that we do not labor alone in building the earth, but always in cooperation with the Lord of the universe. In our work we discover "the knitting together of God and the world." God awaits us in every moment of our daily activity. He "is at the tip of my pen, my spade, my brush, my needle—of my heart and of my thought" (*The Divine Milieu*, p. 64). When our work brings pain and exhaustion, we can identify with the crucified Christ, who was faithful to the end. When

---

"*. . . we must try everything for Christ; we must hope everything for Christ. Nihil intentatum: that is the true Christian attitude. Divinization means not destruction but supercreation. We can never know all that the Incarnation still asks of the world's potentialities. We can never hope for too much from the growing unity of mankind.*"

— Hymn of the Universe

---

our labors bring joy and satisfaction, we can identify with the risen Christ, who is the source of all good gifts. As workers, we are never alone. This is good news, because God's presence does not stifle our activity but, in Teilhard's phrase "sur-animates" it, rendering it holy and full of meaning.

Prayer is our best method of cultivating a deep awareness of God's presence in all our activities. Far from being an escape into the heavenly realm, prayer attunes us to the hidden truths and the mysterious powers which undergird life on this earth. If our work is dull and boring, prayer becomes a self-sacrificing plea for the gift of perseverance. If work is exhilarating and satisfying, prayer flows into a hymn of gratitude. In prayer we come to know in a deeper way Jesus Christ the worker, who continues to illumine and energize our labors today. Prayer, which sharpens our awareness of the divine presence, provides focus in a world of work which oscillates between boredom and frenzied activity. Furthermore, Teilhard insisted that reflections on Scripture should nourish and guide our prayer life. He found special enrichment in the writings of Paul, who taught us that all human activities, including the most humble, should be done for the glory of God. This teaching encourages us to approach our work in a spirit of faith, confident that God can be found in all our legitimate activities.

For Teilhard, effective Christian living in the world also demands a detached-attachment. This dialectical virtue prompts us, first of all, to be passionate about our own personal growth as well as the progress of the whole world.

We can make our own unique contribution to the building up of the Body of Christ only if our talents are developed and our skills honed. In turn, our work serves as an effective catalyst for such self-development. Work can draw us out of our selfishness and laziness by giving us new goals and common projects. It can tap our latent potential and move us to acquire new knowledge and skills. Honest labor can teach us about accepting our limitations and bring us some of the most satisfying joys in life. There is a proper attachment to work which involves care for a job well done and concern for the personal and societal fruits of our labor. Affirming this Teilhardian insight, the Second Vatican Council exhorted Christians "to discharge their earthly duties consciously and in response to the gospel spirit" (*Gaudium et Spes*, 43).

According to Teilhard, genuine attachment to work is part of a larger synthesis which includes renunciation and detachment. Work, by its very nature, detaches us from the calm repose of a self-centered inertia and moves us into the challenging arena of activity. Workers who strive for high standards must renounce laziness and sloppy procedures. Those who have devoted themselves to a worthwhile cause know firsthand the self-sacrifice which such commitment demands. Laborers, whose daily toil is extremely burdensome, are denied the opportunities for personal development provided by more challenging jobs. Those who cannot find meaningful jobs often feel diminished by a loss of self-esteem. Work, which can bring so much fulfillment, also demands a great deal of self-surrender. While Christians are called to fight against all the dehumanizing tendencies connected with work, we also realize that work remains work and that the cross is an inevitable element in human activity.

In Teilhard's vision, attachment and detachment are not mutually exclusive, nor are they simply set side by side. They are, rather, dialectically related like the two phases of our breathing process. In healthy human effort, the apparent opposition between a self-sacrificing and a self-fulfilling mysticism disappears. In all of our endeavors, we are free to strive wholeheartedly for self-actualization as long as the whole effort is placed at the service of God, who gives deeper meaning to all our work. Renunciation is not an end in itself but a means to purify ourselves so that we can function as flexible workers, dedicated to constructing the kingdom. Christians must labor with care and passion in order to build the earth, while always remaining open to the greater work being accomplished by God. The cross of Christ reveals that the final transformation of ourselves and our work lies beyond our time and history. This fundamental truth does not diminish the value of our efforts on this earth, but gives them their ultimate meaning by linking them to the work of the cosmic Christ, who could not be thwarted by death. For Teilhard, the cross is not a symbol of limitation and repression, but an invitation to be adventuresome, "to try everything—to completion," to labor with passion and love to build the earth and complete the Body of Christ.

Workers, Reformers, Co-Creators

MANY CHRISTIANS, CONSCIOUS of oppression and injustice in the world, judge Teilhard's grand vision overly optimistic and question the adequacy of his analysis of work. It is true that most people in the developing world cannot recognize themselves in Teilhard's optimistic descriptions. The unemployed and those who struggle for social reform will find little practical help in his writings. To sober realists, his eloquent statements about work may sound utopian and impractical.

Nevertheless, I think Teilhard has valuable advice and insights for individuals who are trying, in diverse ways, to find greater meaning in their work. He reminds those who labor hard and well without pay or much recognition that their work is indeed valuable, because it makes a unique contribution to the building up of the Body of Christ. His vision suggests direct advice for those who find their work burdensome: try to transform your toil by achieving a positive attitude toward it; learn something from it about the value of fidelity, patience, and perseverance; pray that you may find God in the midst of your tedious tasks; join your toil with the cross of Christ, who transforms the sufferings of life.

Furthermore, Teilhard's own life struggles remind Christians who are trying to reconcile their love of God and their passion for work that all of their honest labor helps create the divine milieu and thus brings them closer to God. He challenges workaholics to destroy the idols they have created by placing their work in a context of love of God and neighbor. Finally, Teilhard de Chardin invites all of us to help construct a viable spirituality of work. For this task he provides a grand vision and some vital building blocks expressed in striking imagery: Omega Point and cosmic Christ, mass on the world and a universal Host, God at the tip of the shovel and the pen, a cross which transforms suffering and unleashes energy. Most of all, this renowned man of courage and faith offers us encouragement and hope by insisting with such eloquence that all of our good efforts to humanize our labors have intrinsic significance and ultimate meaning.

Discussion Questions

1. What is your attitude toward work and how does it relate to your spiritual life?

2. How did Teilhard's war experiences and training in the sciences affect his religious vision?

3. What were Teilhard's major theological insights and how did they influence his outlook on work?

4. How could you apply Teilhard's vision in developing your own spirituality of work?

Suggested Readings

The Divine Milieu (Harper & Row, 1960). His classic work on the spiritual life.

The Phenomenon of Man (Harper & Row, 1959). His masterwork, which can be difficult reading but contains important insights now part of the contemporary mindset.

Hymn of the Universe (Harper & Row, 1969). Contains his famous "Mass Upon the World" and recounts his mystical experience.

Pierre Teilhard de Chardin: Christianity and Evolution (Harcourt Brace Jovanovich, 1969). An excellent collection of essays including "How I Believe."

CHAPTER 19

Martin Buber
recovering the personal dimension of life

WHILE MODERN LIFE has provided us in the Western world with marvelous opportunities for personal development, it has also unleashed a powerful array of depersonalizing forces which threaten to undercut our full humanity. Our industrialized economy, for example, has placed many workers into routine jobs where they feel like mere cogs in a gigantic machine. Bureaucratic organizations tend to stifle individuality and creativity. Our image-conscious culture concentrates more on creating favorable impressions than on revealing the true reality of personal life. The computer age tempts people to understand themselves as nothing more than sophisticated machines. The breakdown of family life and other forms of community makes it harder for individuals to enjoy the sense of belonging and rootedness necessary for genuine personhood.

In our continuing struggle against these and other dehumanizing forces, we find a powerful ally in the pre-eminent Jewish religious thinker of our century, Martin Buber (1878-1965).

The fundamental outlook of this great scholar was shaped by his continuing dialogue with his Jewish heritage. He was born into a middle-class Jewish family in Vienna on February 8, 1887. Through his paternal grandfather, an excellent rabbinic scholar with whom he lived from age 4 to 14, Martin was exposed to an enlightened Jewish piety which stressed the love of learning. During his student years at the Universities of Vienna, Berlin, Leipzig, and Zurich, Martin pursued a rather disjointed course of secular studies, especially philosophy and art history, while generally ignoring any serious study of his Jewish heritage. His interest in Judaism quickly returned, however, when he got involved around the turn of the century in the Zionist movement to establish a Jewish homeland. He rose quickly in the movement, becoming at the age of twenty-three, the editor of the leading journal *"Die Welt."* He was not comfortable, however, with the exclusively political orientation of Theodore Herzl, the movement's leader. Buber argued, on the contrary, for a cultural Zionism which would include the development of Jewish art, folk culture and education. He was convinced that a general renaissance of Jewish spirituality was the best preparation for return to their homeland. For Buber, the establishment of a free Jewish state was not merely a political goal but an act of obedience on the part of Jews to the God who called them to establish a nation which would exemplify genuine community and a just way of life. It was important to Buber that proper means be used in reestablishing a homeland. Thus, he criticized Herzl for his leadership style which did not retain a dialogical relationship between the leader and the others in the movement.

The Wise Teacher

WHEN HE BROKE WITH HERZL IN 1903, Buber did not try to assume leadership of the Zionist movement but chose instead the role of the "wise teacher" who would call the Jewish community to live up to its own high ideals and historical mission. While remaining in Germany, he carried out this informal teaching responsibility by establishing a Jewish publishing house and helping to set up an adult education program designed to help Jews appropriate their religious heritage. He also contributed to the revival of Jewish thought within the academic world by serving as professor for Jewish history of religion and ethics at Frankfurt University from 1923 to 1933, when he was dismissed by the Nazis. In 1938, having been completely silenced by Hitler's regime, Buber accepted the position of professor of social philosophy at the Hebrew University in Jerusalem. From this post which he held until 1951, Buber continued to function as the moral gadfly for Zionism. In one of his more striking political positions, he advocated a bi-national state composed of Jews and Arabs as equal citizens. Even after the establishment of the state of Israel in 1948, he insisted that the Jews must learn to live in peace and harmony with their Arab neighbors. Despite strong opposition from many Israelis, including political leaders such as David Ben-Gurion, Buber maintained this open and tolerant attitude right up to his death on June 13, 1965.

Buber's religious sensibilities were also shaped by his intensive study of Hasidism, the popular mystical movement of East European Jewry begun in Poland in the 18th century by Rabbi Israel Ben-Eliezar (1700-1760), popularly known as Bal Shem-Tov. Though often opposed by traditional Jews, Hasidism spread widely, encompassing at one point almost half of East European Jewry. They formed themselves into small fervent communities under the leadership of their own spiritual master called a "zaddik." The Hasidic tradition was handed on primarily by retelling the stories used by the zaddikim to instruct

"In every sphere in its own way, through each process of becoming that is present to us we look out toward the fringe of the eternal Thou; in each we are aware of a breath from the eternal Thou."

— I and Thou

their communities. Due to his own early interest in Eastern mysticism, as well as the German mystics Meister Eckhart and Jakob Boehme, Buber initially was attracted by the Hasidic emphasis on particular ecstatic moments of union with God. Later, however, he came to interpret the Hasidic stories as invitations to live a joyous community life in the world and to hallow everyday activity. By entering into genuine dialogue with the Hasidic tradition, Buber felt that he was able to uncover the real secret of this religious movement which he considered "the greatest phenomenon in the history of the Spirit" because it created a society which truly lived by faith.

Guided by his distinctive understanding of Hasidism as a joyful communal celebration of God's presence in ordinary life, Buber collected, interpreted, and eventually published many of the stories and legends attributed to the zaddikim, especially the Bel Shem-Tov (cf. *Tales of the Hasidim: The Early Masters*, Schocken Books, 1947). His reading of the Hasidic tradition was, indeed, selective and open to criticism. He concentrated on the golden period of the movement from 1750 to 1825, before it fell into excesses and rigidity. He included in his collection only those legends and stories which supported his interpretation, leaving out those which represented the more mystical aspect of Hasidism. The great historian of the Hasidic movement Gershem Scholem severely criticized Buber for this selective reading which effectively undercut the distinction between the sacred and the profane. Others criticized Buber because his study of Hasidism did not carry over into his public religious practices. He rarely attended the synagogue and generally avoided the Jewish ritual practices although he saw their value, especially for initiating young people into their religious tradition.

"But the separated It of institutions is an animated clod without soul, and the separated I of feelings an uneasily fluttering soul-bird. Neither of them knows man: institutions know only the specimen, feelings only the 'object'; neither knows the person, or mutual life."

— I and Thou

Nevertheless, Buber did uncover and preserve essential aspects of Hasidic spirituality, especially the value of wholehearted participation in a religious community. He understood that this fosters both an awareness of the abiding divine presence and commitment to the task of sanctifying everyday life and transforming the world.

A paraphrase of one of Buber's Hasidic tales gives us the flavor of this worldy spirituality. On the eve of the Day of Atonement, the faithful were gathered for prayer waiting for the rabbi. But time passed and he did not come. One woman took advantage of the delay to return home to check on her child, left alone in the house. When she entered her home, she found the rabbi holding the child in his arms. While on the way to the House of Prayer, he had heard the child crying and stopped to play with it until it fell asleep.

The Scriptures also formed and nourished Buber's religious vision. His efforts to help German Jews rediscover their religious heritage convinced him of the need for a new translation of the Hebrew Scriptures into German. He wanted a version which would reflect the concrete, dynamic, dialogic and oral character of the original text. He began his work in 1925 in collaboration with his very good friend Franz Rosenzweig, who unfortunately died in 1929. Buber persevered, finally completing his critically acclaimed translation in 1961 while living in Israel.

In addition to this translation, Buber produced many commentaries on the Scriptures which expand his central insight that the Bible is a record of Yahweh's meeting with his people in history. His commentaries were designed, not so much as an aid for reading the Bible, but to enable individuals to hear in the Scriptures the voice of the living God who calls us to partnership in establishing holiness and justice in the world.

Buber's biblical studies also brought him to a deep and sympathetic understanding of the Christian Scriptures. For him, Jesus stood clearly within the Jewish tradition, especially Isaiah's notion of the suffering servant. Buber spoke easily of his "deepening fraternal relationship with Jesus" who occupies a great place in Israel's history while transcending the usual categories.

A Grand Vision

As this brief survey suggests, we cannot properly understand Martin Buber apart from his Jewish background. Because he penetrated to the core of his own religious tradition, he became the great interpreter of Judaism to the contemporary gentile world. Out of his spiritual roots he was able to develop a grand vision of human existence which continues to serve as a radical corrective to the depersonalizing trends in our culture. His vast and diverse writings develop and apply his scripturally inspired understanding of the interpersonal dimension of life. Through his open and courageous manner of living, he calls us to the "life of dialogue," characterized by personal involvement and deep respect for everything which constitutes our world. He is a prophet who proclaims the importance of the personal realm, a poet who points to the depths of human existence, a wise teacher who guides us in the quest for authentic personal relationships. We can make the most of Buber's guidance by allowing his exemplary life and grand vision to speak to our hearts as well as our minds.

Buber attempted to describe and explain the central insight at the core of his vision in a variety of ways. Human existence is for him essentially relational. As social creatures we are necessarily related to nature, to other human beings, the cultural products of the human spirit and, most fundamentally, to God. Expressed negatively, we are not in our essential nature isolated individuals searching for relationships, nor are we societal clones striving to discover our individuality. Our personhood, on the contrary, flows precisely from our relationships.

In his classic work, *I and Thou* (Scribners, 1958), first published in 1923, Buber gave poetic expression to his personalistic vision. The primacy of relationship is clear in his repeated phrase, "In the beginning is relation," as well as in his constant theme, "All real living is meeting." Crucial to Buber's central insight is his famous distinction between I-Thou and I-It. These primary words represent two diametrically opposed attitudes or fundamental orientations toward the world of things and persons. Applying this broad distinction to the specific

---

"Only he who knows relation and knows about the presence of the Thou is capable of decision. He who decides is free, for he has approached the Face."

— I and Thou

---

world of personal relationships, we see that the I-It orientation leads to treating others in a detached and objective fashion, without personal involvement. The other person becomes an object to be experienced or used, rather than a subject to be treasured. The relationship itself is planned and calculated rather than spontaneous and free. By way of contrast, I-Thou relationships are inherently involving. They demand wholehearted personal presence and intense engagement. In these relationships we are lifted out of ourselves, while forgetting our own needs, concerns, and projects. The other person is treasured as a gift and respected as a unique subject. By recognizing the freedom and potential of other persons, we overcome the temptation to stereotype, manipulate, and control. Genuine encounters with other persons are direct, open, and intense; they engender a spontaneous sense of immediate presence. Such encounters help create a mutual relationship which enables both parties to actualize their potential. Through this interchange, individuals restricted by their distinctiveness are transformed into genuine persons liberated by the relationship. In the process, the partners come to a deeper awareness of their identity, which always exceeds objective knowledge and defies precise expression.

I-Thou relationships are not self-contained. In genuine encounters the life of the Spirit is unleashed. It is in concrete meetings with other persons that we meet our God. In Buber's phrase: "Every Thou is a glimpse through to the eternal Thou." We cannot know God directly in himself, but he is present in the apparently empty spaces between persons. "The extended lines of relations," according to Buber, "meet in the eternal Thou."

The "Between"

IN SUBSEQUENT WRITINGS, especially the essays collected in *Between Man and Man* (Macmillan, 1965) and *Knowledge of Man* (Harper & Row, 1965), Buber attempted to ground his vision in a personalist philosophy. In order to analyze the universal structures of reality, he developed the category of the "between." While philosophers traditionally concentrated either on the objective world or the individual experiencing that world, Buber insisted that the really real is the "between," that sphere which is created by the interaction among persons. This sphere, which is common to both partners in the relationship, transcends what properly belongs to each of them. The genuine meaning of personal life cannot be found within individuals, nor even within two people in relationship, but only in the "interhuman" which binds them together and makes communication possible. Any talk of the Spirit or the spiritual life must be located in the "between." In Buber's metaphor, the spirit is more like the air we share than like the blood which flows in an individual's veins.

This attempt to describe the universal structures of reality leads Buber to his distinctive understanding of human existence. As human beings, we come to existence only in relationship. Without the Thou there is no I. We have the capacity to distance ourselves from others, but we can also reach out to them in order to encounter them in genuine mutuality. Furthermore, we are unique creatures because we partake of both the finite and the infinite. Though limited by our factual situation, we have the potential to enhance our relational life. As creatures of potential, we are essentially surprising to one another and the source of newness in the world.

While Buber's philosophy is often criticized as vague and undeveloped, it does remind us of the radical character of his vision of personal existence. Even if less than compelling to philosophers, his personalistic anthropology still sharpens our awareness of the relational aspect of our lives. Moreover, by developing his philosophical view of human existence, Buber issues us a summons to a life of dialogue.

The phrase "life of dialogue" suggests an ideal mode of existence in which we participate in our world with passion and reverence. According to this ideal, we are called to respect nature by cultivating an awareness of the "divine sparks" emanating from it; to relate openly with others by respecting their uniqueness; to appropriate significant cultural forms such as religion and art by probing their inner meaning; and to encounter the eternal Thou in everyday life by refining our awareness of the divine presence. Thus, Buber offers both a vision and a program to recover the personal dimension of life in a world filled with depersonalizing forces.

Buber's vision of personal existence will come into clearer focus by examining some significant events in his own life. Before he reached his fourth birthday, Martin experienced one of the decisive events of his life. When he was only three, his mother suddenly disappeared (it was later discovered that she went to Russia and remarried), and Martin was sent to live with his paternal grandparents. Since no one had explained to him that his mother had abandoned him, he presumed that she would return soon.

One day an older girl assigned to look after Martin told him clearly and directly that his mother would never return. Reflecting on that remark years later, Buber noted that he knew immediately that the girl had indeed spoken the truth. This shattering experience of a broken primary relationship led him, according to his account, to a lifelong search for genuine relationships, which would enable him to deal with the insecurity generated by his mother's departure. Far from being paralyzed by this early trauma, Buber responded by pursuing the authentic life of dialogue with both enthusiasm and intelligence.

Analysis of Love

IN THIS QUEST, Buber developed many important relationships. He had significant encounters with famous people, including Albert Einstein, Franz Kafka, Carl Rogers, and Dag Hammarskjöld. He enjoyed an especially enriching relationship with Franz Rosenzweig, who initially collaborated with him on the Scripture translation. Rosenzweig's untimely death forced Buber not only to complete the translation by himself, but to deal again with the insecurity caused by the fragility of human relationships.

In a precarious world, Martin drew much of his security and strength from his wife Paula, an intelligent and talented woman whom he first met in 1899. Although she was a Catholic, she formally converted to Judaism before their marriage and was an active participant in Jewish causes. By his own admission, she supplied the missing maternal element which enabled him to become more self-confident and courageous.   There is no doubt, however, that Paula and Martin shared a deep and mutually enriching love throughout their extremely long life together.

Buber's marital relationship exemplifies elements of his theoretical analysis of love.   Reacting against the prevailing sentimental notions, he insisted that love is not merely the enjoyment of a moment of ecstasy, but "the responsibility

---

"Meeting with God does not come to man in order that he may concern himself with God, but in order that he may confirm that there is meaning in the world."

— I and Thou

---

of an I for a Thou."   Positive feelings naturally accompany love, but they should not be mistaken for the reality.   Love must endure the test of time, which always diminishes romantic feelings. Genuine lovers share a life together, but without smothering each other's individuality.   They do not cling to one another, but walk the path of life side by side.   Love at its best is able to discern the true potential lurking in the heart of the beloved and to encourage its full development with a patient and steadfast care.   Physical intimacy offers the opportunity to enhance and express the best qualities of the marital relationship.   Buber, for example, advises couples in their love-making to imagine the experience from their partner's viewpoint, thus transforming pleasure into love.   In this way, sexual expression becomes a model for the kind of mutuality which should exist in all relationships.

Some critics claim that Buber, the great proponent of authenticity and openness in relationships, was actually quite reserved and closed with all but a handful of intimates.   On the other hand, glowing reports of enriching encounters with him abound. For example, Eugenia Friedman, former wife of Buber's biographer Maurice Friedman, recorded her enthusiastic reactions to a simple encounter with Buber in her home. She described him as "greater than his books because he lives out what he has written." This short, stocky man with his imposing white beard and disarming smile impressed her as a real human being who had suffered much and could still encounter others with openness and understanding.   In the meeting she experienced "a great comforting warmth," and was convinced that she could tell him anything and he would not be shocked or become judgmental. Her account included the telling statement that Buber enabled her to understand for the first time "what it means to be a human being."

From this striking testimony we gain some appreciation of Buber's remarkable interpersonal gifts. The example also leads us to explore some of his advice for establishing such deep relationships. In a culture which puts a premium on image and appearance, Buber reminds us to deal with each other in an "upright way"—not worrying about what impressions we are making but presenting ourselves as we truly are. This is difficult, because our great need for acceptance can easily move us to make unreasonable efforts to impress others, even resorting to deceit. To yield to this temptation, according to Buber, is our "essential cowardice," while to resist it is our "essential courage."

In order to overcome superficiality in our relationships, Buber advises us to avoid an analytical approach to other persons which reduces them to psychological categories or predictable patterns of behavior. We should, rather, be aware of others as whole persons in all their concrete uniqueness. Human beings live out of the power of the Spirit which integrates their personality, enabling them to enter into relationships which are essentially mysterious and beyond logical analysis. We need to cultivate our intuition and imagination, which enables us to accomplish "a bold swinging" into the lives of others so that we can be in touch with their unique spirit. This is possible only if we live in true partnership with the other, opening ourselves to the risk of relationship. Such risk is made possible by "an existential trust," which is ultimately founded on a God who is not only "Wholly Other" but also "Wholly Present" in the concrete encounters of life.

Martin Buber's contacts with other persons did not always produce such positive responses, as one of his more striking autobiographical references illustrates. One afternoon after Buber had experienced a morning of "religious enthusiasm" (we might surmise a type of mystical experience, although he often denied he was a mystic), he was visited by a young man whom he had never met before. He received him in friendly enough fashion but "without being there in spirit." He conversed openly and attentively with him but "omitted to guess the questions which he did not put." Soon after, the young man was dead. Buber later learned from one of the young man's friends that he had come not for a casual chat but for a decision.

The terse way Buber recounts the story led some to conclude that the young man committed suicide. Actually, he died at the front in the First World War.

According to Buber's later interpretation, however, the young soldier suffered from the kind of despair that no longer opposes one's own death. Buber's own commentary on the story suggests that he himself was so caught up in his religious ecstasy that he had failed to discern the deeper questions troubling the young man. Buber's radical response to the whole event was to reject the mystical approaches to God which had been so important to him in his early life. He decided to concentrate instead on everyday existence and on the "fullness of claim and responsibility" found in each hour of our lives.

Evil Urges

BUBER ALSO RECOGNIZED the importance of exploring the darker side of human relationships. He indicated the depth of the problem with his penetrating observation that every Thou must become an It, a sad fact which he described as "the exalted melancholy of our fate." We simply cannot sustain the personal intensity and immediate presence demanded by I-Thou relationships. Our most treasured loved ones at times become a part of the world of things, where planning and usefulness predominate. We should not forget that the world of It is good in itself and serves a necessary role in human life. We recognize the importance, for instance, of the scientist who pursues his research with detachment. However, as the impersonal world has grown ever more swollen and dominant in modern society, we find it more and more difficult to establish and sustain genuine personal relationships. In Buber's distinctive terminology, when It predominates, the Eternal Thou is eclipsed, making it hard to say Thou.

Buber had a deep appreciation of the "evil urges" which inhabit the human heart such as deep rage and secret jealousy. He understood both their destructive power and their potential as energy sources for good. His theory was that we dare not repress these urges but must instead transform them, releasing their powers to enhance our relational life. In mysterious ways, the evil urges are encompassed in the divine plan. We must find creative ways to bring them into the process of creating genuine communities and hallowing our ordinary relationships.

We must also take into account the sin and guilt which inevitably enter into human relationships. In opposition to those who insist that all guilt feelings are neurotic, Buber spoke about a genuine existential guilt which arises from real harm done to relationships and thus to the proper order of the world. Our conscience, which should not be identified with the Freudian superego based on social taboos, gives us the capacity to discern which of our actions harm or enhance our personal relationships. From the theological perspective, the Eternal Thou addresses us in our personal uniqueness with concrete demands which cannot be determined by general societal or religious norms. When we ignore the divine imperative and do harm to other persons, we must admit our fault, accept responsibility, and try to repair the damage.

Crucial to this process for Buber is the "act of illumination," by which we cast a gentle glance into the depths of our hearts, probing the essence and meaning of our faults. If this examination leads to a "mute shudder" of self-recognition or a deeper awareness of ourselves as the bearers of responsibility for our previous sins, then we are prepared to seek God's forgiveness in an authentic way. Having turned to God we can then turn to the difficult task of helping the injured person overcome the lingering consequences of our sinful action. Buber's unequivocal insistence that we courageously confront the possibility of sin and guilt in relationships is a clear challenge to a culture which either ignores sin or reduces it to neurosis.

Throughout his life, Buber engaged in many private dialogues with other scholars and authors. In 1957 at the University of Michigan, he participated in a productive public dialogue with Carl Rogers, the well-known psychotherapist. Responding to Rogers' general notion that therapists should accept their clients just as they are at a given moment, Buber developed his own notion of "confirming the other"—a notion which has general application to all human relationships. In confirming others, we begin by accepting them as real persons with their own unique individuality. Genuine care, however, should take us beyond mere acceptance to a deeper perception of the other person's true potential. Love, far from being blind, reveals something of what the other person can become. While recognizing the factual limits surrounding the potential of other persons, we should strive to help them to develop their unique gifts. This may entail challenging their misperceptions and destructive behavior patterns. We may have to assist them in the "struggle against themselves" so that they can overcome the obstacles to entering into mutually enriching relationships. Human beings are the only creatures with potential. Confirming others means that we help them to develop this potential in order that they may live more fully human lives.

In the course of this public dialogue, the two participants came to a deeper perception of the truth. Buber's comments permitted Rogers to refine his own position, bringing the two of them closer to agreement. Buber, who previously was skeptical about the possibility of public dialogue, became convinced that it was possible and potentially useful.

Buber often returned to the theme of dialogue in his writings. For him, dialogue is rooted in the "between" established by interpersonal relationships. Because the Eternal Thou first addresses us, we are able to communicate with one another. Thus dialogue does not happen in us or to us, but between us. It is made possible by the mutuality of I-Thou relationships. Through a dialogic relationship we enable others to see something new about the world, to broaden their horizons, and to appreciate the potential in their particular situation.

World of Language

DIALOGUE CAN BE WORDLESS, but by its very nature it seeks expression. We want to be heard not by ourselves but by others. A totally self-contained inner dialogue does not have the same power to reveal the truth as does conversation with another person. We benefit from the objectivity provided by speech as well as the surprising insights provided by a dialogue partner.

For genuine dialogue, we need a common world of language within which we can gradually define our own personal understanding of particular words. A living language necessarily involves ambiguities and tensions between various interpretations. This suggests that we should enter dialogue with another recognizing that we do not have exactly the same understanding of particular words. This is especially important to remember when we are using the significant traditional words preserved in our cultural and religious heritages. From this perspective, dialogue has the precise function of helping us to understand and reconcile our different meanings and interpretations while realizing that ambiguities will always exist.

In dialogue we must speak truthfully, in the Hebrew sense of faithfulness. Thus, our speech must demonstrate fidelity to reality, to the uniqueness of our partner, and to our own situation. Candor is not the great virtue in dialogue. Fidelity demands that we be prudent in what we reveal. While deliberate deceit impedes dialogue, respect for the other may demand withholding certain information. We must say what we mean and contribute what is required, but always with prudence.

Genuine dialogue also demands that we turn to the other with an open spirit. Some people find within themselves a certain reserve which prevents them from revealing their true selves and taking the risk of reaching out to another person. Buber insisted that existential trust is essential to overcome this reserve and enter into interpersonal relationships. Such trust is based on the faith conviction that God is the source and center point of our whole relational life.

While aspects of Buber's philosophy have been severely criticized by scholars, his personal vision of human existence maintains its power to challenge the depersonalizing trends in our society. His writings are a rich resource for understanding and improving our personal relationships. Reflecting the spiritual dynamism of his religious heritage, Martin Buber remains the prophet who summons us to a life of dialogue in which every genuine encounter with a Thou does indeed give us a glimpse of the Eternal Thou.

Discussion Questions

1. What depersonalizing forces do you encounter and how do you deal with them?

2. How did Buber's family life and his Jewish heritage help shape his religious vision of life?

3. What did Buber mean by his insistence that all authentic human existence is relational and how did he ground and apply this key insight?

4. How could Buber's ideas help in the effort to restore the personal dimension to contemporary life?

Suggested Readings

I and Thou (Scribner, 1958). His classic work which gives poetic expression to his personalistic vision.

Between Man and Man (Macmillan, 1965). A collection of essays which develop personalistic philosophy as a basis for his religious vision.

The Knowledge of Man (Harper & Row, 1965). Another collection of essays which explain his personalist outlook.

Martin Buber's Life and Work by Maurice Friedman, three vol. (Dutton, 1982-1984). A comprehensive biography by a friend and scholar who gives a feel for the man and relates Buber's thought to his personal life.

CHAPTER 20

Mohandas Gandhi

learning from the east

WE ARE JUSTLY PROUD of the great accomplishments of our Western culture. Its powerful mixture of fundamental meanings and institutional forms provides us with a rich material and spiritual heritage which shapes our worldview as well as our style of social life. The pervasive power of our culture can, however, delude us into assuming that our sense of reality is the only legitimate or valuable way of understanding the world. It can also blind us to the distortions and contradictions which keep our culture from attaining its highest ideals.

One way out of this cultural cocoon is to enter into serious dialogue with a great Eastern culture representing a radically different worldview. Such interaction can broaden our horizons and bring to light the shortcomings of our Western heritage.

The great Indian "holy man" Mohandas K. Gandhi (1868-1948) is an excellent partner for such a dialogue. Although a Hindu by birth and conviction, he was open to the truth and goodness available in other religious traditions. His sense of reality was shaped primarily by Indian culture, but he understood important aspects of the Western world. He functioned as a spokesman for the Indian people, but he was also a "servant of mankind" with a universal message.

Gandhi does not fit easily into our tidy Western categories. He was not a trained theologian, although he did have a remarkable ability to penetrate to the core of religious traditions and did write insightful

contemporary commentaries on the Hindu Scriptures. He was not a professional philosopher, although he wrote cogent analyses of important issues, including the power of love to overcome violence. He was not an elected politician,

"The little fleeting glimpses, therefore, that I have been able to have of Truth can hardly convey an idea of the indescribable lustre of Truth, a million times more intense than that of the sun we see daily with our eyes."

— My Experiments with Truth

but he demonstrated remarkable political acumen in gaining independence for his country. He always denied he was a saint, but he was revered by the multitudes as the "Mahatma," the great souled one who had come close to God through his amazing discipline and genuine compassion.

Perhaps we can best understand Gandhi as a "passionate searcher after truth," the self-interpretation he presented to the public in his revealing book, *An Autobiography: The Story of My Experiments With Truth* (Beacon Press, 1957). Although he searched for truth in a cultural context quite different from our own, we can still identify with the dynamics of his quest. The story of his long and productive life serves as a provocative challenge to many of our cultural assumptions. His distinctive understanding of truth, as well as the precise methods he used in its pursuit, function as a powerful corrective to our Western drive for self-fulfillment and economic success through competitive means.

If we are to absorb the challenge of Gandhi's life and teaching, we must relax our usual thought patterns and enter his world. Indian scholars remind us to approach him as an integrated person with a unified worldview. In passing over to Gandhi's world, we should leave behind the typical Western distinctions between religion and politics, the sacred and the secular, theory and practice, church and state. While we will try to see Gandhi whole in our search for his corrective message, our encounter with him will inevitably reflect our Western style of pursuing truth through analysis and practical application.

Mohandas was born October 2, 1869, in Porbandar, a seacoast town north of Bombay, India. His father was a government official and his mother a deeply religious Hindu who attended temple services daily. As a boy, he was small, quiet, and only an average student. At the age of thirteen, he entered into a traditional arranged marriage with a girl his age named Kasturbai who bore him four sons and remained his devoted wife for sixty-two years until her death in 1944.

After about three years of marriage, Mohandas was called upon to spend a good deal of his time nursing his terminally ill father—a service he rendered with great care and devotion. When his father actually died, however, Mohandas was not at his side but was with his wife in the "grip of lust," as he himself later described it while still laboring under the heavy burden of guilt.

In his penetrating study *Gandhi's Truth* (Norton, 1969), the psychoanalyst, Erik Erikson, suggests that the terrible guilt Mohandas felt over this perceived failure supplied him with motivation for the lifelong care and service he rendered so generously to his country. Whether we accept Erikson's analysis or not, we do find in Gandhi's life truly inspiring examples of compassionate care generously given to the suffering and needy.

In 1888, Gandhi went to England to study law, completing his studies in 1891 when he was admitted to the bar. After a couple of disappointing years attempting to practice law in India, he accepted an offer to represent an Indian business firm in Pretoria, South Africa. While traveling first-class on a train in Natal, Gandhi was thrown off by a constable for refusing to move to the van compartment where Indians, derisively called "coolies," were required by law to ride. As he sat in a bitterly cold waiting room until another train arrived, he made one of the key decisions of his life. With a profound sense of dedication fueled by his own experience, he decided to devote himself to rooting out the disease of social prejudice. Erikson interprets this decisive event as Gandhi's positive resolution of his identity crisis, through which he changed from a shy individual drifting into an ordinary law career to a determined man committed to a life of public service on behalf of his people.

"Satyagraha"

SHORTLY AFTER THIS TRAIN INCIDENT, Gandhi launched his campaign to improve the legal status of Indians in South Africa who suffered from the same discriminatory laws as black people. His efforts included a stringent regimen of self-discipline, designed to purify and strengthen himself for the task of public leadership. He bought a farm in Natal and dedicated himself to a simple lifestyle. He took on the heavy duty of editing and printing the weekly magazine *Indian Opinion*, which enabled him to disseminate his views on current issues. He fasted regularly, allowing himself at most two meager meals of nuts and fruits a day.

"If I found myself entirely absorbed in the service of the community, the reason behind it was my desire for self-realization. I had made the religion of service my own as I felt that God could be realized only through service."

— My Experiments with Truth

In 1906, he made a vow, without consulting his wife, to live a celibate life on the assumption that this would enable him to channel more energy into his life of service. In addition to renouncing the pleasures of wealth, food, and sex, Gandhi also renounced the use of violence. In its place, he developed a positive method of actively fighting injustice which he called "Satyagraha," or truth-force, designed to strengthen the oppressed and change the heart and the policies of the oppressors.

During his time in South Africa, Gandhi's thought developed in dialogue with three important Western thinkers: John Ruskin, whose book *Unto This Last* reinforced Gandhi's desire to care for the spiritual welfare of all, including the least fortunate; Henry David Thoreau, whose notion of civil disobedience became an important tactic in the satyagraha program; and Leo Tolstoy, whose interpretation of the Sermon on the Mount spawned a stimulating correspondence between the two apostles of nonviolence.

In 1907, Gandhi mounted his satyagraha campaign in order to overturn discriminatory laws. He used public protests such as marches to highlight the grievances of the people. His tactics also included illegal strikes and other acts of civil disobedience. In order to train protest leaders and house those displaced by the campaign, Gandhi acquired land about 20 miles outside Johannesburg and founded a cooperative community known as Tolstoy Farm.

After many years of struggle, the nonviolent campaign did succeed in getting the Indian Relief Bill passed in 1914 which, among other things, declared minority marriages valid and abolished the tax on former indentured Indian laborers. In the process of gaining this limited victory, Gandhi also won over General Smuts, the South African leader who opposed him throughout the campaign. The general came to appreciate Gandhi's vision and tactics, praising him for redeeming the nation from "ruthless and brutal forces."

Satisfied that the satyagraha campaign had proven successful by vindicating, at least in principle, racial equality, Gandhi returned to India to continue his work of public service. He now faced the far more challenging task of gaining self-rule for his country and a healthy sense of freedom for his people, especially the most despised social group known as the "untouchables."

His nonviolent tactics, gradually refined under the pressure of events, were designed to induce the British to leave India voluntarily because they could see it was in everyone's best interest, including their own. As a base of operations, Gandhi established "Satyagraha Ashram," near the city of Ahmedabad. This community eventually numbered 230 people, including some untouchables. Though located in a tranquil setting, it was not an escape from the real world, but a training ground for activists in the independence movement. Gandhi also began publishing a new weekly magazine, *Young India*, which helped him spread his message of nonviolence.

In protest against the repressive Rowlatt Acts passed in 1919, Gandhi inaugurated a nationwide work stoppage which proved to be enormously successful in bringing the nation to a halt, but unfortunately, also led to violence. Admitting that the whole campaign was a "Himalayan miscalculation," Gandhi called it off, advising people to undertake a fast instead. The worst violence occurred in Amritsar, a city sacred to the Sikhs, where troops under the command of General Reginald Dyer slaughtered an estimated 379 people and wounded three times that many.

Battling Britain

GANDHI RESPONDED TO THE VIOLENCE by calling for a policy of non-cooperation with the British, combined with a positive effort to achieve Indian self-sufficiency. At the urging of Gandhi, the people began to spin cloth for their own clothing and to rid themselves of clothes made in England. Through this massive effort, the spinning wheel became an important symbol, not only of self-reliance, but of the efficacy of hard work and a simple lifestyle.

In the struggle for freedom, fasting remained an important tactic for Gandhi, but with a crucial modification. In 1918, Gandhi began to support a group of mill workers in Ahmedabad who were striking for decent wages. Sensing that the workers' spirits were flagging after weeks of fruitless negotiations, Gandhi spontaneously announced that he would not take any food until they received a 35 percent increase in pay. This "fast to death" lasted only three days, ending when the mill owners agreed to arbitration which led to a fair settlement. Erikson, who made this event the focal point of his study of Gandhi,

"Inhibitions imposed from without rarely succeed, but when they are self-imposed, they have a decidedly salutary effect."
— My Experiments with Truth

points out that the Mahatma feared that this tactic violated the spirit of satyagraha by unfairly forcing the owners to capitulate. Despite these misgivings, Gandhi employed this "fast until death" tactic on 16 other occasions in the struggle for justice and peace. In 1924, he fasted for 21 days in order to bring the feuding Hindu and Muslim communities closer together—a unity which he considered to be an essential precondition for achieving national independence.

Gandhi also used protest marches as a means of calling attention to unjust laws and strengthening the resolve of his people. The most striking example of this tactic was the 1930 "Salt March," undertaken to protest the British tax on salt which placed an especially heavy burden on the poor. After marching 241 miles in 24 days, Gandhi and thousands of others reached the sea. Following a night of prayer, the Mahatma, in a powerful symbolic gesture, picked up some salt left by the waves, thus breaking the British law which made it a punishable crime to possess salt not purchased from the government monopoly. Inspired by Gandhi, people all over India began to make their own salt, thereby breaking the law and subjecting themselves to imprisonment and, at times, beatings. Despite this treatment, the protesters all over India heeded Gandhi's advice and remained remarkably nonviolent. The great Indian poet and close friend of Gandhi, Rabindranath Tagore, viewed this whole event as the turning point in the struggle for independence, calling it "a great moral defeat" for the Western world.

The struggle, however, continued for 17 more years. Throughout, Gandhi worked tirelessly to reach a political settlement with the British and to prepare his people for a life of self-reliant freedom by instructing them in basic skills. These years also brought heavy crosses to the Mahatma. His oldest son Harilal rejected him and became a derelict. His wife Kasturbai died in 1944. Bloody strife continued in India between the Muslims and the Hindus. Gandhi himself spent a total of almost six years in jail for his various acts of civil disobedience. When national independence finally came on August 15, 1945, Gandhi refused to participate in the celebration because the nation had not heeded his pleas for unity between Muslims and Hindus. Refusing to lose faith, the Mahatma continued to fast and pray for unity and peace. On January 30, 1948, just before the evening service in his ashram, he was shot and killed by a Hindu extremist, Nathuram Godse.

Searching for Truth

GANDHI OFTEN SAID that those who desire to understand his message should examine his actions and not his words. Surely the life of this great man has an amazing power to broaden our horizons, raise our consciousness, and challenge our assumptions.

Nevertheless, his writings can also help us in our effort to grasp and assimilate the deeper meaning of his life. In his autobiography, written when he was in his late fifties and appropriately subtitled *The Story of My Experiments With Truth*, he offers us various formulations which express what his life was all about. He reports, for example, that his encompassing passion is to achieve "self-realization, to see God face to face," to attain salvation. He possesses an "innate passion for truth," which is the "very breath" of his life and the "sole objective" of his quest. "Return good for evil" is his "guiding principle," and nonviolence is his "rule" and the breath of his life. For him, "renunciation became the highest form of religion." "Service of the poor" is his "heart's desire" and the essential condition for "realizing God."

From Gandhi's holistic perspective, these personal statements are not inherently contradictory as a Western analyst might suppose. They represent, rather, various legitimate ways of describing his core passion in life. Depending on the context and circumstances, he placed different but interrelated notions at the center of his self-interpretation—God, truth, self-realization, salvation, nonviolence, renunciation, and service.

Let us examine how these notions fit together by following a path suggested by Gandhi. In the search for truth, we gradually penetrate the illusions which distort our consciousness and thereby move toward a greater self-realization in which we come to know our true self. The truth which attracts us, however, is not merely subjective and partial, but has an objective and absolute character.

Service which is rendered without joy helps neither the servant nor the served. But all other pleasures and possessions pale into nothingness before service which is rendered in a spirit of joy."

— My Experiments with Truth

Believers recognize that this truth is really the God who addresses us through events and calls us to a life of service. We can break through illusions and attain salvation only by responding to the Truth which is God.

Since the search for the truth demands concentration and commitment, we must be people of discipline, able to renounce pleasures for higher goals. Furthermore, we can realize truth only through nonviolence which allows us to identify with all human beings, especially those most deprived. We cannot make this identification, however, unless we are able to reduce our own egos and purify ourselves of enslaving passions. To control ourselves in this way, we must cultivate a life of consistent self-discipline. If we can break through illusions and recognize our fundamental unity with others, then we will have a solid basis for a life of public service, which is the essential condition for attaining salvation and seeing God face to face.

Thus, we see that to follow Gandhi's path draws us into a comprehensive and integrated search for truth which avoids the fragmentation often associated with Western spirituality. According to Gandhi, life is whole and unified so that every action has "spiritual, social and economic implications."

With the holistic character of Gandhi's life and thought clearly in mind, we can examine two specific ways in which he challenges questionable aspects of our Western outlook.

First, the emphasis that Gandhi places on self-realization serves as a powerful corrective to our dominant cultural ideal of self-fulfillment. As Westerners, we tend to think of ourselves as incomplete beings searching for wholeness. Many find themselves driven by a sense of emptiness to seek satisfaction in finite material goods, such as pleasure, power, wealth and prestige. Often this search is conducted without concern for the common good and without explicit reference to God.

By way of contrast, Gandhi, representing a typically Eastern approach, believed that the essential human problem is not incompleteness or emptiness, but rather illusion which leads to bondage. Our fundamental illusion is that we are isolated and autonomous individuals who can find happiness by building up our own egos and acquiring more material possessions. For Gandhi, therefore, the essential solution to the human predicament is not self-fulfillment but self-realization, not acquiring more but seeing the truth about ourselves more clearly. Thus, we need an abiding passion to reduce our inflated ego or empirical self to zero so that we can experience our true self and break out of the prison of selfishness. In this process, we must "grope in the dark" for a truth that can be glimpsed only partially. In seeking the true self, we are seeking God, for "Truth is God," as Gandhi came to formulate his deepest conviction. When we achieve greater self-realization, we bring our divine side to consciousness and come to a deeper appreciation of our "godly character." God is the "Certainty hidden in our uncertainty," the Helper who comes to us when we feel helpless, the Omnipotent One who dwells within us. The God within enables us to control our minds and our passions so that we can maintain the struggle for self-realization. True religion guides and inspires the quest for the true self.

Rooted in Action

FOR GANDHI, THE PROCESS of "turning the searchlight inward" must always be rooted in action and directed toward a life of service. Self-realization should not be sought merely through withdrawal from the world and long hours in contemplation. Certainly regular prayer is important, especially in enabling us to be more responsive to the "inner voice" which offers guidance. We do need to develop inner attitudes such as humility which keeps us open to correction, and fortitude which enables us to withstand social pressures. Gandhi insisted, however, that action was also essential to achieving self-realization. We break through illusions by performing our duties and sticking to our tasks. God speaks to us in the events of life, calling us to become our true selves. Work, especially manual labor, keeps us in touch with reality and provides good therapy for the soul. Compassionate care extended to others reminds us of the unity of the human family and enables us to come "face to face with God and Truth."

As his close friend C.F. Andrews noted, Gandhi was "a saint of action rather than of contemplation." His devotion to truth drove him into politics and a life of public service dedicated to building a new society. Gandhi was interested not only in transforming consciousness, but also in transforming the fundamental relationships among human beings. He was convinced that those who divorce religion from a life of service do not really understand the true nature of religion or its essential connection with self-realization. We can only find ourselves and our God by serving humanity.

Thus, it is clear that Gandhi's broad and organic understanding of self-realization presents a radical challenge to Western notions of self-fulfillment which exalt the individual ego while effectively excluding God and ignoring the common good.

Second, Gandhi's disciplined life, together with his insightful understanding of renunciation, calls into question our Western success ethic based on rugged competition. Our culture tends to prize success more than effort and competition more than cooperation. This has helped to produce an affluent society which trumpets the dream that everyone can and should move up the socio-economic ladder. At its worst, the success ethic suggests that the goal of economic advancement justifies questionable means, that affluence automatically brings happiness, and that competition which rewards the strong and wounds the weak is fundamentally healthy.

The social ethic lived and taught by Gandhi challenges these assumptions and priorities by insisting that effort is more important than success, simplicity more attractive than affluence, and loving cooperation more effective than rugged competition. Gandhi's innovative reinterpretation of a key portion of the Hindu Scriptures known as the *Bhagavad-Gita* provides the key to a healthy social activism. The *Gita*, which he called his "holy mother" and "an infallible guide of conduct," portrays the dilemma of the princely warrior Arjuna as he ponders whether he should enter into battle against an opposing army which includes his kin. Krishna, the most perfect Hindu avatar, incarnated in this story as Arjuna's charioteer, advises him to fight, but to do so without regard to the outcome.

Rather than reading the *Gita* literally or using it as a justification for war, Gandhi interpreted it as offering the "matchless remedy" for the ills of the human condition. Thus, he insists that the essential key to achieving self-realization and to performing effective public service is to "renounce the fruits of action." This means, on the one hand, adopting an attitude of complete detachment from the success or failure of our projects and programs. We must practice "desireless action," refusing to hanker after success or brood over failure.

Renouncing the fruits of action will keep us from being puffed up by praise and deflated by criticism. It prompts us to act serenely without impatience and to avoid using unethical means to achieve our goals. In short, we are called to dedicate our actions to God, entrusting the results to his loving care.

On the other hand, Gandhi insists that we give great attention to making an appropriate effort in all situations. Hence, we should be "wholly engrossed in the due fulfillment" of our tasks. We need to plan intelligently and execute efficiently. Knowledge of circumstances and attention to expected results are crucial. Renunciation of the fruits of action does not mean passivity, indifference or halfhearted work. It does mean that we concentrate on making a good effort, while restraining our desire to control the outcome.

Gandhi's fundamental insight into renunciation is organically connected with his whole teaching on discipline. Regular fasting, sexual abstinence, voluntary poverty, simple living, and daily exercise all play a role in attaining the true self and creating energy for a life of service. For him, voluntary self-restraint is not masochistic or debilitating, but rather, wholesome and even essential to a full human life.

Renouncing Violence

GANDHI GAVE SPECIAL PROMINENCE to the renunciation of violence which he considered to be the chief malady of our century, especially as manifested in unjust economic systems and Western imperialism. As an antidote, he advocated the traditional Hindu precept of "Ahimsa," which means nonviolence, and inaugurated his campaign of satyagraha or truth-force which employed nonviolent direct action to achieve social justice and national independence. According to Gandhi, nonviolence does not mean passivity or even passive resistance, but rather suggests a whole way of life in which we act in harmony with the "ground plan" of the universe. Persons who have adopted a nonviolent attitude respect all forms of life and treat others with civility, gentleness and compassion. While they pit their whole soul against their oppressors, they do not try to destroy, defeat or humiliate them, but rather seek reconciliation and the good of all concerned.

Influenced by Tolstoy's interpretation of the Sermon on the Mount, Gandi taught that nonviolence calls us to the kind of "universal love" manifested by Jesus whom he called the "prince of satyagrahis." Such mature love demands arduous self-sacrifice and a willingness to suffer for truth. Nonviolence releases love-force by renouncing brute-force. Gandhi taught that love is "the subtlest force in the world," with an amazing power to elicit love in return, break down barriers and achieve reconciliation. Nonviolent love is based on the conviction that we are all children of the same Creator, possessing within us the divine powers which demand respect. Hence, we are called to love our oppressors and opponents while hating their destructive deeds.

Contrary to popular opinion, Gandhi was not an absolute pacifist. He often repeated that "when there is only a choice between cowardice and violence, I would advise violence." This may be one of the reasons he supported various British wars including the Boer War and World War I. However, this should not obscure his clear preference for nonviolence, manifested in his successful satyagraha campaigns, his consistent teaching to live by love and not force and especially, his willingness to forgive his enemies. His witness for nonviolence challenges not only our success ethic, but also the destructive forms of competition which fuel it.

It is difficult for Westerners to engage in an effective intellectual critique of Gandhi because some of his fundamental presuppositions, rooted in an Eastern worldview, appear foreign to us. We all can try, however, to enter his world, allowing his life and teaching to modify and correct our patterns of thought and action. Given a hearing, Mohandas Gandhi can broaden our horizons and inspire our quest for truth by his consistent and courageous effort to achieve self-realization through renunciation and nonviolent love.

Discussion Questions

1. Have you had contact in any way with other cultures and has this challenged the presuppositions of your own culture?

2. What aspects of Gandhi's life story seem most important in the development of his thought?

3. What did Gandhi mean by the pursuit of truth and how did this influence his life and thought?

4. How could Gandhi's example of seeking truth and self-realization through renunciation and nonviolent love help you to be more faithful to your own ideals?

Suggested Readings

An Autobiography: The Story of My Experiments with Truth (Beacon Press, 1957). A readable, fascinating study of a great man's quest for truth and self-realization.

The Gandhi Reader, edited by Homer A. Jock (Grove Press, 1961). Considered by some to be the best available selection of his writings.

Gandhi: Selected Writings, edited by Ronald Duncan (Harper & Row, 1971). Another collection of his writings including many of his religious ideas and his reinterpretation of the *Gita*.

Gandhi's Truth, by Erik Erikson (Norton, 1969). A penetrating study of Gandhi from the viewpoint of a Western psychoanalyst.

postscript

AFTER EXAMINING THESE INDIVIDUAL AUTHORS, it seems natural and useful to search for patterns, trends, connections, differences and similarities among these very diverse shapers of 20th-century religious thought. Various categorizations, typologies and models are available. Drawing on Bernard Lonergan's work, we can distinguish a classical methodology which begins with biblical or church teaching and applies it to real-life situations, from a contemporary approach which begins with human experience and draws on the Christian tradition to illuminate its true depths and essential meaning. From this viewpoint, Barth and Balthasar appear as representative classicists Whitehead and Macquarrie as contemporary thinkers.

Karl Rahner's distinction between cosmocentric and anthropocentric approaches enables us to perceive essential differences between Maritain's neo-Thomism, which examines the world or cosmos for necessary and universal principles, and Lonergan's transcendental Thomism, which probes the process of human knowing in search of invariable patterns and necessary conditions. Johann Metz accepts Rahner's distinction between the neo-Thomists and the transcendental Thomists but adds a third category which he calls "post-idealist." The political theologians who fit in this category take seriously the social character of human existence, emphasizing the power of ecclesial, political and economic systems to influence our consciousness and behavior. According to this typology, Gutierrez, Ruether, King, and Metz himself are classed as political theologians and distinguished from Rahner and Lonergan, the transcendental Thomists, who analyze the dynamics of human knowing and loving without giving much attention to the social context.

While stressing the public character of all theology, David Tracy has distinguished three audiences addressed by theologians: society as a whole, the academy, and the church. Although theologians address all three publics, at least implicitly, they can be classified according to their dominant audience. Thus Niebuhr, Murray, and to some extent, Tillich, have spoken to the general public; Lonergan and Whitehead have made an impact on the academic world through their methodologies and interdisciplinary work; and Küng, Balthasar, Schillebeeckx, Macquarrie, and Rahner have directed their message primarily to those with ties to the church.

We can also classify religious thinkers according to the specific group they address either explicitly or implicitly. For instance, Teilhard and Whitehead have a special message for scientists; Barth and Küng speak to troubled church members; Rahner and Tillich address the concerns of non-believers; Murray and Niebuhr have a message for those concerned with public affairs; Maritain and Balthasar appeal to traditional Catholics; Buber and Macquarrie touch the lives of those struggling with relationships; King and Ruether speak to the dispossessed in our own country; and Gandhi and Gutierrez respond to those treated as non-persons in the Third World.

As we sort through these standard ways of categorizing theologians, we should remember that among our twenty religious thinkers only a few have been so influential that they generated a movement or school of thought. The clearest example is Karl Barth who spawned the neo-orthodox movement which dominated the Protestant world and continues to be a powerful force. Barth becomes an even more impressive figure when we recall the indirect influence he has had on the Catholic community, especially through Küng and Balthasar. The philosopher Whitehead also belongs on the list of the most prominent because he provided the thrust and direction for the distinctive movement known as process theology. Lonergan has inspired many influential thinkers ranging from David Tracy to Michael Novak and supplied the impetus for important conferences gathered around his ideas. The influence of Rahner is more diffused but also more pervasive. He has not produced a school of disciples or a clearly defined movement. However, through his many interpreters and popularizers, he continues to be the dominant force shaping the postconciliar renewal in the Catholic Church.

In his book *The Nature of Doctrine*, Yale theologian George Lindebeck has proposed a new model to guide religion and theology in the post-liberal world. He believes we must move beyond the dominant liberal or "experiential-expressive" approach (most clearly represented by Rahner among our authors) which speaks of Christianity as articulating the deeper levels of human experience. Lindebeck's positive appeal is for a post-liberal theology which recognizes that Christianity is a "cultural-linguistic" phenomenon which shapes our consciousness and creates a distinctive religious world. Among our religious thinkers, Balthasar is the clearest representative of this "cultural-linguistic" model.

Pastoral Ministry

THE TWENTIETH-CENTURY religious thinkers can also be analyzed according to their impact on pastoral ministry and the spiritual lives of believers. Most of these authors have tried to be responsive to the needs of the Christian community. Karl Barth, for instance, initially rejected liberal theology and began developing his neo-orthodox approach in order to preach more effectively to his working-class congregation in Safenwil, Switzerland. In both theory and practice, Karl Rahner always worked on the principle that the more scientific theology is, the more pastorally effective it will be. Bernard Lonergan explicitly invited his readers to use his method to deepen their self-awareness as part of an integrated conversion process.

My own interest in these authors grew out of the demands of my pastoral ministry. Perhaps recounting parts of that story will not only strike some responsive chords but also set the stage for further generalizations.

When I began serving as a priest over 25 years ago, it was immediately apparent that the manualist approach to theology which predominated in the seminary was not very helpful in preaching, teaching, and counseling. The theology of Aquinas which I was privileged to encounter directly in special courses was obviously richer and more balanced than the manualists, but I still had difficulty applying it to my pastoral work. The neo-Thomists led by Jacques Maritain were still busy at that time trying to relate the thought of Aquinas to the concerns of the modern world. For me, however, their approach did not feel comfortable. My impression was that they were trying to force the experience of individuals into a preformed system which did not accord with the way ordinary people understood themselves and their world.

My search for a more effective theology took me to authors I had never read in the seminary. On one occasion, I had to give a talk to the Kiwanis and had no idea what to say. Randomly paging through Karl Rahner's *Theology for Renewal*, I found a chapter dealing with male spirituality. Although parts of the article seemed obscure, I was struck by his analysis of the reticence that males feel concerning the deeper aspects of experience, including their relationship to God. The talk, which expanded this point, was well received and led to some private healing conversations with individual members of the group. This was my introduction to the pastoral relevance of Rahner's thought. From then on, his writings became increasingly important to my ministry. Books such as *Biblical Homilies* and *The Eternal Year* regularly supplied seminal ideas for preaching. His popular books, such as *Opportunities for Faith*, as well as the more scholarly *Theological Investigations*, became a prime source for preparing classes and lectures.

My teaching responsibilities also gave me an appreciation for the work of Edward Schillebeeckx. His excellent *Christ the Sacrament of Encounter* provided an overview of sacramentology which helped in teaching liturgy to sophomores in high school. His scholarly work *Marriage: Human Reality and Saving Mystery* suggested an outline and important insights for a course on marriage that I taught in a local nursing school. The historical approach to theology used so effectively by Schillebeeckx in much of his work helped me appreciate the value of approaching current questions in the light of the whole of Christian tradition.

After the Council

AFTER THE SECOND VATICAN COUNCIL, parish leaders had the responsibility of initiating and explaining the changes in the church. For me, the progressive ecclesiology proposed by Hans Küng offered encouragement and direction in implementing these reforms. Reading Küng not only provided background information which thinking parishioners needed, but also put me in contact with a kindred spirit who was passionate and courageous in expressing the progressive view.

Shortly after the council, David Tracy made me aware of the work of Bernard Lonergan, especially his distinction between a classical mindset with its static viewpoint and commitment to timeless truth, and a contemporary mindset with its evolving viewpoint and understanding of truth as historically, culturally, and personally conditioned. This distinction enabled me to understand the diverse reactions to the conciliar reforms among my parishioners and became the centerpiece of numerous lectures explaining the changes. In addition, Lonergan's book *Insight* made me more conscious of the experiential approach to preaching and teaching which I had already instinctively adopted.

My attempts to teach high school religion solidified for me the developing conviction that I needed more education to improve my ministry. Two years of study at Fordham University in New York led to a master's degree in religious education and exposed me to outstanding scholars, including John Macquarrie and Hans Küng. From Macquarrie I learned to take the existential philosophers seriously because they opened up important areas of common human experience which often remain hidden. He also gave me an initial feel for the diversity of modern religious thought as well as some ways of making it more accessible for the ministry. During this time, I also studied with Gabriel Moran, a brilliant teacher who reenforced my belief that Rahner's thought could be used creatively for improving religious education.

After completing my studies, I taught at Mount St. Mary's Seminary in Cincinnati for a year. An important part of my task was to convince the seminarians that theology could be an ally in the pastoral ministry. My strategy was to immerse them in Rahner's theology, but always with a slant toward the practical problems encountered in parish life. I was well aware of my limitations in developing a truly pastoral theology, although subsequent feedback from some of my students suggested that we were on the right track because the material did prove helpful in their ministry.

From the seminary, I went to Bowling Green State University in Ohio where I served full time as a campus minister and did some part-time teaching. I found myself especially challenged by a course entitled "Belief and Unbelief" which I team-taught with a brilliant agnostic professor who was an expert on 19th- and 20th-century intellectual history. In this exciting setting, my colleague skillfully mobilized the arguments of the great critics of religion such as Nietzsche, Freud, and Sartre to challenge the theistic position I was defending. My response was to add Teilhard and Tillich to my Rahnerian resources in order to present a broadly-based case for theism. Teilhard proved helpful for the students who identified with his struggles to reconcile the Christian faith with the modern scientific world view. Tillich's explicit dialogues with Freud and the existentialist philosophers exemplified the way a believer could enter into creative dialogue with the critics while maintaining fidelity to the Christian tradition. Rahner's universalism and salvation optimism provided a broad framework which enabled me to respect my colleague's agnostic position, thus avoiding any compulsive urges to convert him and the students.

Teaching this course convinced me that I needed to return once more to theological studies in order to minister effectively in the world of higher education. To meet the kind of serious challenges presented by my agnostic teaching partner, I needed a wider knowledge of the modern debates over religion and a deeper grounding in a particular theology.

Pursuing this conviction, I investigated various theological systems, searching for one to study in greater depth. An adequate system for me had to resonate with my own religious sensibilities and provide a solid and comprehensive framework for dealing with the secular mentality prevailing in the university. Teilhard's broad vision was appealing, but the springtime mood of his writing, if not of his rather depressing life experience, was overly optimistic for my melancholic temperament. The great value of Lonergan's methodology in promoting systematic personal growth was clear to me, but his precise categorizing of the modes of consciousness and the process of growth seemed too rigid and confining for analyzing our experience which is ultimately mysterious and beyond rational calculation. Although the systematic thought of Paul Tillich held great appeal because of its open engagement with a broad range of cultural concerns, his theoretical explanation of the method of correlation struck me as overly restrictive and negative. His claim that the culture can only pose questions to Christians and never provide any answers or insights simply did not accord with my own experience of the positive aspects of the secular world. My limited reading of Reinhold Niebuhr gave me the impression that he had some important things to say about religion and politics but did not have the kind of comprehensive approach I needed. It was only later that I discovered the broad and insightful anthropology contained in his *Nature and Destiny of Man*. I never seriously considered Karl Barth's neo-orthodoxy since its negative view of philosophy, reason, culture, and the world religions was totally opposed to my own instincts and training.

By process of elimination, I was back to Rahner's transcendental Thomism. His "wintery piety" matched my own sense of reality. His anthropology resonated with my experience of the longings of the human heart. His methodology was open to the valid insights of the culture, the secular disciplines, and the great religious traditions. Finally, Rahner's theology was organic and comprehensive, providing a solid foundation for dialogue with the diverse strains of thought in the academic community.

Satisfied that Rahner would be the best guide for my ministry, I went to Oxford to study his theology in greater depth under the direction of John Macquarrie, whose scholarship and personal integrity I admired and trusted. It quickly became apparent to me that Rahner's notion of "mystagogy" was the key to the pastoral dimension of his theology. For Rahner, the mystagogical task is to help people in a secular culture uncover the mystery dimension of their ordinary experience and to relate this deeper perception to the illuminating power of the Christian tradition. In my dissertation, I tried to show that Rahner's mystagogical method could help us discern the mystery dimension of our knowing and loving as a base for vindicating a theistic position. Through this study,

I was developing a way of responding to my agnostic friends in the academic world. Rahner's key insight that we are oriented to mystery appeared to me like a powerful searchlight which could illumine the mystery dimension of the full range of human experience.

Pastoral Applications

WITH MY DOCTORAL STUDIES COMPLETED, I returned to the United States and my responsibilities as a campus minister. My dominant concern was not to write scholarly articles but to apply the fruits of my learning to my pastoral work. My continuing dialogue with the secular community went well, in part because the mystagogical approach had become for me a more refined instrument.

New challenges, however, were evident in the late 1970s on our campus. The fundamentalist Christian groups were more active and encounters with aggressive proselytizers multiplied. The mystagogical method was not of much help in dealing with these zealous Christians. The classical theology of Karl Barth, who was biblically oriented without falling into fundamentalism, seemed to offer some sort of bridge to these people, but I was never very successful in working this out in practice. The challenge of relating to the fundamentalists has continued. My Rahnerian outlook reminds me that arguments over specific biblical texts are generally fruitless, and that we must first discuss our different perceptions of the divine-human relationship and the role of inspiration in the Bible. Beyond the theological world, I also find enlightenment in the psychological analyses which suggest the connection between biblical inerrancy and the drive for security.

New challenges also arose in the area of social justice. The general apathy over social causes which prevails in our individualistic society became more evident once the momentum of the 1960s movements waned. This made it increasingly important for pastoral ministers to point out the injustices existing in society and to make the case for the social dimension of the gospel. Recognizing the limitations of Rahner's theology in this regard, I turned to the political and liberation theologians for help in meeting this ongoing responsibility. For example, Metz's insistence on the power of the institutional church for accomplishing social change provided theoretical support for our parish social justice committee, as well as national programs such as the Campaign for Human Development. The liberation spirituality developed by Gutierrez proved to be a rich resource for homilies and spiritual direction. Ruether helped me understand not only the pervasive power of patriarchy but also why it is important for women themselves to shape the debate over specific feminist issues. Martin Luther King provided inspiration and guidance for me in preaching the social dimension of the gospel. His practical understanding of the dynamics of social change taught me the importance of forming coalitions and drawing on the best instincts of our citizens in the struggle for peace and justice.

With the publication of the bishops' pastoral letters on peace, the economy, and women's concerns, the demands for a compelling defense and clear explanation of Catholic social teaching have increased. Again, the liberation theologians provide a context and an orientation which has proven to be very helpful when adapted to the specific situation in the United States.

In making extensive use of liberation and political theology I have felt no need to abandon Rahner's comprehensive theology for another system. Rather, the new and important insights of the liberationists can be placed within the Rahnerian framework as elaborations of themes already present in his thought. Rahner's anthropology is open to a detailed analysis of the precise social, political, and economic situation of individual human beings, including those who must learn to question the injustice which imprisons them and to take greater charge of their own lives. His Christology embraces the notion of Jesus Christ the liberator, and his moral theology encourages detailed analyses of social sin. For me, Rahner's comprehensive theology is not restrictive, but rather encourages the pastoral use of the themes and insights developed by the liberation theologians and other schools of thought.

The ecumenical situation has also taken on a different tone in the last decade, losing some of its earlier enthusiasm and momentum. Yves Congar, who had been helpful to me in the 1960s on questions of church renewal and the role of the laity, has also provided some historical perspective and encouragement in the search for ways to continue our progress toward unity. In ecumenical settings, I often echo Rahner's impatient call for reunion based on the conviction that, in principle, all the theological differences between Catholics and mainline Protestants are solved. At the same time, I try to remember Congar's more patient approach, which gives greater attention to the history of the disputes as well as the need to resolve them in precise detail.

The political campaigns of the last decade have taken me back to the thought of Murray and Niebuhr. On the volatile abortion question, Murray's analysis of the role of the "public consensus" in reform legislation suggested a viable position for those who are opposed to abortion, but are convinced that a constitutional amendment would do more harm than good at this time. Rather than settling for a disastrous split between private morality and public policy, such individuals should work actively to shape the public consensus so that it will eventually include the unborn among those deserving protection under the law. Such an approach is an effective pro-life position, because it prepares the way for a workable public policy. It would function more like the successful civil rights legislation which reflected a growing public consensus than prohibition which failed because it did not have popular support. This position, inspired by Murray, has been helpful to some of my parishioners searching for a middle ground in this divisive debate. It could also benefit candidates for political office who find themselves under attack by pro-life activists. Moreover, Murray's broad understanding of the proper role of religion in our pluralistic society provides a constructive critique of the political tactics employed by the Moral Majority.

Niebuhr's biblical realism solidified my conviction that the peace movement must work to form broad-based coalitions which increase the chances of electing peace candidates for national office. No doubt, my lectures on peace issues and my own active involvement in the movement reflect this collaborative strategy which prefers inclusive electoral politics to divisive symbolic action.

A Reverent Mood

SEVEN YEARS AGO I left Bowling Green State University and came to the University of Toledo as co-pastor of the university parish. Our staff has worked hard to improve our liturgy but we recognize the need to make further progress. In this effort, I am taking more seriously these days the position of Balthasar, who insists that the sacraments not only make visible what God does always and everywhere, but that they also form a sacred world which shapes our consciousness and forms our imagination. His encouragement to develop a contemplative spirit and a prayerful attitude before the glory of the Lord suggests that we put more effort into creating a reverent mood in our liturgy.

Finally, interfaith dialogue continues to be an important part of ministry in the university environment. Maritain is still helpful on relations with the Jewish community. Gandhi has generally functioned for me as a good bridge to the Eastern world. The expanding concerns of Hans Küng are instructive on this question of interfaith dialogue. Küng's ecumenical interests have always been behind his work on the renewal of the church as well as his writings on the essence of the Christian life, the existence of God, and the hope of eternal life. Recently, he has turned his attentions to the religions of the world, publishing, in 1984, his lectures on Islam, Buddhism, and Hinduism under the title *Christianity and the World Religions* (Doubleday, 1986). With his current studies on Chinese religions, he is preparing himself to write a systematic theology which will take into account the global perspective formed by the growing interdependence of the world's great religious traditions. Küng proceeds on the conviction that interfaith dialogue is crucial to the task of achieving and maintaining world peace. The potential importance of his project is immediately evident to me as I reflect on the large numbers of international students on our campus and the importance of improving dialogue among the diverse nationalities. Küng's work has already been helpful to me in preparing for some stimulating dialogues with large groups of Muslim students.

Adopting an Interpretation

THIS PERSONAL SURVEY, which has purposely excluded biblical scholars and moral theologians, not only indicates the impact on my ministry of the twenty authors treated in this book, but also prompts some more general observations on contemporary religious thought from a pastoral perspective. Such an analysis should be of interest, not only to those explicitly engaged in ministry, but to all who are serious about personal development and deepening their spirituality.

Pastoral ministers have the responsibility of relating the Christian tradition to the needs of the people they serve. In our culture, this task often includes uncovering the depth dimension of ordinary experience by illuminating the important needs and questions which are so easily neglected. We must gain the attention and interest of our people before we can proclaim the good news to them. Furthermore, we need to have a working knowledge of the vast and diverse Christian tradition in order to make it available to our people as they sort out their experience and work to spread the kingdom in the world. Those of us involved in pastoral leadership bring very pragmatic concerns to our reading of the great religious thinkers and the professional theologians. Our eyes are open for insights into human nature and cultural analyses which help us understand ourselves and our people better. We want fresh readings, significant retrievals, and creative applications of Christian teachings so that we can use them in our pastoral work. As parish ministers we realize our responsibility to help our people make the precise correlations between particular Christian doctrines and their existential concerns.

Many pastoral ministers burdened by demands on their time and their energy and discouraged by the difficult prose and esoteric character of some academic theology turn to the popularizers for guidance and support. For these leaders, the thought of the great religious thinkers is not encountered directly, but is filtered into their pastoral practice through the interpretations of others. These ministers have little or no interest in the differences between Rahner and Barth, but they are concerned with new insights which can enrich their preaching and teaching. They know theology, not as a speculative academic discipline, but in a more intuitive mode as Christian reflection which illuminates experience.

Pastoral concerns tend to make ministers eclectic and pragmatic in their use of the influential religious thinkers and their popularizers. It is true that individuals who study theology in depth usually find a particular author who resonates more with their experience and generally provides more illumination and encouragement than others. A few ministers may totally embrace a particular author, making him or her a complete resource for their pastoral work. Most pastoral leaders, however, adopt a more flexible approach, borrowing from other authors when they are beneficial and selectively using material which fits the needs of their people. Given the eclectic approach to theology dictated by the active ministry, the truth claims of competing theological systems are decided more according to pragmatic criteria than through scientific analysis. In Rahnerian terms, ministers employ a "first level reflection" which attempts to discern the best theology for them in a given situation based on converging probabilities and an intuitive sense of what works.

Furthermore, those of us who explicitly adopt a theological system do so because it feels right, illumines our experience, resonates with our sensibilities and guides our work while offering some measure of hope and encouragement. We also choose to read books by certain popularizers for practical reasons. For instance, they put into clearer language what we have known intuitively or point out ways to serve the community better. We turn to particular authors in certain pastoral situations because their work constructively addresses the real needs of the people we serve.

Classical Thought

FROM THIS PASTORAL PERSPECTIVE which remains pragmatic and eclectic, we can organize twentieth-century religious thought into five categories or models: classical, experiential, liberation, public, and interfaith.

The classicists represented most clearly by Barth and Balthasar reconstruct

Christian thought and make it available for current pastoral usage. Their clear teaching on the transcendence of God, the centrality of Christ, and the normative character of the Christian tradition as found in the Bible or church teaching, provide pastoral leaders with a definite package to communicate and clear criteria for making judgments about contemporary culture. On the other hand, the classical emphasis on the unique truth found in Christianity makes it harder to find common ground in dialogue with other religions and the modern world. The classical authors do not put much effort into elucidating the mystery dimension of human experience and of correlating this with the Christian message. The top-down approach used by these theologians offers little direct guidance for pastoral ministers trying to make applications to the real concerns of their people.

For pastoral ministers, the so-called post-liberal theology represented by Lindbeck's distinct "cultural-linguistic" model still functions in the same way as the traditional classical approach. Although theologians pursuing this project are attempting to respond creatively to the specific needs of the post-liberal age, they still employ the traditional top-down approach. Their project may provide ministers with a reformulated theological package, emphasizing the shaping power of the Christian message, but their methodology still leaves the challenge of application in the hands of the preachers and teachers. If Balthasar does, indeed, represent the "cultural-linguistic" model, he still remains a classicist. Ministers who sample his trilogy *The Glory of the Lord* will surely discover profound ideas beautifully expressed. On the other hand, they will find little direct guidance on how to relate this material to the existential concerns of their people.

Experiential Thinkers

IN RECENT DECADES, pastoral ministers in the United States have moved away from the classical approach in an effort to overcome the split between real life and the gospel. They do not want to give answers, even beautiful and coherent ones, to questions that no one is asking. The classical methodology which begins with the message is not well designed to stir up interest and tap the existential concerns of the potential hearers of the word. Although classical theology in both its traditional and contemporary forms is strong on the transcendence of God and the uniqueness of the Christian message, it is less helpful for finding God in ordinary experience and applying Christian teachings to real life.

From the pastoral viewpoint, we can discern a second group of religious thinkers who fit into the experiential model. In responding to the needs of people today, these authors reverse the classical methodology by beginning in human experience and using the Christian tradition to reveal its true meaning and depth. Among our authors, Rahner, Tillich, Whitehead, Lonergan, and Macquarrie clearly represent this model and Küng has steadily moved in this direction since his early Barthian period.

Pastoral ministers who serve people influenced by the modern secular mood find the methodology of this model helpful because it makes common human concerns the focus of discussion. Those who have serious doubts about traditional Christian doctrines still must wrestle with the great questions of identity, meaning, and purpose. Selective Catholics who tune out the undesirable pronouncements of church leaders still are looking for resources in their heritage which will help them cope with the modern world. Parishioners who are serious about their faith want guidance in relating Christian truths to their everyday experience. The experience-oriented religious thinkers recognize these concerns and present the Christian message as a response to them. In the last couple of decades, ministers serving the affluent and the educated as well as middle-class working people have turned more and more to the experience-centered authors and their popularizers for help in communicating the gospel to their people. The practice of religious educators in the United States represents this trend. In Catholic circles, the experiential approach of Rahner popularized by creative authors such as Gabriel Moran has come to dominate religious education at all levels from children to adults. Our admitted failures in catechetics since the council are not due to the experience-oriented methodology. They result, rather, from a failure to follow through with a clear and cogent presentation of the content of the Christian message which remains rooted in experience.

As the example from the world of religious education suggests, the current problem for ministers is not only to discern the linkage points with common experience, but also to find reformulations of the Christian tradition which are intelligible and credible to people today. The experiential theologians provide us with a wide variety of options, including Rahner's "from below" Christology, Tillich's existential interpretation of sin, Lonergan's penetrating analysis of grace, and Macquarrie's dialectical treatment of God. Contrary to the claims of some neoconservatives, pastoral leaders serving in average congregations in the United States are not faced with a choice between a post-liberal classicism which will restore a sense of transcendent uniqueness of Christianity and a liberal theology strong on method but weak in content. The real challenge is to make the vast resources of the Christian tradition available to our people without ignoring the vital linkages with their experience. From this viewpoint, the new classical model should not become the dominant paradigm for pastoral ministry, although it could function as a valuable corrective, reminding us that the immanent God is transcendent, that Jesus the man for others is the risen Lord, that the servant church is the sign of the kingdom, and that the sacraments which make grace visible also create a sacred world. At times, the classical methodology may fit a specific pastoral need. For example, priests who use an experiential approach in their weekend homilies may, at weekday masses, simply develop a theme found in the Scripture readings, allowing the interested and committed parishioners present to make their own applications. I can recall preaching in a black Pentecostal church where a classical top-down methodology seemed entirely appropriate because of the congregation's familiarity with the Scriptures and their evident interest in the exposition of the text. Despite exceptions of this kind, ministers serving congregations influenced by the modern secular mood must work hard at uncovering the depth dimension of experience and relating the gospel to existential concerns. The experience-oriented religious thinkers remain our best guides for this task.

The Liberation Model

SPECIFIC PASTORAL CONCERNS have also dictated the development of a distinctive style of theology represented by the liberation model. The theologians who fit into this category have responded to the cries of the poor and oppressed by exposing the unjust social structures which imprison them and by mobilizing the liberating power of the Judeo-Christian tradition in the struggle for justice. From our list of authors, Gutierrez, Ruether, Metz, and King have explicitly addressed the concerns of particular oppressed groups by focusing attention on neglected resources in our religious heritage which can empower those relegated to the margins of society. While Niebuhr cannot be comfortably confined in this model, he does share important concerns with these authors. He has provided us, for example, with a penetrating analysis of the use of power in the struggle for justice and has also helped us understand the sinful character of institutions. Martin Luther King had this aspect of his thought in mind when he commented that he learned more from Niebuhr than from Gandhi. In the later stages of his career, Schillebeeckx moved closer to this model by adopting a liberation perspective in his writings. This was a shift from his earlier work which employed a classical methodology and his middle period which is closer to the experiential model.

In the United States, the liberation model is especially attractive to those who work with minority groups and are sensitive to the concerns of women. When these ministers take the concerns of their people seriously, they have to face the pervasive influence of oppressive systems. In responding, they need to show that the Christian tradition has resources to encourage and guide their people in the struggle for emancipation. Some of those serving the oppressed found that the writings of the experiential theologians, which had moved them to listen more attentively to their people, could not supply them with the social analyses and the scriptural guidance they needed. When these ministers encountered the thought of the Latin American theologians, including our representative figure Gustavo Gutierrez, they often felt an immediate sense of kinship. They recognized, for instance, that the Exodus theme and the image of Jesus Christ the Liberator developed by the Latin Americans would enrich their preaching.

This shift in perspective is exemplified in the experience of a priest friend of mine who was the pastor of an inner-city parish located in a black neighborhood. As part of his continuing education, he sat in on a course I was teaching in a Protestant seminary on Karl Rahner's theology. For him personally, the course was intellectually stimulating and resonated with aspects of his own experience. From a pastoral viewpoint, however, it proved to be frustrating because the material was not immediately relevant for his people. About a year later, my friend heard a series of lectures by Gregory Baum on liberation theology and sensed immediately that this material would, indeed, enrich his ability to inspire and guide his people. He went on to take a summer course in liberation theology, discovering in the process a distinctive spirituality which spoke to his own experience as well as his parishioners.

In order to become even more useful to pastoral ministers in the United States, the liberation model must include the work of theologians immersed in our own culture. We need social analyses which illumine the strengths and weaknesses of our distinctive political and economic systems. Rather than continuing to borrow from Latin America, we need theologians to follow the lead of Martin Luther King in working out an indigenous liberation theology. Because of his refocusing of scriptural themes, his courageous and insightful defense of nonviolence, and his remarkable analysis of the dynamics of social change in our democratic country, King is an excellent exemplar for liberation theology in the United States. It is unfortunate that he is so seldom mentioned in discussions of liberation theology. We will all benefit when his fundamental ideas begin to play a more prominent role in the development of an indigenous theology which reflects the liberating power of the gospel. Rosemary Ruether is another example of a liberation theologian rooted in our culture. She is especially helpful to ministers responding to the concerns of women because of her radical analysis of the roots of patriarchy and her retrieval of the prophetic tradition which calls women to take charge of their own lives.

For many of us who find our ministry nourished mainly by the experiential religious thinkers, the liberationists serve as a corrective. They remind us that we human beings who seek answers and long for love are always influenced by our socio-economic context. This helps us understand the concern our relatively well-off parishioners often express in response to the bishops' economics pastoral. The social analysis offered by liberation theology forces us to look at the bias in our thinking and the way our sins can foster injustice. Their spirituality calls us to a simpler lifestyle. Finally, they provide us with scriptural and theological arguments for greater involvement in the quest for peace and justice in our world.

Public Theologians

THE PASTORAL PERSPECTIVE links together Niebuhr, Murray, and King as major representatives of the public model. Public theologians are visibly involved in the affairs of the world, attempting to influence public policy and to shape the national consensus according to gospel values. Their approach reminds ministers that the parishioners they serve are also citizens of the country. Their active participation in public life teaches us that spreading the kingdom cannot be confined to church renewal, but must also involve the humanization of society. They give us concrete examples of how to mobilize the resources of the Christian tradition for the common good. Finally, their witness encourages ministers to proclaim with vigor and courage the social dimension of the gospel.

With the passing of Martin Luther King we have lost the last of the obvious representatives of the public model. Some say that we will never have such influential theologians again because our media-dominated culture cannot tolerate carefully reasoned and ethically-oriented positions on social questions. Others claim that leading theologians today work more behind the scenes, influencing leaders and policies more indirectly while leaving the responsibility for public witness to the bishops. It seems to me that pastoral ministry would be strengthened if our leading theologians were more visible and carried more weight in the debates over public policy. They are free to advocate more creative and radical solutions to societal problems than those suggested by official church leaders. Their personal interaction with public officials and policy makers could, in some cases, achieve positive results which cannot be accomplished through official church pronouncements. A theologian appearing again on the cover of *Time* magazine as did Niebuhr, Murray, and King could be a graphic reminder of the importance of religion for the health of the nation, as well as the value of filtering the distinctive American experience into the church. Such publicity might also remind pastoral leaders that theology can, indeed, make a difference in the real world.

The Interfaith Model

FINALLY, FROM THE PASTORAL VIEWPOINT, Gandhi and Buber, religious thinkers representing diverse traditions, can be joined in a fifth category called the interfaith model. This model encompasses not only the leading thinkers representing diverse religious traditions, but also the popular interpreters of the world religions who write for a predominantly Christian audience. These religious thinkers challenge our narrowness and help us build bridges to other world views. They enrich our ministry by expanding our horizons and enlarging our sense of reality. While they cannot provide us with an encompassing vision or a total system, they do make us aware of the limitations of our own theological position. Thus, Gandhi opens up the riches of Eastern thought for us and instructs us in the power of active nonviolence. Buber puts us in touch with the core of the Jewish tradition and offers valuable advice for deepening our human relationships.

A theological typology which ignores these religious thinkers will fail to account for significant influences on pastoral practice today. For instance, Buber in his reinterpretation of Judaism helped foster a personalistic approach to the ministry which is widely accepted today. The popularizers of Eastern religions have broadened our understanding of mysticism and taught us practical meditation techniques. Various expressions of the creation-oriented spirituality of the American Indians are now available as we reflect on environmental problems. Christian interpreters such as Thomas Merton have supplied us with thought-provoking parables of the Buddha and stories representing Chinese wisdom.

A growing number of Christian ministers, true to their pragmatic orientation and eclectic approach, are now open to such influences from other traditions. By organizing twentieth-century religious thought according to pastoral considerations, we can find a proper place for those authors who do not totally share our Christian view or fit neatly into models of academic theology, but who do have the power to expand our vision and improve our pastoral practice.

Categories and models are always limited instruments for sorting out the complexities of the religious world. Some of our twentieth-century thinkers do not fall easily into any of the five models; classical, experiential, liberation, public or interfaith. Others seem to be representative of more than one. Even limiting ourselves to the pastoral perspective, we could imagine other ways of organizing contemporary religious thought. Nevertheless, our attempt to relate and compare these thinkers does reveal important patterns and trends in the midst of great diversity. Our analysis reminds us that contemporary religious thought does have a definite and often explicit pastoral orientation. In various pastoral situations, ministers can choose between the classical top-down mode of proclaiming the gospel and the contemporary experience-centered method of relating real life concerns to the Christian message. The liberation theologians are an increasingly powerful ally in challenging the individualism and apathy which impede the task of spreading the kingdom of peace and justice. Fresh ideas and surprising insights are available from our own culture and other religious traditions which can enrich our preaching and teaching. Collectively, these writers constitute a vast and rich resource which provides a solid foundation for pastoral ministry and the spiritual life.

This book functions best as an invitation to enter into genuine dialogue with these contemporary authors by bringing our important concerns to an open-minded encounter with their thought. This dialogue is not only personally stimulating, but prepares us to make our own unique, if limited, contribution to the great conversation.

NOTES

NOTES

NOTES

NOTES